THE TAO OF
I CHING
Way to Divination

Jou, Tsung Hwa.

易　經

占卜之道

Tai Chi Foundation

II

First Printing in Taiwan March 1983

Third Printing in Taiwan January 1986

Fifth Printing in Taiwan December 1991

Sixth Printing June 2000

ISBN 0-8048-1423-1

Published by

Tai Chi Foundation

7199 E. Shea Blvd. Ste 109-225

Scottsdale, AZ 85254

Dedicated to:

Tai Chi Foundation

THE TAO SERIES
by Jou, Tsung Hwa

1. **The Tao of Tai Chi Chuan**

   Way to Rejuvenation

   Third revised edition is available

2. **The Tao of Meditation**

   Way to Enlightenment

   Shows you how to open your mind and spirit. For the frist time in English, the Way to enlightenment

3. **The Tao of I Ching**

   Way to Divination

   A new and refreshing way to understand and utilize the I Ching.

More informations on page 405, 406, 407 and 408.

CONTENTS

Chapter Three: THE CRADLE OF CHINESE CULTURE

It is my intention that this book will encourage students to pursue a course of self-development and to study life and nature, as it was the pursuit and study of these things that led to the creation of the I Ching in the first place. Most English translations of the I Ching emphasize academic approach and therefore highlight the Judgments of the 64 hexagrams and their individual lines or Yao. In such books, divination is simplistically explained and the student uses coins or yarrow stalks to derive a reading consisting of general advice with respect to the hexagrams and lines selected.

Although students using the I Ching in such a manner may receive useful information and advice, the reading is very often general and composed of archaic language. More often, students are left with doubts regarding proper interpretation and cannot use their own intelligence to determine the true meaning. In addition, serious students have unanswered questions, such as the following:

"How were the hexagrams derived and their meaning determined?

What is Yin and Yang and what relation do these concepts have to the hexagrams?

Why does divination work and for what purpose?

What relation does the I Ching have to my life?

How can I learn to divinate better? "

Finally, the student puts all of his or her questions together and summarizes as follows:

"The I Ching claims to be derived from nature in the simplest way, yet I do not find it simple. If the principles are simple, why can I not use the same principles to understand my life better?" Anyone who has encountered these roadblocks and asked these questions will find the answers in this book. I would like to give some hints here on the approach to understanding the I Ching that will be most effective.

First in order to understand the I Ching, we must be free of a scientific or regimented type of thinking. Taoist philosophy, in general, and the I Ching, particularly, are very different from modern science. The philosophy of the I Ching goes beyond the scope of "science." The goal of the traditional scientist is to achieve standards of knowledge and then expand upon those standards. To standardize, the scientist uses a "scientific method." That which cannot be measured, demonstrated in rigidly controlled experiments, or proven by meticulous observation cannot be used by the scientist to expand his knowledge. A scientific study is a careful exploration of what is popularly called the "five senses." Through ingenuity, a scientist may find it possible to measure the "invisible," however, even this must be done with tools that are perceived by the five senses.

Taoism, like science, approaches life with this type of curiosity and desire for knowledge, but it goes beyond the limits of scientific standardization. Taoism recognizes that there is no single standard, of a scientific sort, for some of the most important and humanly meaningful things in life. The I Ching describes spheres that are a great deal more intangible than the five senses; they are most often referred to as the "mental" or "spiritual".

The I Ching reveals the great wisdom and understanding of the ancient Chinese philosophers. They looked at the world around them and sought to understand why and how change occurs. They did not look beyond reality or ascribe all events to the "hand of God." Instead, they found enlightenment through the very practical process of examining the concepts of space and time.

By understanding time and the cycle of life, they could explain all events. Because they did not assume that everything was caused by God, they sought to find the explanation of change in the person, thing, or event itself.

Second, the I Ching deals with that which is intangible. Therefore, the mental and spiritual preoccupation of the individual using the I Ching will necessarily influence the meaning to be derived. In studying the I Ching's methods of interpreting life, one must keep this in mind. For example, suppose two people look at the full moon and appreciate the atmosphere and energy it creates. Although one person may feel awed by a sense of the beauty and peace and feel a boundless gratitude and happiness towards life; another person may appreciate the power of the moon, but be moved to misery and tears. Why? He may be saddened by the memory of a friend that died and how they had once enjoyed full moon evenings together. Everything has this quality. A man may lose all of his possessions and laugh carelessly, only because he has just come from the doctor and learned that he does not have a fatal disease after all. Another man may cry at good luck because the bad luck that preceded has devastated him. Because of this fundamental fact, whenever there is an event, one must relate it to the existing situation in a thorough way to truly understand its meaning.

The same principle is true for the divination of Yin and Yang lines. Consider the following simple divination: a broken line is drawn (yin), meaning presently unfavorable, and a solid line is drawn (yang) meaning very active right now, a time to move. One person may draw yang and interpret it to mean "it is time to ask the boss for a raise." Another person may draw yang and decide that it is finally the right time for him to climb that mountain in China he had alway wanted to try. Another person may draw yang and uses it for guidance in a major business decision. Thus, the same simple line has given self-guidance to three people in totally different situations. The philosophy of the I Ching is that this multiplicity and variety is a natural part of life, and that if we want to learn to live more effectively, we need only study the I Ching and work with it.

The third point, and perhaps most important thing, I can make about the I Ching is that you will understand nothing unless you spend time researching the meaning of the I Ching for yourself. In addition, you will gain nothing if you do not like to exercise your judgment and imagination; that is, if you always expect someone else to tell you what is right and how to do things. The person who has some insight and is willing to take personal initiative can use the I Ching to make work more effective and enjoy life more fully.

This book is a concrete example of what I mean by an open-minded approach to change. I have written it for a person with a western background. My student Louis and I evolved a simple approach to translating the I Ching from a western perspective. After Sunday Tai Chi class, we would meet at a diner and I would describe the work for the week. Louis would take notes and my handwritten English translations. The following week he would produce a typewritten text for editing. His questions and suggestions told me exactly what needed to be explained more fully for a western mind.

Because of his help, I was able to proceed with this book rapidly while continuing a great many other activities. Louis is a good example of a student's progress. As the work progressed, he not only helped me find the right words, but took up his own studies. Although he had lived in a rural and scenic area all of his life, he began to appreciate the natural beauty of his surroundings that he had always taken for granted. He used nature to define the meanings of the energies described in the I Ching and to make his understanding direct rather than a matter of memorized words. When he took up divination he asked "How can I be sure I am learning to do this well?" He decided to study developing news events and then compare what actually happened with the explicit "judgments" he divinated. Finally, he worked at seeing some of the things in his everyday life in terms of Yin and Yang and the I Ching. I believe that Louis presently knows a little bit about the I Ching. It is only the beginning, but it is something real, and it is becoming part of his skills as a person.

Would he know as much if he had studied as a scholar for twenty years, but could only quote hundreds of different fine points of interpretation? If he had troubles in everyday life would this knowledge be any use to him? If he had good fortune, could he use his knowledge to make the most of it for himself and others? The answer is simply, never.

On the basis of the foregoing, I warn you against the specialized scholarly approach. It is valuable, but too limited for a person to live with. To depend upon another person's interpretations is an example of letting someone else decide your life. You alone must live your life. Consider the following: the four great men of the I Ching are Fu Hsi, its originator; King Wen, who interpreted the hexagrams, the Duke of Chou, who wrote on the lines; and Confucius, who reviewed the whole. One can spend years studying the lore of these men yet learn nothing. It is far better to use only the first, Fu Hsi, as your inspiration. Remember that he had no one to teach him and no one to tell him what to do, therefore, he found his answers by taking life itself as his teacher. When studing these teachers, follow the spirit of their teaching, but always remember to accommodate the message to your personal circumstance.

An example of following the Spirit of the I Ching can be found in the interpretation of the seasons. Athough the study of the times and the season are deeply related to the I Ching in traditional Chinese culture, it is too complex and specialized to describe fully here. Instead I use the open-minded spirit of "change" and give the basics for the student to use. January has definite meanings in the I Ching cycles, since it is mid-winter, but if you live in Australia, you had better not study January if you want to learn about winter. You must take the initiative to turn things completely around and study July instead.

Likewise, when we read the inspiring translations of the I Ching's scholars, it is important to consider their original meaning. Consider the following translation: "It is time to cross the great river." Try to feel the meaning and spirit of this advice. Cross the Great River? Get on a ferry boat? Get your feet wet? Look at the water and be inspired? Remember, when these words were written the world was a primitive and unsettled and often dangerous place. The simple act of fording a wide river by boat could end in disaster if one was careless or unskilled. Thus, the real meaning becomes, "the times are good for undertaking difficult things."

Again, consider the terse comment: "There are no fish in the bag". Ask yourself what would Confucius say if he lived today. He'd probably pen something like this: "There is no money in the checking account!"

Do this with everything you meet, and you will be a true student of the I Ching by learning to understand yourself and others. The material I have put together for you covers a wide field of study. Sometimes I have found it preferable not to explain everything fully, in order to show basic principles and give enough guidance for you to do your own work.

Following is some of the information you will find in this book:

* A description of how the Tai Chi diagram creates the meaning of Yin and Yang, and the basic principles of their alternation. The material will show how a student can evolve the meanings of the trigrams directly from this central concept. Further material shows how the hexagrams develop directly Ying to Yang.
* The method of divination using yarrow stalks or coins is presented along with other more dynamic methods by which you can divinate directly from life and events around you.
* The use of a three part divination is explained, and how the principles of the five elements can be used for interpretation. There are some specific examples here to help you start.
* A traditional picture for each hexagram that summarizes its qualities visually instead of with words is given. This will help you learn to use non-verbal creative concepts in understanding advanced concepts. The pictures are old-fashioned. What can you do about this, can you tell me?
* The material with the hexagrams shows how translation of the traditional meanings can be taken the next step into relevant personal translations. Included here are also many details on the lore of divination as applied to the specific hexagrams and their line, or Yao.

There is much more. And there is no reason why you should not get a loose-leaf notebook, number it, and begin jotting down your own notes on each hexagram immediately. Get to work!

In a more serious tone, we must each evolve our own feeling for what these activities mean. When we divinate we are going further than our five senses, and we are appealing to the spiritual world that surrounds and pervades everything for our guidance. This will differ for each of us. I belive the principle for each of us is that the I Ching and its divinations is a blueprint from the "fourth dimension" to guide us in leading our lives in this third dimensional world. The concept of our evolving relationship with the fourth dimensional world is more fully described in my book, "The Tao of Meditation." Meditation is still another way of approaching this fourth dimensional world and developing our place in it.

Some may ask, "Which is best, Meditation, the I Ching or Tai Chi

Chuan?" The question is like asking whether warm is better than cool. You may find that studying meditation or Tai Chi Chuan gives you a simpler and more direct understanding of the I Ching. Alternatively, you may find that your study of the I Ching is directly helping your progress in meditation and Tai Chi Chuan.

Since the I Ching was first translated into German and other languages, it has awakened great interest and fascinated countless people. Yet, I believe this interest is only a fraction of the attention it deserves when it is used in the way it was created to be used. I wish everyone the best of fortunes in their studies. Remember, this is not a book on Chinese culture or philosophy. This is a book about things no more exclusively Chinese than a lake, a person or the sky.

There are a number of people who have been helpful in the writing of this book. Without their advice, assistance and encouragement. Writing this book would have been much more difficult.

I would especially like to thank of the following: Louis Kovi, Mindy Sheps, Marsha Rosa, Paul, Albe, Susanna Thompson, Victor Franco. And, I extend a very special gratitude to Dr. Shoshana Adler for her help in proofreading the first half of the text at the workshop in Eureka Springs, Arkansas.

Jou, Tsung Hwa
December, 10th, 1983

Chapter One:
RAISING THE VEIL OF MYSTERY

1-1 Returning to the Roots

The I Ching (易 經), or Book of Changes, is the most ancient book in China and perhaps in the world. It represents both the source of Chinese culture, and a key to the understanding of Chinese history, even in its most turbulent stages.

This is notable during the reign of Chin Shih-Huang(秦始皇 see figure 1-1a), the first emperor of the Chin Dynasty(秦朝 221-207 B.C.), who succeeded in unifying six other kingdoms of the country. Chin adopted a series of strict measures to unify the country. The most lasting of these was the adoption of a single language. He also evolved a tyrannical system of suppression that he thought would establish his dynasty forever. His strategy was the destruction of all learning in order to keep people in an ignorant and submissive state. Thus in 215 B.C. he ordered all the scholars buried alive to humiliate them, and searched out and destroyed all of the country's works of literature and philosophy, including the most revered classics.

However, Chin saved one book, the I Ching. He and his officials needed it for political guidance and divination.

Thus the I Ching has been transmitted to us from the past without

Figure 1-1a

any serious interruption.   There was a gradual evolution and three different I Chings have been developed. In the Hsia Dynasty (夏朝 2205-1766 B.C.), the Tui trigram (兌卦), which was the image of lake, was doubled and became the first hexagram in the series of 64. This arrangement was called Lien Shan (連山). In the Shang Dynasty (商朝 1766-1150 B.C.), the trigram Kun (坤卦), which symbolizes the receptive earth, was doubled and became the first hexagram. This arrangement was called Kuei Tsang (歸藏).   Finally, in the Chou Dynasty (周朝 1150-249 B.C.), Chien (乾卦) the symbol of creativity and heaven, was doubled to make the first hexagram. This arrangement was called Chou I (周易).   Since written language was not well-developed during the Hsia and the Shang Dynasties (in fact, records were kept on tortoise shells) knowledge of the Lien Shan and Kuei Tsang was largely extinct by the time of the Chin Dynasty.   What remains today is the Chou I, which we call the I Ching, or simply I.

The Chinese character for the word I is created by combining the symbols for the sun (⊙) and the moon (☽), and this combination presents the most fundamental perception of Chinese philosophy towards experience and life. Later we will see these formalized into the symbols of Yin and Yang, but before the symbols there is the observable actuality.

First, the sun and moon are alternating qualities that follow each other in a circular path. The sun rises and comes to its zenith, and begins to decline. It disappears below the horizon, and the moon appears. The moon is followed by the sun, and then follows the sun again. First one dominates, then the other.

There is also the opposition of the sun and moon in their qualities. The sun is huge, yet distant beyond imagination. Its tremendous energy brings the warmth and light that is responsible for all life on earth. The moon is smaller even than the earth, yet it is closer to the earth than the sun, so it raises powerful tides in the oceans and also – as scientists are beginning to study – in the tissues of all living things. The moon is dark and has no light, yet it shines brightly and dimly and brightly again with the light of the sun. The moon changes the quality of the sun through polarization. Together, the opposing qualities of the sun and moon create a complex and always changing series of influences on the life of our planet.

As we observe the interaction of their opposition, we come to another perception – that their contrasts and the contrasts of similar energies here on earth are what make our life. Thus we can say that they not only oppose each other, but also complement each other.

To understand this, we need only consider a photo. It is shades of light and darkness. Take away all the darkness, and what do we have? Take away all the light, and what do we have?

The study of the I Ching considers all the things we experience, do, say, feel, and deal with, and finds this same contrast of qualities. Without it, there is nothing. With it, anything in our world may be seen and described. Our world and life are based on the activity and changes of complements.

But this only happens because within the changes there is always constancy. To imagine this, think of a light burning brightly forever, with no shadow. This is one kind of constancy. It is easy to imagine.

Now imagine a light fluctuating with darkness forever in a way that has no pattern and no order. We might perceive this, yet the perception would have no meaning. Just as we might act, yet never know the meaning of our acts if there were no stable conditions to reflect that meaning to us.

Finally, consider a light that grows bright and then dims to darkness and then brightens again in an endless cycle.

Now the repetition of the contrasting parts of light and darkness has become a constant cycle. Because it moves and shows detail of shadow and light, we have perceptions. Because it goes through the same cycle again and again, the perceptions follow patterns that we come to learn, until finally the whole richness and complexity of our world and our lives appears.

Thus the constancy of cycles that repeat themselves faithfully makes possible all that we experience and do. These cycles always bring us change and the freedom to change, and at the same time create the unchanging foundation of our life and world.

Out of this, we analyze the word I to have three distinct qualities: Chien I (簡易) or easy and simple, reflects on how easy and simple our world is in its make-up; Pien I (變易) refers to its aspect of continuous change; and Pu I (不易) refers to its constancy.

Thus the book I starts with this precise observation of universal phenomena and of our daily life. These primary data of life are simple and easy to understand. As it is said in Ta Chuan (大篆):

> Chien (乾) knows through the easy
> Kun (坤) does things simply
> What is easy is easy to know
> What is simple is simple to follow
> He who is easy to know makes friends
> He who is simple to follow attains good works
> He who possesses friends can endure forever
> He who performs good works can become great.

1-2 Ancient Chinese Wisdom

A specific description of how the I Ching was created is given in the Ta Chuan (大篆) or Great Treatise:

"In the I Ching there is the Tai Chi or Grand Terminus (太極), which generates the two forms or Liung Yi (兩儀). Those two forms generate the four symbols of Ssu Hsiang (四象), and those four create the eight trigrams or Pa Kua (八卦)."

This passage obviously tells us that if we intend to study the book of the I Ching, we have to follow a logical progression, first understanding the meaning of Tai Chi and then how this meaning progresses to Liung Yi, Ssu Hsiang, and Pa Kua.

If we simply read the judgments and images of the hexagrams, we are like a person who tries to learn about the nature of a large forest without studying its surroundings. This person sees a profusion of meanings, first one thing, then another, but he never looks beyond the forest. He comes away with vague impressions. He never knows that through the thick cover of leaves overhead there is the sky, or that in one direction the edge of the forest is a short distance away, while in another direction are dense thickets.

So we must first know the Tai Chi. But here the I Ching is reticent, for it does not state where the Tai Chi comes from. Its origin, however, is discussed in ancient Chinese philosophy, and given the name Wu Chi (無極) or Hsien Tien (先天). Wu Chi means "what there is before the universe comes into being." Can we imagine this? We can begin by considering smaller examples of Wu Chi in everyday life. For in Chinese philosophy, we say that every part of life operates the same as the Tao or universe as a whole. The microcosm faithfully follows the macrocosm.

First we need to know what the concept of *change* is, as defined by Wu Chi. If there is no change, then nothing came out of Wu Chi. If there is change or even the possibility of change, we say then that the situation of Tai Chi is beginning. That is why the I Ching is also referred to by another name: "The Book of Changes."

We can see the change from Wu Chi to Tai Chi in an apple. Imagine that the apple is in a state of Wu Chi. It simply is there. But then bacteria develop in the apple and it starts to spoil. At first there is only a tiny part spoiling, too small to be seen. Then it becomes visible, the size of a pinhead. By stages it grows larger and progresses until finally the whole apple is gone.

As long as it was an apple, it was Wu Chi. But the moment the bacteria began spoiling it, the stage of Tai Chi began.

The same is seen in the formation of a tornado. At first there are only gentle breezes, no tornado, or Wu Chi. Then there is an acceleration of the breezes, and they begin to travel in circular motions instead of just randomly flowing. This is now the Tai Chi of the tornado. The breezes grow stronger and a definite circular wind is created that picks up loose leaves and twigs from the ground and throws them high in the air in circular patterns. Finally all the wind energy from the surrounding area becomes funnelled into this circular motion, and tremendous forces begin to build up. Now people cry "tornado" and hide in the cellar. The tornado moves slowly along with the sound of a dozen express trains and tears loose everything it touches. Houses, trees, and rocks are drawn up into its vortex and cast away. At some point, however, the tornado starts to lose its force and slow down. Soon it has only moderate force. Finally, it cannot be detected at all. It is gone, and Tai Chi has returned to Wu Chi.

All we observe in life, including ourselves, follows this pattern. Before we exist in this world, we are Wu Chi. When we are born, we begin the stage of Tai Chi. At first we are small and weak. Slowly we grow strong and live our mature years. Finally we die, and the matter that formed our bodies is dispersed like the breezes that formed the tornado. We have returned to Wu Chi.

When Wu Chi changes to Tai Chi and a thing exists and can be observed, a duality begins. At any time that a thing exists, part of it is changing and part remains unchanged. Like the apple, part of it is still good and can be eaten and part is spoiled. Or the tornado, part of the atmosphere is drawn into it and part is unaffected.

We call the unchanging part Yin and the changing part Yang. Chinese philosophers use a circle (O) to represent Yang and a solid black circle (●) to represent Yin. Another notation is a broken line – – for Yin and a solid line —— for Yang. It does not matter which symbol stands for Yin and which for Yang, and we can also reverse the process. The important thing is to understand the major characteristic of the duality: where there is Yin, there is also Yang, and vice-versa.

For example, there are men and women. We can say a man's character is vigorous and intense like fire; and that a woman's is tender and gentle like water. Since we link man and fire together, we say they are both Yang qualities, and likewise that women and water are Yin.

This points out another quality of Yin and Yang: we can apply them to any object or process we observe in our world. They are not to describe some particular object, but are for all dualities, and refer to all of them. Thus Lao Tzu said: "A single Yin cannot be born, and a single Yang cannot be grown." (孤陰不生 , 孤陽不長).

We can see how there must always be Yin where there is Yang

by considering electricity. Light and power come from energy flowing across positive and negative poles. If there is only one pole, we find nothing.

We can see another principle by observing how the positive and negative charges are named. If we have only one particle of charge, it cannot be given a name. We can only name it by comparing it to another particle to see if they attract or repel. If they repel, they are identical charges, but if they attract, one is positive and one is negative. Which is which? It does not matter. We simply give our test particle a name and the other particle the opposite name. This corresponds with the I Ching commentary: "One Yin and one Yang make the Tao." (一陰一陽之謂道).

What we have discussed so far can be illustrated in the following way as shown in figure 1-2a.

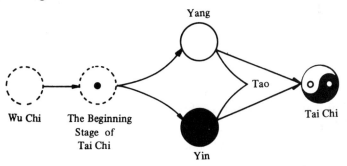

Figure 1-2a

In this diagram we see Wu Chi giving birth to a Tai Chi state. If there is no movement in the beginning stage of Tai Chi, then its Yin and Yang are combined, as in a storage battery for electricity. But if there is movement, then Yin and Yang separate and become distinct, just as the battery uses opposite ends of the pole to produce heat, energy, and light.

In this separation of the Tai Chi, the two symbols of Liung Yi are created. These basic first steps later evolve into the I Ching trigrams and hexagrams. This philosophy of Yin and Yang within the I Ching has three basic aspects:

1. Hsiang (象) or symbol. This is based on the symbols ● and ○, the Tai Chi diagram ◑ , and the symbols – – and ——, arranged in various combinations: four symbols, eight trigrams, or sixty-four hexagrams.

2. Li (理) or philosophy. This deals in accurate forecasting, and includes the writings, judgments and images of the I Ching — what we have from the four sages Fu Hsi, King Wen, Duke of Chou, and Confucius.

3. Shu (數) or number. Here numbers are used to deduce the likelihood of future events by reviewing what has happened in the past. In modern computers a binary system is used that creates numbers by using two opposed elements, just as we have Yin and Yang in the I Ching. And just as we say that Yin and Yang can picture our whole world, we find that a computer can produce an abstract formulation of any words, logic, pictures, or calculations using only these two symbols.

These three aspects are specialized parts of the whole I Ching. To understand the I Ching, we need to learn about each of them. In Chinese history, there have been various schools of study, each emphasizing one of the these three aspects. For example:

1. The philosophical theories of the scholars of the Han Dynasty (206 B.C. — 219 A.D.) or the Ni Li School (義理派). Studying, emphasizing, following, and explaining the texts of the four sages Fu Hsi, King Wen, Duke of Chou, and Confucius.

2. Philosophical theories of the scholars of the Sung Dynasty, (960-1279) or Hsiang Shu School (象數派). Researching and studying the trigrams and hexagrams and how they relate to mathematical symbols and philosophy.

3. The Taoist School (道家). Using the philosophy and principles of I Ching to develop Tai Chi Chuan and meditation techniques, etc. For Tai Chi, the inner trigram represents one's state of mind and the outer one the condition of one's body. These two sets of trigrams have been translated into a series of continuous movements, incorporating the constant changing between Yin and Yang. For meditation, the hexagrams indicate how the chi flows in the body during meditation. A famous book *Gen Tung Chi* (參同契) discusses this process in detail.

Ironically, my interest in the I Ching came after my interest and experience in Tai Chi and meditation. By studying the I Ching I gained greater understanding of Tai Chi and meditation because I could see more clearly how they were created and developed.

4. Chan Pu School (占卜派) or divination. Using the inductive and deductive methods to predict the future. (This method will be emphasized in this book.)

These various schools of study are not contradictory. They are simply different ways of approaching and understanding the I Ching as a building and each school as a window, each giving a different view. Whatever window you look through influences what you will see, but you are still in the I Ching "building".

1-3 The Four Symbols

The I Ching uses the arrangement of lines in a sequence. The places that the lines fill in the sequence are called Yao (爻). A Yao may be filled with either a solid or broken line. The line indicates Yin or Yang. All dualities, all contrasts of any sort, can be characterized as Yin for one of the pair, and Yang for the other.

If we call darkness Yin, then light is Yang. If we call cold Yin, then hot is Yang. And so on.

By using several Yao we may summarize a very complicated situation, filling in the spaces with either Yin or Yang lines. For example we can take each Yao to represent a period of time. We have a cup of very hot coffee which eventually becomes cold. We express this with two Yaos. The starting Yao is the bottom line and indicates hot. The top Yao indicates cold. The Yaos are always read from bottom to top. Reading the Yaos can be compared to reading a sign on the highway. The name of the coming exit, for example "South", would appear under the name of the following exit, for example "North". The driver of a vehicle would read the sign from bottom to top to find out which exit comes first, which comes second, and so on. See figure 1-3a below:

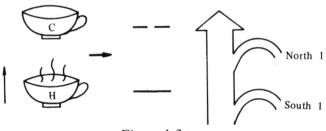

Figure 1-3a

The set of two lines used to describe "the cup of coffee in time" is one of the four symbols. We can use the Tai Chi diagram to derive these four symbols in an orderly way, or tree system, as seen in figure 1-3b. Next to this diagram, we see another way of generating the four symbols by reading the quarters of two concentric circles, beginning from the inside, to generate the four symbols as shown in figure 1-3c.

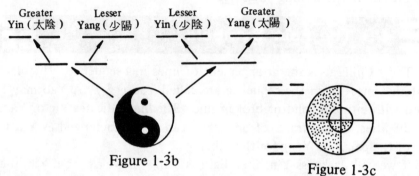

Figure 1-3b

Figure 1-3c

We need to learn how the four symbols can logically follow one another in events, and we can observe an example of this by looking at our moon. The moon is a whole like the Tai Chi sphere, and when we add time to our observation of it, it begins to separate into Yin and Yang. Thus we have the New Moon and the Full Moon, and this is like ● and ○, or Yin (– –) and Yang (——). We also name the halfway points between New and Full the First Quarter and Last Quarter. Below we can see how this naming is exactly the same as a circular sequence of the four symbols as shown in figure 1-3d.

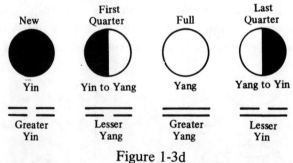

Figure 1-3d

Still another use of the four symbols is to describe our seasons as shown in figure 1-3e.

Winter	Spring	Summer	Fall
▬▬ ▬▬	▬▬▬	▬▬▬	▬ ▬
very cold	from cold to warm	very hot	from hot to cold

Figure 1-3e

If we assign north as Yin and south as Yang, we can easily work out how the directions of the compass can be indicated with the four symbols. In fact the use of the lines has a wide applicability in geometry and mathematics. If we consider Yang as going along a line from the original point 0 to the right, and Yin from 0 to the left, we can see from this basic definition how easily the two dimensional graph of plane geometry is set up as shown in figure 1-3f and 1-3g.

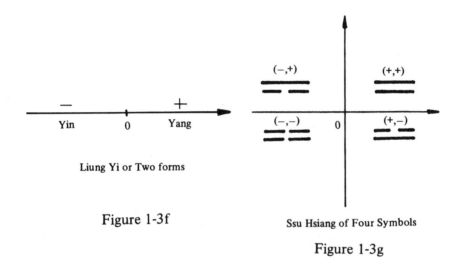

Liung Yi or Two forms

Figure 1-3f

Ssu Hsiang of Four Symbols

Figure 1-3g

In this system, the bottom line of the symbol is the horizontal axis and the top line represents the vertical axis. If we wish to add a third Yao, we can go on to a three dimensional graph for solid geometry. In mathematics, we can assign Yang as zero and Yin as one and thus derive a binary system.

The four symbols can describe not only the moon's phases, but also a man's destiny, or that of a society. The Greater Yin is like a person who is not established in anything. In societies we might compare this with the emerging nations of Africa. Here a person or nation must take what little they know and plan and work with it. The next stage is Lesser Yang. This is like a young man just rising in the world, or a nation like China that is just establishing itself. Here there are great challenges and activities and constant changes to be met. Then we have the Greater Yang. This is like a successful businessman or a nation like America that is strongly established and powerful. Here the need is to always use great care to maintain things, for otherwise decline will come rapidly. Finally in Lesser Yin we find a person or nation that has passed its peak of development and has begun to decline. Since this is like the fall of the year, its major quality is that it must harvest its riches from the past with good judgment in order to endure the coming winter.

In this kind of investigation we can see clearly what part of the cycle a person or society occupies. We can look at ourselves this way and decide how to be. A person who has high standards and wants good things from life, for example, never says, "Oh, everything is fine now, I don't have to worry or pay attention", even when he achieves success. If he says and believes such things, he immediately leads himself into a decline. Instead, he will say, "I want to do better." Thus he is always learning something new, always taking himself back to the stage of Greater Yin to start anew and recreate himself.

We can see this simple cycle in still another way: the cycle of our day. When a man is asleep, he is Greater Yin. Then he awakes and gets going with the morning preparations. This is Lesser Yang. Finally, he gets to work and is using his full powers. This is Greater Yang. Then he goes home and relaxes, resting from serious things, and doing less demanding things. Here he is at Lesser Yin. Finally, he goes to bed and the cycle begins again.

The Yin-Yang balance is crucial to understanding. In some situations, Yin may be more desirable. In others, Yang may be more desirable. We must seek one and avoid the other. But even this we must do by following the observation in the I Ching that Yin always begets Yang and Yang always begets Yin. We must study this movement and reciprocity and follow it wisely.

We can see from these simple examples how people seriously using the I Ching can greatly enhance their understanding of themselves or the world. A person who has not considered this need of personal initiative might say, "This is too simple! A child can understand it." But a child lacks the breadth of knowledge and maturity of an adult. And adults vary in the amount of maturity and ability they have developed. These traits are derived directly from the initiative they have taken to develop themselves. Those who have interest and initiative in their lives can use the I Ching to great benefit.

One of the most important philosophical uses of the I Ching is in developing our emotions. The poet Shelley speaks with foreboding of the wild west wind and the cruel winter changes it is bringing. Then, after developing this image through his whole poem, he concludes: "Oh Wind, if winter comes, can Spring be far behind?"

Thus, if some event or emotion happens to bring with it great distress and unhappiness for us, we need not be like the unknowing child who thinks "Oh, everything is all over for me!" We can look to the changing cycle that must occur in every event, and see that even bad feelings cannot last forever. New opportunities will be coming for us, which we may develop successfully.

All of these philosophical and other observations can be seen in the simple foundation of the Tai Chi model. That model comes from Wu Chi and splits into Yin and Yang, and then the four symbols. But to learn about the sixty-four hexagrams of the I Ching we must understand the final derivation of the eight trigrams.

1-4 The Eight Trigrams: Heaven, Earth and Humanity

I Ching history tells us that the evolution of the trigrams comes from the first Emperor, Fu Hsi (伏羲 2953-2838 B.C. see figure 1-4a) It is said that Fu Hsi set out to study all of heaven and earth. He turned his eyes to the heavens and studied astronomy as well as the movements of the sun, the stars, the moon, and the planets. He turned back to earth and observed the flat, the rolling, and the mountainous land. How some soil was good for tilling and other soil was not. He studied the weather, the tides, the storms, and the regular changes of the seasons. Natural

Figure 1-4a

history claimed his interest, and he watched the birds and the animals, and deciphered their languages.

Finally he turned to observe and study within himself. Out of this he created the eight trigrams as a method to commune with the spiritual and invisible world, and a way to be part of everything within the visible world. He also used it to represent the relationships of everything in our three dimensional world and to build images of anything in our world.

We can see here how important human experience and exploration are in the foundation of the I Ching. The trigrams were developed by a man of relentless curiosity who wished to understand all things.

We can begin to study the eight trigrams by observing how simply they are derived from the Tai Chi. Two different methods are used to describe this process in figures below. One uses a rectangular block formation, see in figure 1-4b the other uses a tree diagram as shown in figure 1-4c.

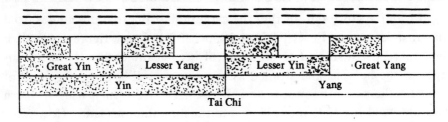

Figure 1-4b

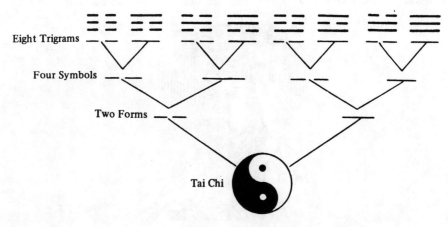

Figure 1-4c

				Pinyin
乾	☰	Chien	or	Qián
兌	☱	Tui		Dui
離	☲	Li		Lí
震	☳	Chen		Zhèn
巽	☴	Sun		Sūn
坎	☵	Kan		Kǎn
艮	☶	Ken		Yin
坤	☷	Kun		Kǔn

The circular form below is another method of visualizing the generation of the eight trigrams. It is created by taking the rectangular blocks and forming them into a circle as shown in figure 1-4d.

Figure 1-4d

If we want to easily recall the eight trigrams, we can use an ancient menmonic using four pairs. One member of the pair is generated by changing the lines of the other:

Symbol		Chinese Name	Sharp	Order
Chien	☰	乾	Three Continuous	1
Kun	☷	坤	Three Broken	8
Chen	☳	震	Upwards Cup	4
Ken	☶	艮	Overturned Bowl	7
Li	☲	離	Empty Middle	3
Kan	☵	坎	Full Middle	6
Tui	☱	兌	Deficient Top	2
Sun	☴	巽	Broken Bottom	5

In another method, we can look at the four fingers of our hand, and imagine a set of trigrams, one on the upper and one on the lower joint. Note that each set is symmetrical with of Yin and Yang reversed, and that the order of one to eight follows that derived with the rectangular bars as shown in figure 1-4e.

Figure 1-4e

If we are familiar with the binary system of enumeration, we may recall the eight trigrams simply by reading off the numbers 0 through 7 using the 0 to represent a Yang line and the 1 to represent a Yin line, or vice-versa. For example:

Tui   ☱   is the same as 001 or 1

Kan   ☵   is the same as 101 or 5

All eight are written as follows:

Trigram	Symbol	Binary System	Decimal System	Order
Chien	☰	000	0	1
Tui	☱	001	1	2
Li	☲	010	2	3
Chen	☳	011	3	4
Sun	☴	100	4	5
Kan	☵	101	5	6
Ken	☶	110	6	7
Kun	☷	111	7	8

(Note: Normally, binary and decimal numbers are read from right to left. However, I recommend reversing the order of reading to avoid confusion. Always read from left to right to derive the eight trigrams. For example, "001" is read Yang, Yang, Yin, or —, —, – –.)

Finally, if we take our Tai-Chi symbol and rotate its center a little to more visibly symbolize the intermingling of Yin and Yang, we can read the eight trigrams in it by taking eight sections as shown in figure 1-4f.

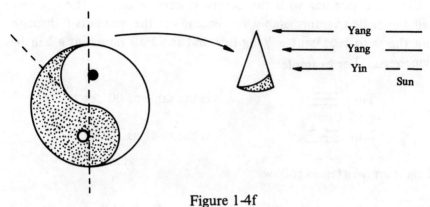

Figure 1-4f

By reading the eight sections from the Tai Chi symbol, we arrive at an arrangement like this as shown in figure 1-4g.

Figure 1-4g

This arrangement is called the Hsien Tien (先天) arrangement, and it is believed to have been developed by Fu Hsi.

In addition to this Hsien Tien circular arrangement there is another called the Hu Tien (後天) that is traditionally credited to Chou Wen

Wang (周文王) who founded the Chou Dynasty circa 1143 B.C., as shown in figure 1-4h.

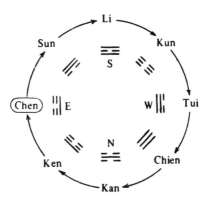

Figure 1-4h

The eight trigrams of Hu Tien are based on the I Ching passage that reads:

"The ruler comes forth in Chen with his creation. He completes the work in Sun. He causes things to see one another in Li and to serve one another in Kun. He rejoices in Tui and battles in Chien. He is comforted and rests in Kan, and then finishes the work of the year in Ken."

We can see how this cycle begins in the east and the spring of the year and proceeds in a clockwise cycle. This sequence of trigrams was used to explain the principle of the movement and cycles of the universe, and the Chinese calendar was created from it. Later on we will explain in detail how the Hsien Tien and the Hu Tien are interrelated for use in divination.

Once we have arrived at eight trigrams, we then have three lines for each. With Yin and Yang we have two, and the addition of a third line symbolizes creation, particularly the creation of humanity by heaven and earth. Just as man and woman create a child through their relationship; heaven and earth, Yin and Yang are seen as not only existing apart, but as interacting and producing a new, third quality. This is called Three Powers or San Tsai (三才), as shown in figure 1-4i.

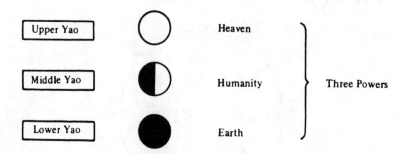

Figure 1-4i

We see in the diagram of the trigram that the first and bottom line is the Yao of earth, the middle line is the Yao of humanity, and the top line the Yao of heaven. When we look at a hexagram, we take the first two bottom lines as the Yaos of earth, the next two as the Yaos of humanity, and the top two as those of heaven.

The addition of the third quality locates humanity within the universe in a meaningful way. Because humanity's relation to the Tao is of the most vital interest, one of the important uses of the eight trigrams is to describe social relations. The simplest society is that of the family of father, mother, and child. The father is identified with Chien (乾), the mother with Kun (坤), and the remaining six trigrams are the three sons and three daughters.

To derive the three sons, we imagine the Chien intermingling with the Kun, and giving it one of its solid lines as shown in figure 1-4j.

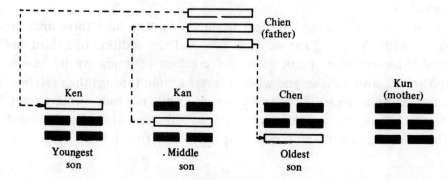

Figure 1-4j

In the derivation of the three daughters, we imagine Kun intermingling with Chien and giving one of its lines as shown in figure 1-4k.

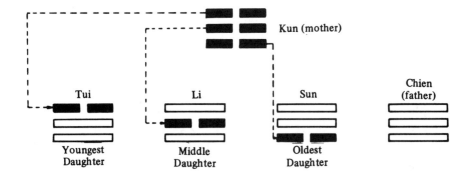

Figure 1-4k

To eventually understand the hexagrams, we must first assign meanings to each of the eight trigrams. The evolution of these meanings can be understood if we consider the Hu Tien arrangement that was used to evolve the Chinese calendar. Each season of the year has a trigram. If we look about during each season at the different things happening and the influence on our lives and moods, then we can give a meaning to each one.

Thus, if Chien stands for the late fall and early winter, we can imagine a tree that has grown all summer and has now dropped its leaves and withdrawn its sap into its roots. If we look at this and other late fall phenomenon we can evolve an image of strength and resourcefulness. We can call this Chien.

If we go back a step to early fall, we may think of the farm family working to bring in the rich harvest of crops during the warm Indian summer. From this we can sense a mood of energetic joyfulness, and call it Tui.

If we go a step forward from Chien, we can imagine the dead of winter, a time of hidden dangers for the unwary person — like the motorist whose car runs out of gas in a storm and who almost freezes to death. We can call this phase Kan.

In the following table, some of the traditional attributes of the eight trigrams that have been developed are given, along with the inner relations — parts of the body, season, time and so on. The different tables are not arbitrary inventions, but have evolved over the centuries in a trial-and-error way through observation, and we should expect to find modern parallels. For example, Kun tends to represent activity of a responsive sort, such as "work." Its time is from 1 to 5 p.m. Modern scientists of body rhythms, paying no attention to the I Ching, have independently discovered that the time of day when a person is "most able to cope" is this same period.

The student should memorize the tables and also work out individually each part of the table to develop themselves, A wild pig, for example, would tend to attack a traveller by rushing from concealment in a fast dangerous charge. Thus it is represented by Kan. Dogs for thousands of years have been guards and protectors of the home, hence it is easy to see how they are related to Ken. Some of the attributes — such as liver and Chen — relate to specialized branches of knowledge that are not clear unless we have studied them. However, most can be figured out with common sense and will train us to develop our perceptions. The more we study the basic symbols and how they work, and then relate other things to them, the more we will begin to learn.

In studying, we must keep an open mind and not look for a single solution that never changes. A hotel, for instance, means Ken, because it is where people stop for the night and are inactive. But if it has a nightclub in it, then we are looking at the Tui aspect of it.

Trigram	☰	☱	☲	☳
	Chien	Tui	Li	Chen
Symbol	Heaven	Lake	Fire	Thunder
Virtue	Tough a Strong	Joy	Magnificence	Stimulus to Movement
Animal	Horse	Sheep	Pheasant	Dragon
Trigram	☴	☵	☶	☷
	Sun	Kan	Ken	Kun
Symbol	Wind	Water	Mountain	Earth
Virtue	Penetration	To Entrap	Stop	Obedient
Animal	Chicken	Pig	Dog	Ox

Trigram	☰ Chien	☱ Tui	☲ Li	☳ Chen
Human Body	Head	Mouth	Eyes	Feet
Human Affairs	Father	Youngest daughter	Middle daughter	eldest son
Season	early October mid-December	mid-September mid-October	early June early July	early March early April
Time	7 p.m. to 10 p.m.	5 p.m. to 7 p.m.	11 a.m. to 1 p.m.	5 a.m. to 7 a.m.
Direction	South or Northwest	Southeast or west	Eastor South	Northeast or East

Trigram	☴ Sun	☵ Kan	☶ Ken	☷ Kun
Human Body	Thigh	Ears	Hands	Abdoman
Human affairs	eldest daughter	middle son	youngest son	mother
Season	early april early june	early december early january	early february early march	early july early september
Time	7 a.m. to 11 a.m.	10 p.m. to 1 a.m.	1 a.m. to 5 a.m.	1 p.m. to 5 p.m.
Direction	southwest or southeast	west or south	northwest or northeast	north or northwest

Miscellaneous:

☰ Chien — A circle, ruler, jade, metal, cold, ice, deep red, serious, bone, large city, resort, car, sky-scraper, cogwheel, clock, machine, huge.

☱ Tui — A bar-girl, female singer, bank employee, restaurant, bird, bill, sword, coffee, kitchen, mouth and tongue, concubine.

☲ Li

A teacher, artist, library, beauty salon, church, TV, gun, camera, operation, sun, lightning, armor and helmet, spear and sword, tutle and crab. Referring to personal qualities, it suggests a large belly.

☳ Chen

Blue and sand stone (玄黃), great highway, young fellow, announcer, operator, the liver, broadcast, telephone.

☴ Sun

White, long, lofty, advancing and receding, deficiency of hair, wide forehead, postman, salesman, airport, harbor, air conditioner, electric fan, travel.

☵ Kan

Channels, ditches, bow, wheel, increase of anxiety, distress of mind, pain in the ears, red, moon, thief, boatman, waterfall, restroom, bar, gas, tryst, sleep, pen.

☶ Ken

A by-path, small rock, gateway, fruits, porter, rat, family, hotel, warehouse, secona floor, bridge, beef.

☷ Kun

Cloth, caldron, frugality, large wagon, multitude, handle or support, black soil, old woman, farmer, village, antiques.

1-5 The Structure of the I Ching

The structure of the I Ching evolved over several thousand years, with four individuals making the major contributions. The first was Fu Hsi (伏羲 2953-2838 B.C.) who created and named the hexagrams. King Wen (文王), founder of the Chou Dynasty (1150-249 B.C.), then gave an explanation of each of the 64 hexagrams. A brief text accompanies each hexagram and contains a decision or judgment. The text is called Kua Tsi (卦辭). King Wen's son, Duke Chou (周公), then added a text in which the meaning of each of the six lines is individually examined. This is called the Yao Tsi (爻辭). Finally, Confucius (孔子 550-478 B.C.) made a lifelong study of the existing work and added both general comments on the philosophy and specific comments on the hexagrams. His work is called the Chuan (傳) or Appendices, of Ten Wings (十翼).

Here is a sample of the first hexagram of the I Ching.

---

1. Chien (乾)   (symbol)
                                            Hexagram created and named
                                            by Fu Hsi.

2. Kua Tsi (文王卦辭)

乾，元亨利貞。

These four Chinese characters are King Wen's explanation of the meaning of the hexagram Chien.

3. Yao Tsi (爻辭)

The following are the Duke of Chou's explanations of the meaning of each Yao.

初九：潛龍勿用。
九二：見龍在田，利見大人。
九三：君子終日乾乾，夕惕若，厲无咎。
九四：或躍在淵，无咎。
九五：飛龍在天，利見大人。
上九：亢龍有悔。
用九：見羣龍无首，吉。

The entire text of the I Ching contains explanations of each of the 64 hexagrams.

When we study the I Ching, our teacher is life and nature, not the writings of other persons. If we really understand the I Ching, we do not need to refer to or quote the writings of others. An example of this is Confucius' greatest follower, Mencius, who in his written work never discussed the I Ching and yet all of his work is developed from the principles of the I Ching. This is the kind of person who truly knows the I Ching. Such a person is like the poet Shelley, quoted earlier. Shelley never heard about or learned of the I Ching, yet he understood its approach.

If we study different ways of deriving the 8 trigrams and the 64 hexagrams from the original Tai Chi sphere, then we will begin to understand the way they are grouped and their meanings will become clearer. We have already seen this in the simple way the four symbols describe the phases of the moon or a person's development. Each taken alone, the four symbols are useful, but when put in a series that follows a cycle, they become many times more informative.

We have also seen how the 4 symbols and the 8 trigrams can be derived by a simple splitting of Yin and Yang that develops like the branches of a tree or the veins of a leaf. Obviously this process can be continued till we reach the 64 hexagrams.

Still another method of derivation is best understood through noting its similarity to modern algebra. We will take Yin and Yang together, and multiply that by itself as shown in figure 1-5a.

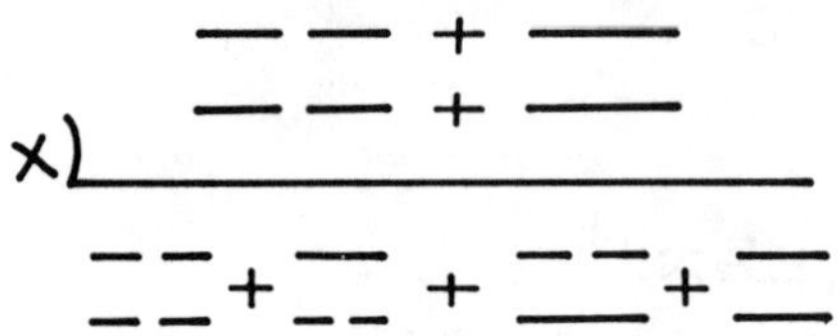

If a represent ——
b represent — —

from $(b + a)^2 = b^2 + ba + ab + a^2$

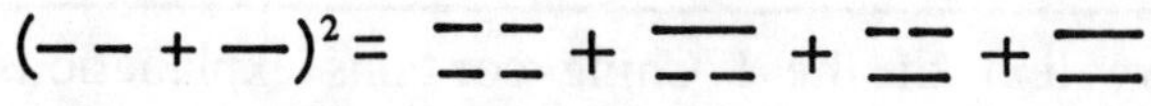

$$(-- + —)^2 = \equiv + \equiv + \equiv + \equiv$$

Figure 1-5a

We can see how similar this is to multiplying (a + b) times (a + b). The only difference being that in algebra ab and ba are put together as a single term, 2ab, whether the a or b comes first. But in deriving the lines, ab and ba have different meanings and are kept separate.

(Yin plus Yang)² gives us the four symbols we already know. If we multiply this by another (Yin plus Yang), we will get a more complex term as shown in figure 1-5b.

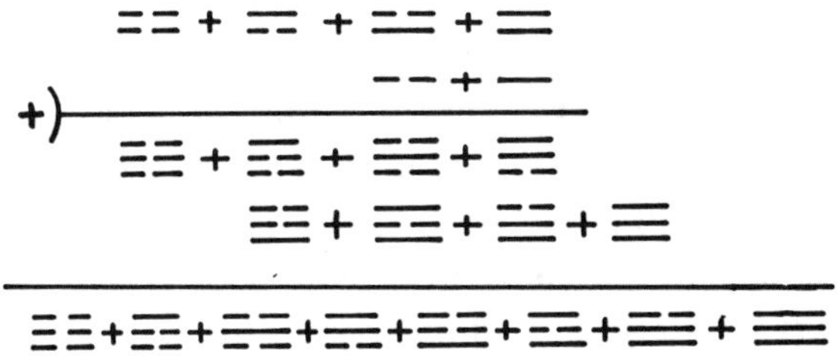

$$⚏ + ⚍ + ⚎ + ⚌$$
$$⚏ + ⚌$$
$$+) \overline{}$$
$$⚏ + ⚍ + ⚎ + ⚌$$
$$⚏ + ⚍ + ⚎ + ⚌$$
$$\overline{}$$
$$⚏ + ⚍ + ⚎ + ⚎ + ⚍ + ⚌ + ⚌ + ⚌$$

or

$(b^2 + ba + ab + a^2)\ (b + a)$

$= (b + a)^3 = b^3 + 3b^2 a + 3ba^2 + a^3$

$= b^3 + b^2 a + b^2 a + b^2 a + ba^2 + ba^2 + ba^2 + a^3$

$= ⚏ + ⚍ + ⚎ + ⚎ + ⚍ + ⚍ + ⚎ + ⚌$

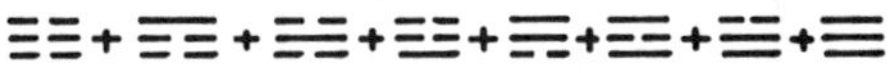

Figure 1-5b

Note that the bottom line of a series of Yaos always is the first element, so that a Yin Yang translates to $⚍$. We can see how (Yin plus Yang)^3 results in the eight trigrams.

Finally, if we take (Yin plus Yang)^6 we will arrive at the 64 hexagrams. If a = Yin and b = Yang, we can use this formula:

$(a + b)^6 = a^6 + 6a^5 b + 15a^4 b^2 + 20a^3 b^3 + 15a^2 b^4 + 6ab^5 + b^6.$

or $(Yin + Yang)^6 = Yin^6 + 6Yin^5 Yang + 15Yin^4 Yang^2$
$+ 20Yin^3 Yang^3 + 15Yin^2 Yang^4$
$+ 6Yin\ Yang^5 + Yang^6$

This condensation gives us a picture of how many hexagrams have a particular proportion of Yin to Yang in the lines: 6 Yin, no Yang; 5 Yin, 1 Yang; 4 Yin, 2 Yang; and so on. If we think of the hexagrams as a thorough picture of the world, we can see that 20 parts of the 64 part map show a world where there is an even balance of 3 and 3, and 50 of the 64 parts are either even or close to it ($20Yin^3 Yang^3$,

15Yin^{4}Yang^2, 15Yin^{2}Yang^4).   As we go further out to all Yin and all Yang, we see how rapidly these become very small in proportion to the whole picture. We can liken this to a person's life and how it has its rare moments of great ecstasy or intense unhappiness. We all sense that we would not be whole without moments such as these. Most of the time, however, life is more balanced and our emotional experiences are moderate. Still, they have a complexity and richness that make them just as meaningful as the extreme high points and low points of life. Students of statistics will recognize in the distribution of the hexagrams a variation of the standard bell curve, which is used statistically to categorize all events. (See figure 1-5c and 1-5d.)

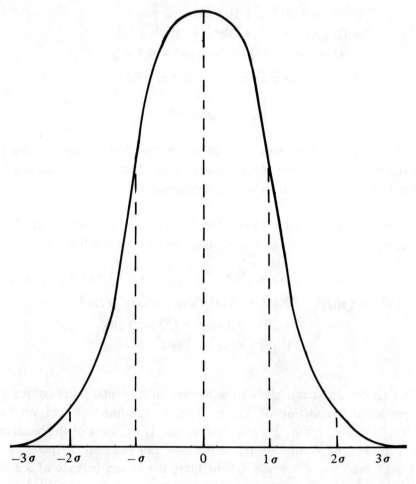

The normal curve

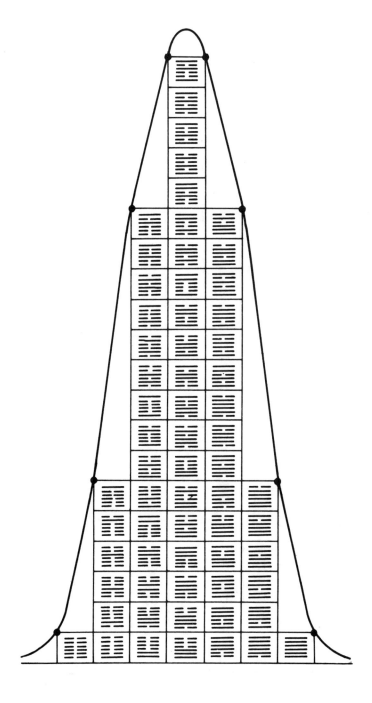

Figure 1-5c

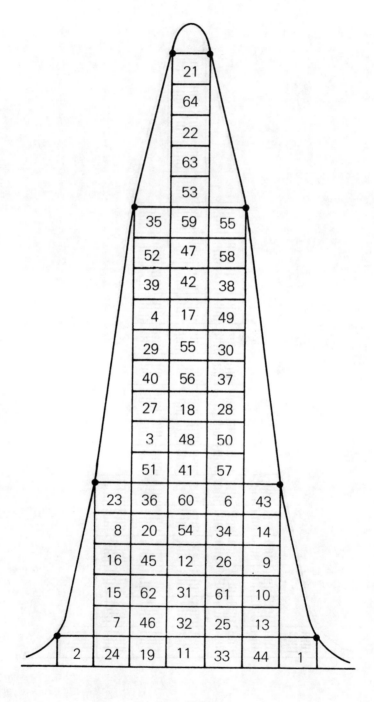

Figure 1-5d

The above diagram shows the distribution of the hexagrams in groups that occurs if we think of Yin plus Yang raised to the sixth power. The diagram shows that the traditional methods of deriving the order of the 64 hexagrams are not the only ones, and that new and modern derivations can be evolved. A student of mathematical statistics might note the similarity of the diagram to the standard curves used in statistics to predict events, and find many new things from the study of the hexagram. Those of us who apply it to everyday life can easily find as many things. Suppose for example we take a Yin line as being a day when our intelligence and intuition is most dominant, and a Yang line as a day when our sense of action and effective action is most dominant. Then we can read each hexagram as the 6 days of a week. In this study, we'll find less than one week a year when our intelligence is totally dominant, and the same for our ability to act. Weeks when all but one day is dominant one way or the other will occur 6 times a year for each possibility. Finally we have the weeks where the two are evenly balanced or close to it; these will occur 78 percent of the time, or about 4 weeks in every 5.

We are now at the core of the I Ching — its 64 hexagrams. Each hexagram contains six Yaos, and people always ask the question, "A trigram has three Yaos, why don't they use four for the next step? Or for that matter, five? Or seven? Why six?"

This question was occasionally a controversial point even in ancient times. But it was largely a waste of energy; the equivalent of medieval Christian theologians arguing about how many angels can dance on the head of a pin.

To understand why six Yaos are used, ask yourself the following: Why does a foot have 12 inches? Why does a meter have 100 centimeters? Why does an hour have 60 minutes? Why isn't our week nine days instead of seven?"

All we can say in reply is that experience shows that a foot is a very convenient way to solve most problems of measurement in daily life. True, if we need to measure the diameter of a hair or the distance between New York and Boston, we need a "special" division of measurement, but otherwise a foot will do fine.

The same is true of the hexagrams using six Yaos. Six Yaos can solve most of our daily problems, but we are free to use what is useful

for us. It is not hard to imagine that we might make up a series of
seven lined figures, and use them to study our weekly activities.

We can see how different numbers of Yaos are useful by our studies
of the moon — we can use Yin and Yang, or ● and ○, or - - and — to
talk about the new and full periods. This is one Yao. Then if we begin
to talk about the quarters, we need to use the four symbols, which
are built with two Yaos. If we want still more detail, we can use the
eight trigrams with three Yaos and the hexagrams with six Yaos as
shown in figure 1-5e and 1-5f.

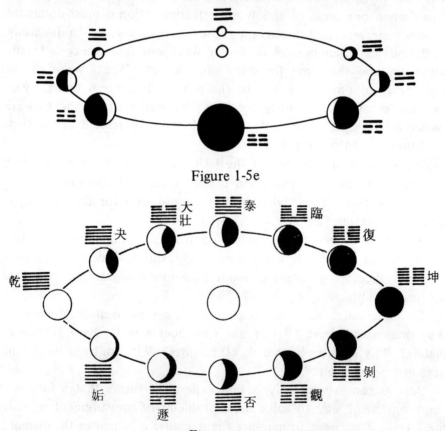

Figure 1-5e

Figure 1-5f

Of course, this concept can apply to many things. If we take the
circle in the center to be the sun and imagine the outer sphere to be
the earth, then we are studying the seasons. We can study the career
of an individual or a nation. And it is clear we can use even more than

six lines if we want. For example, someone can make up a seven Yao symbol and use it to study the course of the week. So we repeat: six lines can show clearly what we need to know about most problems of daily life, but we can sometimes use fewer or more lines.

Another important matter is the ordering of the 64 hexagrams. We saw how Fu Hsi and others arranged the 8 trigrams into a complete cycle and used this order in a logical way. How do we arrange the 64 hexagrams in a circle that makes sense? One way is the example of $(Yin + Yang)^6$, which generates a mathematical sequence. In the Chou Dynasty, mathematics had not yet developed to this degree of sophistication in algebra. Instead, the Chinese used an ingenious visual method. First they arranged the eight trigrams in the Fu Hsi arrangement as shown in figure 1-5g.

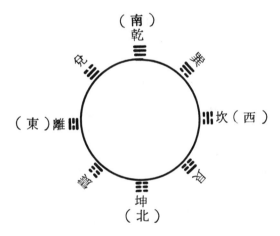

Figure 1-5g

Note that in these diagrams, the "bottom" line is the one closest to the circle, which stands for the earth.

To develop the 64 hexagrams from the eight trigrams, they expanded each trigram further out from the center and drew a circle around it. Now all they had to do was put another eight trigrams around each circle. To read a hexagram, we read first the inner trigram, and then the series of outer trigrams circling it. We have eight hexagrams. Then we go on to the next circled trigram in the diagram and get another eight, and so on, as shown in figure 1-5h.

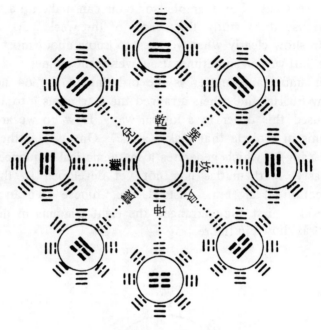

Figure 1-5h

The final result of this kind of computation by diagram is a wheel like the one shown below. The one shown here is derived using a circular order that follows the pattern of the eight trigrams we derived by branching Yin and Yang as shown in figure 1-5i.

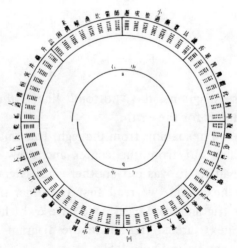

Figure 1-5i

The ancient students of the I Ching also invented a grid pattern for developing the 64 hexagrams in an orderly manner. If we study the block below we will see that the inner (bottom) trigrams are always the same in each file going across, while the outer (upper) trigrams are the same in each vertical row as shown in Figure 1-5j.

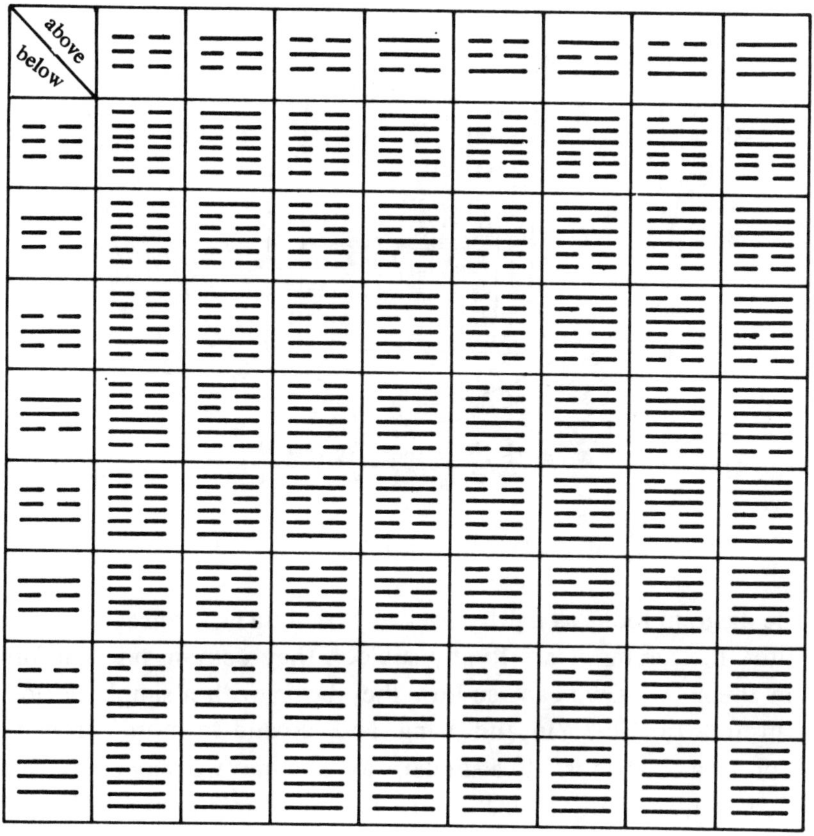

Figure 1-5j

If we combine the wheel and the grid we get this frequently re-produced diagram as shown in figure 1-5k.

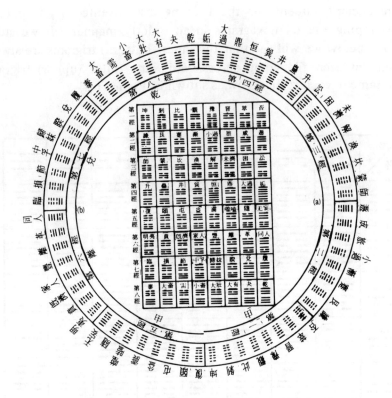

Figure 1-5k

The diagram looks as tightly packed with data as a railroad timetable. Since the hexagrams relate to any subject, they contain much information in them. Yet we can see how they begin with a simple notion of Wu Chi and Tai Chi, Yin and Yang, and expand to more complicated situation in a few steps. In a similar way, at times we may be in a mood to see that all human actions begin with the simple relationship of one person to another, and at other times marvel at the complexity and richness of our human social world, which seems unbounded.

The order of Yao in a hexagram is read from bottom to top. The image of this is the earth below with things growing up out of it to the sky. The simple order of Yao from the bottom is first, second, third, fourth, fifth, and top Yao. For each of these Yaos in a hexagram there is a text or judgment giving the meaning of the Yao.

We also use the odd number 9 to represent a Yang quality occupying a Yao and the even number 6 to represent a Yin quality occupying it.

A sample is shown in figure 1-51.

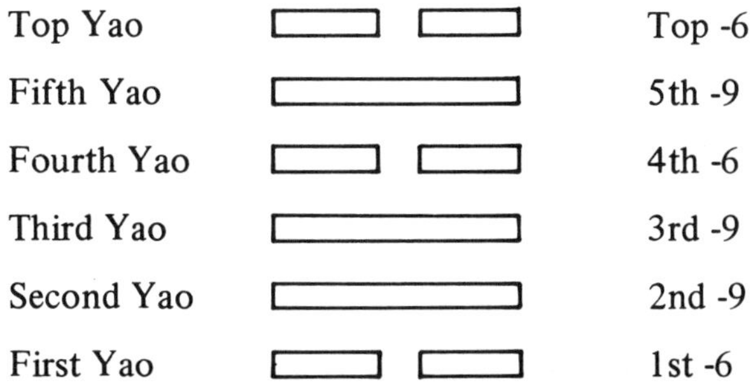

Top Yao	⬛ ⬛	Top -6
Fifth Yao	⬛	5th -9
Fourth Yao	⬛ ⬛	4th -6
Third Yao	⬛	3rd -9
Second Yao	⬛	2nd -9
First Yao	⬛ ⬛	1st -6

Figure 1-5e

The first and second Yao are the beginning stages, or an omen of an event or phenomena. The fifth and top Yao indicate its conclusion and fulfillment. These are the beginning and end of the six Yaos. Also, the inner trigram represents the past and the outer one the future. Their combination represents our present. We must keep in mind that the notions of past, present, and future are among the most complex and mysterious perceptions we have. We do not perceive the past and future in everyday life and experience, but a kind of continuous present that is perceived without a beginning or end. And yet, without notions of past and future, we could not organize our lives and the world in which we live. Further, we can easily imagine how the past affects the future, but how can the future change the past? Consider two men who have separately been working towards some goal for three years to date. Next year the work will be completed, and one man will fail completely, and the other will succeed. Next year one man will say, "That three years of work was a waste of time" and the other will say, "Those were the most productive three years of my life."

Yet right now the three years do not have meaning for either of the two men. We look at them and see that they are both the same. In this case, the future will give the past its meaning. In the same way, we find ourselves making experiments in living and later saying "that was stupid" or "that was smart." Yet, as we make these experiments in the present, we can only give them our best efforts without always knowing their meaning until some future time.

The positions of the Yao also represent the rank and social roles of people:

The first Yao represents all people as a mass (庶民).

The second Yao represents the scholar (士).
Today we might call them the technician, scientist, skilled worker.

The third Yao represents the official (士大夫).
Today we might say bureaucrat, politician, or administrator.

The fourth Yao represents the high ranking officer (公卿).
Today we might say cabinet minister, or presidential advisor.

The fifth Yao represents the King (天子).
Today we might say president, prime minister, or leader.

The sixth Yao represents the hermit of virtue and talent (賢人).
Today we might say the person of talent who has cultivated and realized it to the most advanced degree.

These positions were evolved before or during the Hsia Dynasty (2205-1766 B.C.).

It is important to note that God is not part of this series of ranks; it is a human summary. It is also very important to note that the top rank of human value is not the king or the person in power. It goes to the person who uses talents to good effect in life and culture. This is because a person can become "king" by fortune or birth, even if lacking merit as a person. Thus, the person who combines fortune with an active will and out of this reaches useful achievements is the most worthy. Throughout recorded history, kings tried to make one of their children king. The role was usually defined by heredity. However, if we go back to the earliest times, when the ordering and regulating of human society was just beginning and was much more difficult, we find the "king" or "leader" was chosen according to merit. And even today, while fortune and social status at birth determine the lives of most people, we still have the "self-made man" or woman who achieves success through merit only.

The six Yaos can also apply to the study of the human body: the first Yao, the feet; the second Yao, the calves; the third Yao, the waist and thighs; the fourth Yao, the abdomen; the fifth Yao, the chest; and the top Yao, the neck and head. This is illustrated in figure 1-5m.

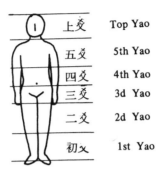

Figure 1-5m

Similarly, we may study the face using the Yaos: the first Yao, the jaw; the second Yao, the cheeks; the third Yao, the nose; the fourth Yao, the ears; the fifth Yao, the eyes; and the top Yao, the forehead. This is illustrated in figure 1-5n.

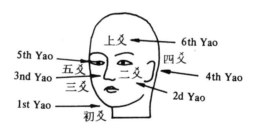

Figure 1-5n

We may wonder how this kind of study could possibly yield important knowledge of the human body or head. Without going into detail, we can say that the nature of our earth, with its gravity, must necessarily order the way the body is formed in a very complete way that extends to every detail of design and use. If this is so, then when we study this ordering, we will begin to find out fundamental things about the way the body and mind work. For a humorous example, if our head was on the ground and our legs in the air, our bodies would not work very well.

Chapter Two:

THE MIRACLE OF DIVINATION

2-1 The Rationale for Divination

Now we come to the following questions. Why do we divinate? How does it work? Why do we use six lines? Why is the time important?

We can begin to understand the answers to questions like these by reviewing the Tai Chi diagram and seeing how simply it can describe our world. First we have Wu Chi, no change; hen we have the Tai Chi Stage, where there is a little change. Since now we have changed and unchanged, we have duality, the two forms called the Liung Yi. If we want to describe our world this way, we can draw a line as in figure 2-1a.

Figure 2-1a

We can see on the line that from a point of origin there are two directions. We can call these plus and minus. By using these two forms, we can describe any place on the line in relation to its origin. We need one Yao to do this, and we can call our line one dimensional. Though we may rarely think of it this way, we frequently use one-dimensional thought. For example, in travelling from one town to another, we consider only one dimension. If we have a goal we are working towards, we picture a line from where we are to where the goal is and say things like "today I took a step backwards!" or "I am nearly there!".

If we take two of these lines and place them at right angles to each other, however, we begin to create a diagram that is more recognizable to us as the flat plane or Descartes Coordinants as shown in figure 2-1b.

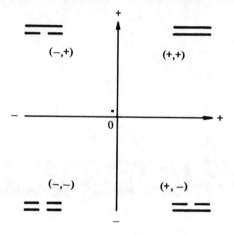

Figure 2-1b

If we examine this diagram closely, we can see how we now require two lines — call them length and width — to describe any place on the plane. With these two Yao, we can locate any point in relation to the origin at the center. Since each Yao can take a plus or minus, we have the four symbols we can see in the diagram. Even though we live in three dimensions, we often use two-dimensional maps to describe the surface of our earth, the floor plan of a house, and so on.

But now we add a third line at right angles to the first two lines, and we have three dimensions or space coordinants, with a Yao for each, as shown in figure 2-1c.

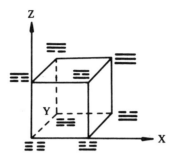

Figure 2-1c

We can see how this creates a division of all space into eight sections, and how the minus or plus of each X, Y, Z coordinante in each section will create a different trigram. If we use a sphere instead of a grid, we have another useful diagram: each segment is a triangle with three sides. We can analyze our spherical earth's surface with Yaos representing each side of the triangle as shown in figure 2-1d.

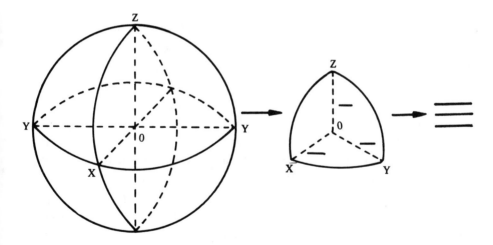

Figure 2-1d

We experience our world partly as space. Though a child may never think "it is all three dimensions" the moment it is explained to him in school, he understands. Why? Because it is the simplest description. If we try to use less, we fall short of describing space thoroughly. If we use more, then part of it is not needed and wastes our time.

Then we may ask, why six lines? The answer is that there is another aspect to our world that physical dimensions do not describe. We call it "time" and we also link it with mental and spiritual qualities. (See chapter Two, The Tao of meditation, Way to Enlightenment by Jou, Tsung Hwa, 1983.)

We might call this a fourth dimension. If we could be aware of all four dimensions then we would be in a godlike state, for the fourth dimension contains all past, present and future. But here we are stopped, for there is no place to add a fourth line to our diagram of space.

So we use our imagination and observation. What do we know about time? What do we know about the spiritual dimension? The answers that come to us are paradoxes. Time is with us constantly and part of everything we do, yet we have no idea how to describe it. Furthermore, all our space lines go forwards or backwards, but we see time only goes one way — past, present, future. Even more, we only occupy a tiny point on the time line, the present.

We find similar paradoxes when we try to look at the spiritual dimension. We are sure there are things, such as our soul, our spirit, our feelings, our will, that we cannot see, touch or hear in the physical world. Most of us can agree on the existence of phenomena. For example, the color yellow is yellow. However, in the spiritual dimension, we find agreements harder to reach, and perhaps only the poet or the mystic can say very much at all.

All of this creates a sense of mystery in life. Perhaps we are a little like shadows who are used to living on a two dimensional surface that is part of a three dimensional world. A child with a ball on a string drops it among the shadows. Its appearance is a complete mystery. The child pulls the ball away with the string. Its disappearance is likewise totally incomprehensible. We live and breathe and take our nourishment from a four dimensional world, yet we have only three dimensions with which to talk about it. Even if we make a clock to show time, it is like a reflection of the fourth dimension in the three dimensional world — if we take the hands of the clock and turn them backwards, time does not go back!

Yet, this does not close the issue. We all have links with this greater world in our everyday living. We have all had the kind of experience we first call "coincidence". Perhaps we are thinking of a friend, and just as the thought of him enters our mind, the phone rings and it's him.

We ponder someone we know in our work lives. Everything seems fine with them, yet somehow we think "something is happening"; even though there is no visible sign. Suddenly, we have a "brainstorm"; we snap our fingers and say, "I bet I know why she seems different. She's thinking of getting married." We look over the details and see nothing explicit. Yet we sense that there is a subtle change in her attitude and actions that shows this. We say "It is as if everything a person does and is appears in their everyday behaviour." We feel no surprise when she introduces her fiance to friends at the office the following week.

Or perhaps we have a spouse or an old friend we see frequently. Another old friend shows up and says "how is he?" And we find ourselves giving a detailled description of their explicit feelings and plans. Then we think, and realize, that he has never described any of these things fully to us in words. Yet, from a vague gesture, a tone of voice, a few words, we know everything.

If we cultivate our awareness of these "coincidences", we find them happening more and more just as anything we give our attention to seems to increase. Finally, we stop using the word "coincidence," and call it intuition.

And we think: "Well, I can't control it. It just happens." But then we think some more. We remember that when we became curious about it, it happened more often. So we do control it, indirectly, by nurturing it.

Perhaps then we remember our school biology class and how we learned that all living things evolve: first creatures with only a dim sense of energy and warmth, then something like a starfish that can sense light, then later a creature with eyes that focus and distinguish objects.

Perhaps we think if life in general evolves, then it must be true that we have the opportunity to evolve as individuals. We begin with our five senses and now and then these "coincidences" occur. If we cultivate them, we begin to evolve more of them. We remember how bright and complete our sense impression of the world looked when we were children, and, if we are sensitive, it still looks bright and complete. Somehow, however, our appreciation of its complexity is more intense as we grow older. We begin to sense that our body and spirit are not static.

Divination is one of the ways we cultivate ourselves in this way. It deals with a sense we may someday develop a sense that we may perceive directly, with control — provided that we are willing to endlessly and patiently follow the modest and humble methods of nurturing it in ourselves.

Whereas our three Yaos of space are explicit and definite, we must add something to them that recognizes the other perceptions we have of things we do not know how to describe so finally: time and the world of spirit. By adding a place for these to the Yaos, we will be focusing our attention upon the whole of our world when we divinate.

Why we are able to take yarrow sticks, coins, omens and time, and systematically derive a meaning from them, is a research area for a specialist. Now and then we read in a newspaper article how scientists discover that people have incredible powers under hypnotism, and so forth. This tells us that we truly do not know the true scope of our perceptions and actions. In the philosophy of the I Ching, we say that our living can be in harmony with all heaven and earth, and all our actions guided by them.

When we add our special Yaos to our ones for space, another line will not suffice, This fourth dimension we speak of has qualities that are not completely like the dimensional Yao, and we sense this. So we look back to the Liung Yi with its two forms, and we take time as a second form, and add not one Yao, but a set of three to match the first three.

Perhaps we may find other meanings to put into these three Yao if our understanding grows with time, but we begin quite simply by calling the first, past, the second, present, and the third, future. These represent our clearest simple understandings of time, and just as humanity is placed between heaven and earth, so our present comes between past and future, as shown in figure 2-1e.

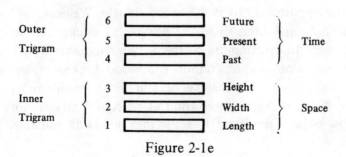

Figure 2-1e

We now have an empty "diagram" of six Yaos that describes our entire sense of our world. Sixty-four hexagrams can fit into this diagram, and only 64. One or the other will give us an exact and specific direction to look for understanding. Since this combination covers all events, we can examine situations in our life that are superficially unrelated, but are described by the same hexagram. Then we can do things like take a sure knowledge we have in one situation, and work at carrying it over into another with the assurance the knowledge will be equally workable there. By studying these 64, we are simultaneously studying our own lives in a thorough and systematic way.

Since our whole life is involved as we study the I Ching, our knowledge will increase slowly in many areas rather than rapidly in a few. For example, when we ask for a hexagram in divination, we are studying discernment. To extend this discernment in everyday life is a large area of study. Yet we must have the complement of discernment, which is to be able to act effectively and successfully with the information we gain. This, too, is a large area, and we study this using the structure of the hexagrams as a guide.

Sometimes we may study actively, by making the Hu Tien arrangement of trigrams to improve our understanding of the trigrams. At times we may guide ourselves through personal events of the greatest seriousness. At other times we may study with light-hearted zeal and imagine ourselves like the fictional detective Sherlock Holmes who could patiently ferret out the densest mysteries with only a few clues.

If we have great ambitions in either a specific or general area, the I Ching can guide us in our development. We should never limit ourselves by the accomplishments of a figure of the past. For they made the beginnings of a value that has evolved as it has come down to us in time. It is left to us to take it and develop it further.

Wherever we are in life, the I Ching can always show us that there is great opportunity open to us, and how to look for it. But to achieve real improvements in our life and enjoyment of it, we need to keep a basic approach firmly in mind — look for the answer by finding appropriate ways to correct our conduct or improve its quality. This carries over to the spirit of modesty in asking for guidance from heaven. It is a simple and easy approach that always works towards harmony. We may also consider this approach when we want to influence others —

instead of considering direct approaches or criticism, we ask ourselves how we may improve our conduct so the harmony of its example is hard to ignore. The effectiveness of this simple attitude and approach can only be understood when we actually try it for ourselves over a period of time and examine the results.

2-2 The Traditional Approach

Now we come to the actual rituals of divining with the I Ching. It should be remembered that a ritual is not a series of meaningless superstitions carried out without any sense of their meaning. It is a process that we can see in all human activity, even in something as informal as two people greeting each other. And it has the effect of focusing our attention on the importance and meaning of what we are doing.

The traditional rituals of divination are recommended even to the modern student. Where it is not practicable to follow them completely, we can evolve our own modern translation of the spirit of them. By doing this, we reap the benefits of following tradition wherever possible, and we also recognize that change is part of the tradition of the Book of Changes.

When we can, we set aside a room that is used exclusively for divination and study. If we do not do this, then perhaps we find a place that we can set up to use temporarily in this way. We store our physical tools of divination carefully, and bring them out when we divinate. We choose a time and situation where we will be undisturbed, away from noise and distraction.

On the wall, we hang a picture of Fu Hsi, King Wen, the Duke of Chou, Confucius and the Great Yu (大禹 , An ancient Chinese King who dug canals prevent flood.) See figure 2-2a.

We have a low, square table, large enough to accommodate our work. Behind this we have a smaller, long, narrow table for holding the incense burner and materials when not in use.

We have a bundle of 50 yarrow stalks, 15 to 20 inches long. In storage, these are wrapped in light red silk. The wrapped stalks are then put in a black silk bag. · Finally, this is put in a Tu (櫝), which is a cylinder made of bamboo or hardwood. It is about three inches in diameter and has a cover that fits over the top.

Figure 2-2a

The Tu is placed at the back of the square table, and in front of it we place two Sen Kua (聖筶). Sen Kua is a curved bamboo shell, about the size and shape of the cupped palm of a hand. In front of the Sen Kua we place an ancient Chinese jug, made of China or brass, to hold a stalk when we divinate. In front of the jug, we place an incense burner.

For recording our work, we use "the four treasures of a study room": a writing brush (筆), an inkslab (硯), an ink stick (墨), and writing papers. We have six Yao bars. A Yao bar is a wood plate a half inch thick and about one inch by ten inches. On one side we have carved in the bar, the sign of Yin (− −) in black. On the other side we have the sign of Yang (—) in red.

Before we begin our divination, we arrange these Yao on the table to form the hexagram Tai (地天泰), as shown in figure 2-2b.

All of these items comprise the tools of divination. Our large table should be set up in front of a window facing South. We now come to

Hexagram Tai

Figure 2-2b

the preparations and rituals. Here, there is no substitution or simplification — second best is not good enough! — for we are concerned with developing our inner attitude and its proper expression.

First, we purify ourselves in advance by observing rules of fasting and abstinence, and then by bathing. For example, we might rise in the morning, bathe, and then go to our divination without having any breakfast.

We burn incense and light candles as an outward sign of our sincerity in consulting the I Ching.

Now we consider our question. We divine to give ourselves a direction out of confusion. We consider our concerns quietly. If we find that we can see a clear way of acting and dealing with things, then we do not divine. We have already seen the answer in our inner selves directly. The purpose of divination is to cultivate this personal meditation and help it along only when it has foundered.

If we decide on divination, then we kneel on the ground which has a seat cushion and pray. The Chinese prayer is given here. We can make up a prayer in our own language that follows it spirit. "Heaven is silent and nature goes its hidden ways without words. Yet I believe this side of nature can be felt, and I believe that when I ask sincerely, heaven will communicate a reply to me. In this matter I am considering, I do not know what actions will bring good fortune or ill fortune. I do not see my way and I ask for guidance and clarity."

If we go on to make a divination and find we do not like it and forget it or do something else, then there is no point in divining at all. We are only following random impulses. If the divination is hard to accept, this only means our imagination has become narrowly caught up in a corner. We can correct this by looking at things with new and positive attitudes and freeing ourselves thereby to use our imagination effectively to carry things out.

After the prayer, we then throw the two Sen Kua upon the ground. If both come to rest face up or both face down, then it is not the right time. We then sit quietly and wait a while and throw again. Perhaps if they repeatedly say no, we conclude our ritual and come back another time. If one Sen Kua is up and the other down, then it is the time. We open the Tu and remove the yarrow stalks from the black bag and the red silk. We hold the 50 stalks in both hands and make a circle in the air above the incense.

We then draw one of the 50 stalks and place it in the jug. This act symbolizes the change from Wu Chi to Tai Chi. The one stalk represents the state of Tai Chi, the source of Yin and Yang and all the changes that come from it. We do not move this stalk until our divinations are completed. We then divide the remaining 49 stalks into two bundles. We do this not by counting, but by simply holding some stalks in the right hand and some in the left hand. We then lay the left hand bundle to the left of the jug and the right hand burndle to the right of the jug. These two piles represent the two symbols, or the Liung Yi. as shown in figure 2-2c.

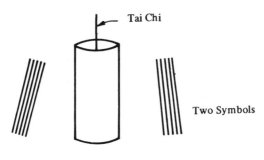

Figure 2-2c

Now draw one stalk from the right pile and place this between the little finger and the ring finger of the left hand. From the right pile we now take two stalks at a time till we have four piles of two stalks for a total of eight stalks. The two stalks represent the two forms, Yin and Yang. The four piles of two each represent the four symbols. The complete group of eight represents the eight trigrams.

After we have separated the first eight in this way, we repeat the procedure again making four piles of two for our total of eight. We do this until we have a remainder of from "zero" to "seven" stalks; not enough to make four piles of two. To this remainder we add one (for the stalk in our hand) and the total gives us the number of our inner trigram (from one to eight).

To find the trigram that corresponds to this number, we use the following cycle of trigrams:

1. ☰ Chien.   2. ☱ Tui.   3. ☲ Li.   4. ☳ Chen.

5. ☴ Sun.   6. ☵ Kan.   7. ☶ Ken.   8. ☷ Kun.

For example, if we have a remainder of 2 stalks and add the one stalk in our left hand, our number is "3". By consulting the cycle of trigrams we determine that our inner trigram is Li (☲).

We then arrange the three bottom Yao bars accordingly from the hexagram Tai on the table as shown in figure 2-2d.

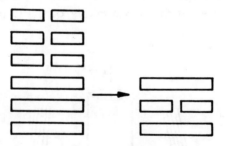

Figure 2-2d

Once we have our inner trigram, we pick up all 49 sticks and repeat the process. This time, however, we choose our sticks from the left-hand pile. After putting one stick from the left-hand pile between the little finger and the ring finger of the left hand, we start counting the sticks by twos, until we have made as many groups of eight (four piles of two each) as possible. Again, our remainder plus the stick in our hand will give us a number from one to eight. This number determines our outer trigram. For example, if our remainder is six, we add this to the one in our hand and our number is "7". We consult the cycle of trigrams and determine that our outer trigram is Ken (艮). We then arrange the three top Yaos accordingly as shown in figure 2-2e.

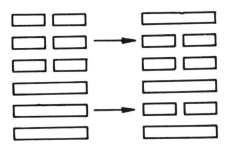

Figure 2-2e

We now have our hexagram. Pick up the 49 stalks a third time. Again we separate them and make two piles, one to the left and the other to the right of the jug. This time, choosing from the right pile, we count by twos again, but only arranging groups of six (three piles in each group). We make as many groups of six as possible, until we have a remainder of "zero" to "five". That number plus the one stick in our hand gives us the "moving Yao" or Pien Yao (變爻).

The Pien Yao tells us which Yao will change to its opposite. When the change is made, a new hexagram is formed, and this is called the Shih hexagram (之卦) of the original.

For example, if our remainder is "four" and we add the one in our hand, our Pien Yao is "5". Therefore, we change the fifth Yao in our hexagram as shown in figure 2-2f.

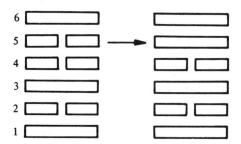

Figure 2-2f

We now have the two hexagrams that give us our divination. We have asked and nature has answered.

We may then use our writing materials to record the reading for our study. In studying the reading and considering its relation to us, we use the same quiet and serious approach we followed throughout the divination.

During the early Han Dynasty period of 206 B.C. to 24 A.D., Ching Wong (京房) brought into use another method of divination using three Chinese coins; as shown in figure 2-2g.

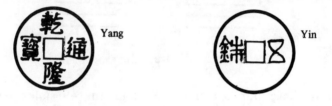

Figure 2-2g

In this method we use three Chinese coins or select other coins. Perhaps we use new coins or take our coins and clean and polish them to prepare them for their new use. The coins are placed in a cylindrical container with a tightly fitting cover. Its size is three to four inches in diameter and four to six inches high. Again we follow the same ritual but instead of picking up the Tu, we pick up the container of coins. To read, we shake the container and pour out the coins. We interpret the coins as follows:

Two tails are called Che (拆), write down " 、 ", meaning Yang

Two heads are called Tau (單), write " ㄟ ", meaning Yin

Three heads are called Chiao (交), write " × ", meaning old Yin moving to Yang

Three tails are called Chung (重), write "○", meaning old Yang moving to Yin

The first throw determines the first Yao, and so on. For example:

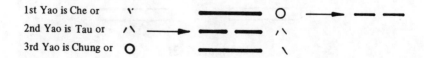

After three throws, we have our inner trigram, and we stop and repeat our prayer. Then we complete the outer trigram and study.

We can see that this method can sometimes give us only one hexagram to study with no Pien Yao, and sometimes it can give us two hexagrams with up to all six Yaos changing. Generally, we receive a result that is much more complex and requires more careful thought and study than the reading from the stalks.

The most highly advanced students of the I Ching would extend this classical divination by using added indicators of divination called the Ten Celestial Stems (天干), the Twelve Earth Branches (地支), and the Five Elements (五行). These involve the use of calendars, months and days of the year, and still other factors. Knowledge of these methods is relatively rare, even among the Chinese people. It is comparable to high level calculus contrasted with simple arithmetic. Since we can answer our questions a simpler way, we do not use a more complicated one. These advanced forms, however, do show us how the derivation of a reading from the Tai Chi sphere can be carried to any degree of complexity.

2-3 The Master-key to Sound Judgment

Now we come to how we judge the meaning of our divination in relation to the question we asked. For this, we begin with the Kwa Tsi of King Wen and the Yao Tsi of the Duke of Chou.

These works are like sketches or outlines of a drama, rather than a detailed explanation. This kind of sketchy outline is actually very common in our lives. However, we may forget that we have been learning all our lives to read these "sketches". For example, turn on the TV and we hear the newscaster summarize: "Youth rescues drowning swimmer." Immediately we know a lot about the story. We come to the office and see the boss's wife glaring at the pretty new secretary. No one needs to tell us what is happening. We look across the street and see two men facing each other with rigid postures, one with his fist raised, and we know what we are seeing. Every day we pass through many situations where a glance at things tells us "something is happening" and where we read enough of the meaning to satisfy our needs − or perhaps we don't read the situation correctly and find we get into trouble as a result.

In fact, when we look at our troubles, we may often find that they come from our not being alert and reading the signs carefully. Divination with the I Ching teaches us to do this in a thorough and systematic way. Since it speaks of the future, it also teaches us to use our imagination to prepare ourselves effectively.

To illustrate this, let us look at the process of divination. We will call the hexagram we divine the Pen Kua (本卦), which means "original hexagram." We will use the first hexagram, Chien, as an example:

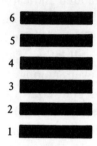

From our Kwa Tsi we know that Chien is creativity or heaven. Its image is six dragons that govern the heavens. Its symbol is the all-inclusive. Then we go to the Yao Tsi and observe the reading for the changing Yao. If the first line is the changing Yao, we read "The dragon is lying under the water." We know the dragon is active in the sky, and it is easy to interpret "here at the beginning, the time is not good for any activity." So we will wait alertly, like the cat watching for a mouse, until we see signs that things are opening up for us.

If the second Yao were changing instead of the first, we would read "The dragon is in the field. The time is good to have a meeting with an influential person." Then we know that the whole situation is good and it is time to become active.

Our interpretations must stay close to what is suggested, yet also apply to our situation. If we are looking for a job, it is easy to see with the second Yao that it is time to go out for job interviews. But suppose we have a personal creative project where we work totally alone. Who is the influential person? Here, that "person" is our own sense of inner creativity — a quality that we have excellent acess to at some times, and at other times do not. This is just like an influential person who may or may not be receptive to what we want.

We can see from these two Yaos how a slight change creates a totally different situation for us.   Once we have our hexagram and changing Yao, our stage is set for the drama to unfold.

Every situation has a beginning, a middle where everything is active, and finally a conclusion.   To find the active middle, we create a new hexagram called the Hu Kua (互卦). We literally take our old hexagram apart, using the lines two, three and four for our lower trigram, and the lines three, four and five for our upper trigram as shown in picture 2-3a.

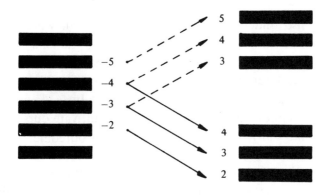

Figure 2-3a

Since the Hu Kua is made by taking the four inner lines of the Pen Kua and expanding them, there can only be sixteen different Hu Kua which is the total number of combinations possible using those four lines.   The Hu Kua is important if we consider that the third and fourth lines of the Pen Kua are for humanity, and they are expanded to form four of the six lines of the Hu Kua.   The Yin-Yang of the second and third Yaos of the Hu Kua is the same as the Yin-Yang of the fourth and fifth Yaos, since both correspond to lines three and four of the Pen Kua or original hexagram.

With the Hu Kua that we derive from Chien, we have an unusual situation — the Hu Kua is the same as the Pen Kua.   This is very good in general, but very poor for asking about health conditions.

The Hu Kua may suggest an "inner situation" that is much different from the clearly described beginning.   This is like when one sees a clearly defined situation, decides to get involved with it, and the moment one becomes involved, everything shifts around and is changed. This is because one has entered the situation and added something new to it.

Here in the middle we follow the suggestions of the Hu Kua. But we must also keep in mind that it is a transitional stage. For example it may be a poor hexagram — yet the rest of the divination tells us the overall reading is good. Then we know we should be patient and not "throw away our chance." Perhaps we begin our day and feel our opening plans collapse, and we think the day will accomplish little, but we work along, and then in the evening we look back and realize that somehow things "cleared up" and we did quite well because we persevered.

We can also understand the opposite situation, where all seems to be going well in the middle, then we find at the end all sorts of reverses. This is like a Hu Kua that is good while the final part of the divination is poor. Since we know this, we do not lose even more by being shocked and taken aback when the fortunes change. Instead, we "make hay while the sun shines" and use the middle to cultivate ourselves in a long range way that will not be limited by the poor outcome. And when the fortunes do become poor, we relax our positive efforts quickly, and adapt ourselves to the wisest way of handling the difficulties. In this way we may do better with a poor fortune than someone with a much better fortune who wastes most of it through carelessness or intemperate feelings.

We find our final stage of the divination by using the moving Yao to generate a new hexagram, which we call the Shih Kua (之卦). We arrange all three hexagrams in order, as shown in figure 2-3b.

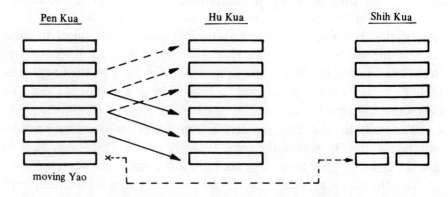

Figure 2-3b

With these three hexagrams we have a complete reading, and we can interpret it by referring to the judgments for each hexagram and for the moving Yao. But there are other methods of Taoist thought we can add to the divination to give greater understanding and detail.

To begin with, we can study a unique principle of interrelationship called the Five Elements. The Five Elements diagrammed below were described by the Chinese Naturalist School over 2,000 years ago. They were called the Wu Hsing (五行) and were not looked on in their passive roles, but rather in the dynamic processes that each one involved.

Thus water is observed as having properties of soaking and descending. Fire heats and moves upward. Wood shapes physical masses in curved and straight forms. Metal can be put in molds as a liquid and then hardens. Earth nurtures the sowing and reaping of plant life, and provides a ground for all.

The Five Elements may be used to classify active phenomena just as we use the eight trigrams to classify all things in our divination. They have also been used to symbolize the active energies in a complex, interrelated system. For example, in Chinese medicine, the five element model describes the interrelations of different organs and parts of the body, showing how a weakness or excess in one organ can cause illness and disruption in an entirely different place. The use of the Five Elements to describe something as complex as a living person should remind us always that the diagrams represent an organized but constantly fluctuating system. We can begin to gain a modest understanding of such a system by studying the four major principles involved as shown in figure 2-3c.

These four processes are summarized by the arrows in the diagram. In the principle of Mutual Creation (相生), one element serves to nurture and sustain the adjoining element in the clockwise circle. We can see how wood nurtures fire, and fire creates new earth with ashes; how earth is the source of metals, and how metal brings dew in the form of condensed droplets of water − these simple examples can help as memorize the relations of Mutual Creation, which we call Sheng (生).

To complement Mutual Creation, we have the principle of Mutual Closeness (相親). Here we are saying that an elements becomes close to the one that sustains it in much the same way as a child becomes close to its mother.

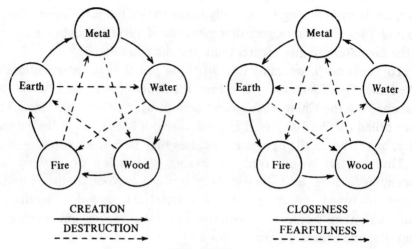

Figure 2-3c

The principle of Mutual Destruction or Ke (尅) describes how one element limits, controls, or completely destroys the process of another. For this we can imagine how water destroys fire, how wood grows and its roots split apart earth, how fire by its heat melts metal, how earth in dams halts water from flowing, and how metal axes cut wood. The complement to Mutual Destruction is the principle of Mutual Fearfulness (相懼) or respect.

When we study real life examples, we must imagine a variety of possible meanings for Ke or destruction and for Sheng or creation and choose an appropriate one. By considering practical examples and using our imagination, we can slowly develop an understanding.

Ke, for example, can be complete destruction. It can also be milder and represent one person who blocks another but does not destroy them. It can be milder still and represent a person who can inhibit another's behaviour, yet in a good way like the mother who applies Ke to her child to prevent him from wandering into the public road where he will meet a much worse Ke.

Her motivation is Sheng, love and protectiveness. Yet this actual act is not Sheng. If you think it is, just look at the child, who is crying and angry at being baulked. He is showing the principle of Fearfulness.

Suppose in divination you find that a specific person has the power of Ke over you in part of the situation. What kind of Ke is this?

You will not find the answer in the divination, because you already have it in yourself. You know what the person is like, and what they are likely to do when they have power over you, from actual experience.

To apply the Five Elements in this way to our divination we add another principle of relationships, that we call Ti and Yung. To understand what Ti and Yung are, we need only consider a few examples.

In general, the bottom, inner trigram, is identified as having the quality Ti (體) and the upper, outer trigram, that of Yung (用). We can begin to have an understanding of these terms by considering a few examples.

Consider a framework of steel with a motor, wheels, steering device, and other controls — an auto chassis. This is Ti.

We can put various bodies on this chassis; one body and it becomes an armored tank, another body and it is an ambulance, another and it is a racy sports car, another and it is a sedate family station wagon. This is the Yung of the auto chassis.

By comparing these two qualities, we notice that the Ti part is always relatively simple, and that the Yung can be multiple and complex.

Another example: Ti is what we have at birth or natural, Yung is what we have now or man-made. This Yung came from the culture we live in and also from our free actions and the habits we built out of them. We all begin with about the same simple Ti; we all have a very different Yung. (See the Tao of Meditation by Jou, Tsung Hwa, 1983)

Ti obviously makes Yung possible, but Yung affects Ti, as well. If the auto chassis must hold a tank, we strengthen the frame; if it must hold a sports car, we use light aircraft metals. One way to look at this is to see Ti as the leading role in a drama, and Yung as all the supporting roles. Without a Ti, the Yung loses most of its meaning and focus. Yet the actions of the Yung determine what directions the Ti goes in as it leads the drama and the development of the plot.

Ti and Yung used in another way become very important in divination, because they may or may not harmonize, as we can see in the following examples:

Ti	Yung	Relationship
Water	Fish	Good
Water	Fire	Conflict
Water	Drinking Glass	Appropriate
Water	Sewage Line	Complements

We may say in a literal way, "But the water goes in the glass, so why isn't the glass Ti?" This is true. But when we consider the situation more thoroughly, we see that water came first, and the glass is part of the Yung that surrounds the water. If we want to study glasses, we can make the glass Ti, and have water, wine, and other substances as its Yung.

When we apply Ti and Yung to our six trigram divination, in organizes all the forces into two parts. To do this, we select one of the trigrams of the first Pen Kua or the original hexagram, to be Ti.

When there are no moving Yao, the inner trigram is always Ti. When there are an equal number of moving Yao in each trigram, the inner trigram is again Ti shown in figure 2-3d.

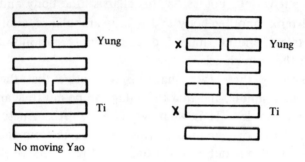

Figure 2-3d

When one of the trigrams has more moving Yao than the other trigram, we select the quietest trigram as shown in figure 2-3e.

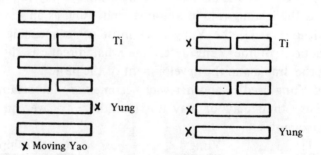

Figure 2-3e

The Ti Kua is the leading force in our divination. It is us, if we are concerned in the divination, or is the major group or person if we consider something outside our personal concern.

Once we have our Ti Kua, we label all the other trigrams as Yung Kua as in figure 2-3f.

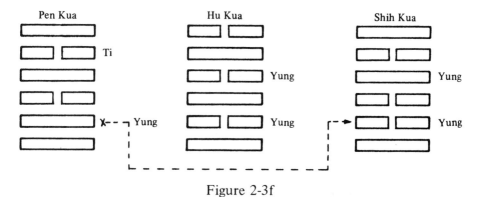

Figure 2-3f

Look at the diagram. The Ti of Li is repeated in the Shih Kua outer trigram of Li. This will always happen, in a one moving Yao divination.

Look again. We see the four other Yung — Li, Kan, Chen, and Li -- are not all different.

We use this comparison for a sign of relative strength of the Ti and Yung forces. Ti has two friends in the Yung of Li. The Yung of Tui has no similar friend. We think of it as having lesser force — that the repetition of a trigram builds up an energy.

If the 5 Yung trigrams were 2 or more of them Tui, we would say the Yung is more forceful than the Ti.

This comparison is useful, but we are going to take it much further by adding the Five Elements. To do this we take the eight trigrams and assign each one to one of the elements as shown in figure 2-3g.

Now we have the eight trigrams dynamically interrelated. First of all there are the ones that are paired with the same element — Kun and Ken, Sun and Chen, Chien and Tui. We think of these as like twins. Each has its own personality, but they go together.

We can see another example with its Ti and Yung and ask the question: Does the Ti have any 'friends' like this? How about the Yung? Here is the answer, you will note we label each trigram by its Five Element position as shown in figure 2-3h.

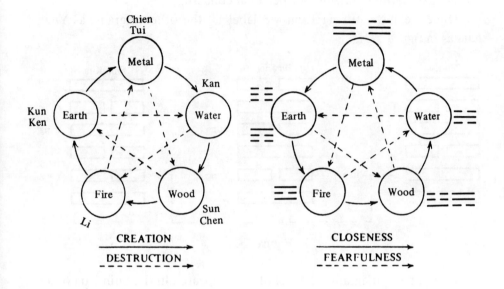

Figure 2-3g

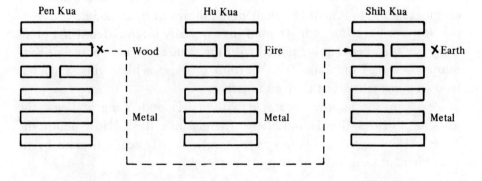

Figure 2-3h

We immediately see that Ti does have friends, and that metal forms a group of three elements. Yung does not combine because there are no common elements. So the Ti is stronger than the Yung.

But we have still another principle coming from our Five Elements Relationships — the Metal Ti destroys the Wood Yung!

This is the relationship of Mutual Destruction, or Ke. We will indicate it by drawing a line -   ·.

When we want to indiate the relationship of Mutual Creation or Sheng, we will draw the line ⁻ ⸱> .

In interpreting these relationships, we consider the following: if the Ti Ke or destroy the Yung, this is good. If the Yung Ke the Ti, this is poor. This simply means that if the Ti finds some influence detracts from its goal, it can remove or neutralize it. If the TV set in the next room is distracting you from your studies, you can shut the door. You Ke the TV set. But if you have no control, if someone can come into the room where you are studying, and turn on a TV set, this is poor.

In terms of Sheng or creation, if the Yung Sheng the Ti, this is good. If the Ti Sheng the Yung, this is poor. Thus if you have helpers available to assist you in your projects, this is certainly good. Suppose instead that, you have obligations to help various other people, and they can call on you and distract you from working on your goals.

Now we may go back to the above example once more, and this time we can see these Ke and Sheng lines added in figure 2-3i.

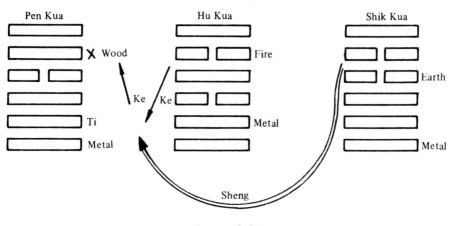

Figure 2-3i

Now we have an entire drama! Pen Kua, Hu Kua, Shih Kua, all have something going on in relation to the Ti.

Not all divinations invoke this special relationship in the Pen Kua, and we can find by simple inspection of the question divinated whether it applies.

Let us assume it applies in the case above, and summarize what our different methods tell us:

1. The Ti is much stronger than the Yung.

2. Pen Kua. Good. The Ti Ke the Yung.

3. Hu Kua, Poor, but not a guaranteed disaster. The Yung Ke the Ti, but the Ti is much stronger, so it has a chance to survive.

4. Shih Kua. Good. The Yung of earth supports the Ti of metal.

All's well that ends well.

Now we can see how to relate the Ti Kua to the different Yung Kua. If the Ti Kua is fire and the Yung Kua is wood, then the Yung Kua creates or sustains the Ti Kua. This is like a person who wants to organize a project, and who finds others ready to support and carry out its purposes. In this situation, the Ti Kua feels a closeness or affection towards Yung Kua.

If the Yung Kua is fire, however, and the Ti Kua is wood, this shows things going the wrong way. It is like giving a knife to an evil man, or like an employer delegating power to an assistant who uses it to benefit himself while he lets the business go to ruin. We note here that the Yung Kua is attracted to the Ti Kua. However, it is like a fox attracted to a farmer's chickens.

If the Ti Kua is fire and the Yung Kua is metal, the Ti Kua controls the Yung Kua. The Yung Kua is like an employee working cooperatively because he knows he can be demoted. Or the Yung Kua can be like a student who is so impressed by the force and energy of his teacher that he respects him highly and pays attention to his teaching.

If these roles are reversed, then the Ti Kua becomes like a man who sets out to ride a horse, and the horse throws him to the ground. We have the influences going in the wrong direction, and whatever the Ti Kua is seeking to accomplish the Yung Kua is weakening and working against.

Since in specific cases a varied set of elements and trigrams are involved, we can apply a great deal of specific detail.

In addition, we may have a combination of good and poor factors. Since they come at different times, we can study how to change with the times. In each case we apply the knowledge to our specific case.

If we plan to start a business and the divination says "very poor at the start, good later on" and we have almost no reserve to start out with, this means we may fail completely at the start and never get to the point of "later on."

If divination shows a poor situation, the details show us exactly what to look out for. If divination shows a very strong situation, we know that success will come to us if we are reasonable. Our success, however, can be spoiled if our conduct is poor. A person given authority over others may be carelessly rude and unfair to them and create a new situation that turns against him. Likewise, if we are offered a strong situation but are too timid to exercise our influence, we will lose it just as surely as if we were overbearing.

But if these things are so, we may ask: "What good is it to have a favorable divination if we feel unequal to carry it out?" We must reflect that if we have weaknesses we also have a potential to correct them. A good divination indicates a time when we may begin to work on these corrections and make something real of them. If we do this over and over again, we will change, and evolve to something better.

We can go back to our Chien reading to see as another example as shown in figure 2-3j.

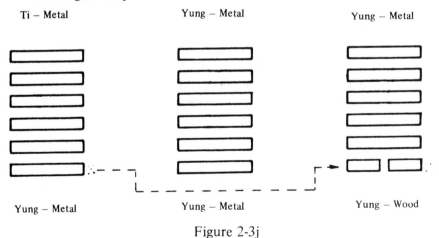

Ti – Metal   Yung – Metal   Yung – Metal

Yung – Metal   Yung – Metal   Yung – Wood

Figure 2-3j

To begin with, the Ti of metal has four other Yungs like it, giving it great strength. In the last trigram, metal controls wood. Thus our overall divination is a favourable one. Here is another example as in figure 2-3k.

We see here the end result is that our Ti of metal is controlled by a Yung of fire. But the Ti has four identical Chiens, making it powerful. With

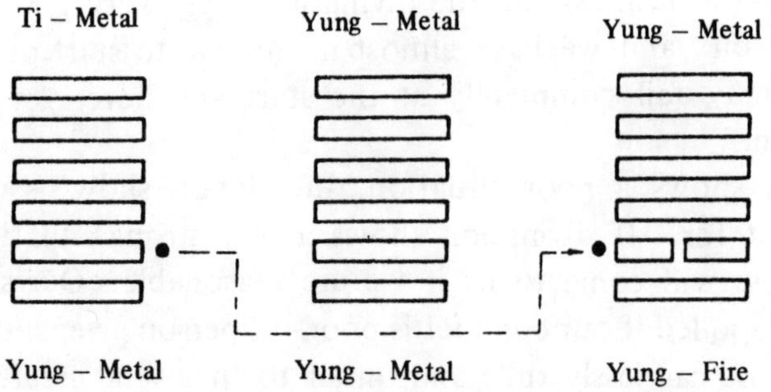

Figure 2-3k

the fire antagonistic and the Chiens very strong, we can predict the likelihood of a battle, with a outcome that can go either way. It is like being in a group of people where almost everyone approves of you except for one very powerful individual who opposes you.

Using this form of divination with imagination can keep us learning new things about how to approach our living for a long time. But with this form, we are working with the final results of work derived by the developers of the I Ching. At some time we will be prepared to undertake a study of how the meanings of the hexagrams and the moving Yao were derived. This is a complex and arduous study, yet its rules are simple and we should know them.

In divination, we use the principle position of a Yao, or "Cheng Wei" (正位). To determine the principle position, we first designate the odd numbers as Yang and the even numbers as Yin. Thus, the 1, 3, or 5 Yaos prefer Yang, and when these are occupied by a Yang line, this is a principle position and means good fortune. When the 1, 3, or 5 Yao is not occupied by a Yang line, it suggests poor fortune. It is the same with the Yin Yaos, the second, fourth, and sixth Yaos. If one of these Yaos is occupied by a Yin line, it is a principle position. We can see this in figure 2-3l:

6.	Yin Yao	▬▬▬	Yang	⟶	Poor	——	Top
5.	Yang Yao	▬▬▬	Yang	⟶	Good	——	5th
4.	Yin Yao	▬ ▬	Yin	⟶	Good	——	4th
3.	Yang Yao	▬▬▬	Yang	⟶	Good	——	3rd
2.	Yin yao	▬▬▬	Yang	⟶	Poor	——	2nd
1.	Yang Yao	▬ ▬	Yin	⟶	Poor	——	1st

Figure 2-3 L

If we look at the above list at the left of the Yaos we find that the first line in the inner trigram is Yang (1) and the first line in the outer is Yin (4), and that this contrast continues with the second line, Yin and Yang (2 and 5), and the third line, Yang and Yin (3 and 6). These contrasts are like electricity, and when they match in an actual hexagram thier mutual attraction indicates good energy. The matching is called Hsiang Yin (相應). In the example A below as shown in figure 2-3m the second Yao is a Yin Yao and the fifth Yao is a Yang Yao. Both are in principle position and match. This is Hsiang Yin. In example B, the Hsiang Yin occurs with the third Yao (Yang) matching the sixth Yao (Yin). Both of these Yaos are in the principle position.

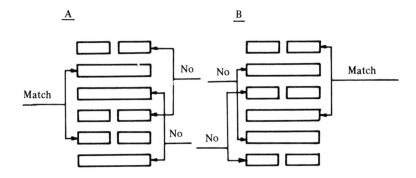

Figure 2-3m

The Middle Position. The second and fifth Yaos occupy the middle positions of the two trigrams. If the line filling them is the principle one and if they match, this indicates very good fortune. Matching and nonmatching examples are given in figure 2-3n.

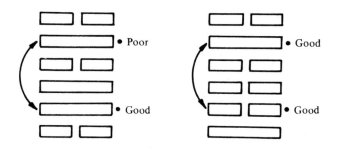

Figure 2-3n

If we think of the three powers (earth, humanity, and heaven) we see immediately why this is so. The second and fifth lines are the lines of humanity for the two trigrams, so they are the most important ones for us. Confucius' major work in philosophy was to develop what we call a 'philosophy of the mean', meaning the middle, the place midway between the two extremes of heaven and earth. As you can see, the I Ching is not a formula that gives simple solutions. We must relate what the trigrams tell us to our own situation. For example, if a trigram has a Yang line in the second Yao and a Yin line in the fifth Yao, we would have a situation where neither Yao is in the principle position, but the two Yaos match together. We must think about how this relates to us. We must decide what is good or bad for us. The situation could be compared to the dilemma of a person who has the opportunity to pursue two occupations. He could be a musician because he enjoys music very much. This is good. He could also work for a large company and make a lot of money. This is also good. The person must decide what is best for himself or herself. Likewise, when consulting the I Ching, we must interpret what it tells us.

We can understand better why these kinds of comparisons are made by referring to the Treatise of Remarks on the Trigrams, or Shuo Kua (少康):

> When the ancient sages designed the *I*, its figures conformed with the principles underlying the nature of men and things, and the ordinances appointed for them by Heaven. They exhibited the way of Heaven, calling the lines Yin and Yang; the way of earth, the weak (soft) and strong (hard); and the way of men, benevolence and righteousness. Each trigram embraced those three powers, and, being repeated, the full form consisted of six lines. A distinction was made between the Yin and Yang lines, which were variously occupied by the strong and weak forms. Thus the figure of each hexagram was completed.

The six Yaos indicate the six stages necessary for the development of phenomenon. According to the traditional commentaries on the I Ching,

> The Yao speaks of the changes.
> The lines of Yao correspond to the movements taking place on earth.
> In the trigrams, these lines are in high and low postions, and we designate them from their component elements, Yang or Yin.
> The lines are mixed together and elegant forms arise. When such forms

are not in their appropriate places, the ideas of good and bad fortune are produced.

We can see by now why the moving Yao is so important. It changes the principle position and the matching lines. We might have a situation that was difficult, but the earth lines of the two trigrams matched, and now the moving Yao destroys the difficult situation.

Or perhaps instead of a complex divination we have taken one hexagram, with one trigram to represent us and the other some person we are concerned with. As we study the two trigrams, we may get a picture of the relationship and its conflicts and strong points. Then we add a moving Yao, and see immediately how a change in our circumstances or the other person's circumstances, creates an entirely new situation that may be better or poorer. This might be like the couple where the husband gets a new job that involves travelling a lot, and the marriage begins to disintegrate. Or it could be like a couple that is always quarreling and ready to break up, and then they move to a new apartment, and now they are happy and in accord again.

A simple divination requires a much deeper understanding and intuition, and this may suit some of us better than the three part divination. All of us should study it, for at times it will be easier, at times the other more appropriate. And at times, we may find no clear indication we can understand in a three part divination, and then analyze the lines, and see exactly the understanding we are looking for.

The more detail we know about possible paths of divination, the more freedom we have to select a method that fits our subject. Personal emotions, many kinds of business activity, and countless other things in our lives are affected by the seasons, and we can include this factor in our divination.

To do this, we only need to refer to the material on the eight trigrams and see how the Hu Tien cycle is applied to the seasons – the period from March to June, for example is ruled first by Chen and then by Sun, so these are the trigrams for spring.

We can use this to evaluate our Ti Kua and Yung Kua as strong or poor.

Spring is wood. Wood Ke or destroys earth, which is Ken in the winter, and Kun in the early fall. One is already in the past, the other too far in the future to be relevant. If our Ti is wood, and the dominant

Yung is earth, we see that the meaning of these two trigrams either adds to or detracts from the basic divination.

Wood Sheng or creates Li, however, which is fire. This is the month of June, just following. If our Ti is Li, we know this means good things are coming.

We can also test and improve our divination skill by asking the weather, and taking the Ti to indicate it.

For example, if the Ti is:

Chen or   ☳   indicates possible thunder, sudden change;

Sun or   ☴   indicates wind;

Kan or   ☵   indicates rain, wet weather; and

Li or   ☲   indicates sunny weather, etc.

If we consult the I Ching about the weather and get a 44th hexagram Gōu or meeting, Ti Kau is ⟍‗⟍, or thunder

$$\text{Ti} \quad \overline{\overline{\equiv}} \quad \begin{matrix} \text{metal} \\ \text{wood} \end{matrix} \Bigg) \text{Ke}$$

Because Chien, or metal Ke or destroy the Chen or wood, we suspect there will be no thunder.

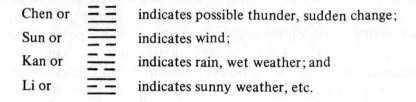

2-4 The Plum Flower Mind I Ching

During the Sung Dynasty (宋朝 960-1279) there lived a government official named Shao, Kang Chieh (邵康節 1011-1077) who began to study the I Ching. So interested did he become in this subject, that he resented his bureaucratic duties because they prevented him from spending all of his time studying the I Ching.

Determined not to be frustrated, Shao finally succeded in obtaining an early retirement from his career on the grounds of poor health, even though his health was excellent. He could now devote all of his time to his studies.

His study of the I Ching became so intense that he did not pay attention to his household responsibilities. When the weather turned cold, he did not even gather firewood to warm his home. As far as Shao was concerned, his normal duties took too much time. He devoted all his time to his continuing study of the I Ching.

He copied all the hexagrams on large cards and placed them on the walls of his home so that they were available for inspection at all times. He made placards with the words to the judgments of each hexagram and placed them on the walls next to the hexagrams.

But no matter how hard and passionately Shao worked to master the wisdom of life through the I Ching, he made very little progress in understanding or achievement.

One day, after working to the point of exhaustion, Shao lay down for a mid-day nap. He was awakened by an unsual sound and saw a large moth fluttering around the cards he had placed on the walls. Angrily, he hurled his pillow at the moth.

However, people at that time used to sleep on pillows made of china because they were cool in hot weather. Shao had forgotten this, and his pillow crashed against the wall. Shao looked at the broken pieces and, to his surprise, found a slip of paper with writing on it that had evidently been hidden inside the pillow. He read the writing on the slip: "In the year 1050 on April 10 in the afternoon this pillow will be destroyed by its being thrown at a moth."

Shao looked at the time. It was the exact date and time written on the slip of paper which had been hidden in the pillow for years. He became very excited and thought to himself, maybe everything has a date! A man is born on a certain date and dies on a certain date, and this is the cycle of his life. A person begins a job on a certain date and retires on a certain date, and this is the cycle of his career. A building is constructed at a certain time in history and at some time in the future is destroyed. It too has a cycle of existence. And even this pillow had a life cycle. It was made on a certain date and just now, on this date, it was destroyed.

Shao quickly realized that this life cycle formula could be applied to every aspect of reality. Every person and thing had a definite date of beginning and a definite date of ending. And, Shao reasoned, if he could learn a method to discover this formula, he could predict the life cycle of anything in the world, as well as all the events of any person's life.

The whole experience seemed like a dream to Shao, but the paper and its message was real. He decided to visit the store where the pillow was purchased, and brought the broken pieces with him. The storekeeper sent him to the wholesaler of pillows, who sent him to the china maker who made the pillow.

At first, the china maker was of no help. He explained that none of his workers could have put the note inside the pillow because none of them could write. At that time in China, only the higher classes were literate. Then the china maker recalled, "There was an old man who was retired and used to come and watch us work. He is very educated and even knows the I Ching. Everyone knows of him. Maybe he put the paper in the pillow."

Feeling he was close to solving the mystery, Shao hurried to the old man's home. He knocked on the door and was greeted by a young man. When Shao gave the name of the old man, the young man replied, "That's my grandfather. He died several years ago."

Shao's hopes were dashed to pieces. However, the young man continued to speak and Shao's hopes were revived. "Before my grandfather died, he gave me a book and told me that on a certain day, month, and year, at a certain time, a person will come to visit, and I should give him that book. It is now that exact time. I am astonished. Wait, and I will get the book for you."

Before his death, the old man had spent many years researching and studying the I Ching. The results of his long study were written in the book. He wanted to pass along this information to someone who was prepared to receive it, and who was devoted to further study. Shao was that person.

Shao took his treasure home and resumed his studies, day and night. He had found the master-key to understanding, and gradually his spiritual enlightenment grew and became complete.

The book contained a method for divination that was more accurate than the traditional yarrow stalks. The new method translated the year, month, day, and time of an event into numbers and then used the numbers to indicate the hexagrams. This new method gave Shao new insight into the concepts of space and time.

The results Shao received using this method were perfectly accurate. In his first judgment, he received the message: there is some gold hidden in the old man's house. Shao went there, and with the grandson, dug out the ground beneath the old man's bed. There they found the gold.

The book Shao received from the young man is called MEI HUA SIN I or The PLUM FLOWER MIND I CHING (梅花心易). It is the source of my book. In studying and using these new methods of divination, we will not just read the written words of the judgments and images. We will study the figures of the trigrams and learn to understand then more directly.

The old man left two methods of divination to Shao, Kang Chieh. He used both methods to reach a mastery of the I Ching. One of the methods is called Hsien Tien (先天), and the other Hu Tien (後天), after the two arrangements of the trigrams in cycles. Tien means Heaven, and the word Hsien refers to our heritage from the past as it affects our present and future. Our genetic make-up and the health and habits of our mother as she carried us before birth, are Hsien Tien.

Divination by the Hsien Tien method is very simple. We get the outer trigram by adding together the year, month, and day of the month, then dividing this number by eight. The remainder will be from one to seven, and if we have no remainder, we count this as eight.

We then use the Hsien Tien numeration of the cycle to assign a trigram: 1 – Chien; 2 – Tui; 3 – Li; 4 – Chen; 5 – Sun; 6 – Kan; 7 – Ken; 8 – Kun.

To find the inner trigram, we add the number of the year, month, day, and the hour. Again we divide by 8 and take the remainder to select the trigram. We number the hours of the day from one to twenty-four for the number of the hour. Thus 10 a.m. is ten; 3 p.m. is 15; and so on. If our clock shows an hour between two hours, such as 10:30, we say this time "covers" the 10 o'clock and count it as 10.

To find the moving Yao, we again use the year, month, day and hour, and this time divide by six. We get a remainder from one to five, or use six if there is no remainder.

But we must assign a number to our year before we can do this. In the traditional Chinese calendar, the years were ordered and named by combining two cycles of time periods called the Ten Celestial Stems or Tien Kan (天干), and the Twelve Terrestrial Branches or Ti Chih (地支). A complex method of derivation was used that is nowadays relatively unknown even to the Chinese. We can think of it in this way: the list of stems was placed with the list of branches to get a set of combinations. Doing this left a remainder of the last two branches, and these were used to start another cycle in the list. When the listing was completed, the combinations numbered 60, and the years were named according to which combination they represented.

In using the spirit of this method in our present-day divinations, we will divide the Western numeration of the year by the number 12. Thus 1,982 divided by twelve gives 165 with a remainder of two. We give 1982 the number 2. We derive any years similarly. We always get a remainder of from 1 to 11, and if there is no remainder we call this 12.

For our month, we count it as the number it follows in the cycle of the year. For example, October is 10. And for our day, we simply take the number of the day of the month.

In divination, we use the time we make the divination. But with careful thought we may use a time that marks the beginning of a subject. We might use the date of our birth, and derive a hexagram that charactarizes our life as a whole. We might take the time we signed the papers for our new house to divine the future surrounding it.

For a specific example of the Hsien Tien method we will consider a date, say April 19th, 1982, at 10:20 a.m.:

> The Year 1982   – – – –2
> The Month April   – – – –4
> The 19th Day   – – –19
>
> Total   25
>
> Divided by 8 = 3 with remainder 1
> 1 equals ☰ Chien, the outer trigram

> The Year 1982   –.– – –2
> The Month April   – – – –4
> The 19th Day   – – –19
> The 10th Hour   – – –10
>
> Total   35
>
> Divided by 8 = 4 with remainder 3
> 3 equals ☲ Li, the inner trigram

> The Year, Month, Day, Hour   is   35
> Divided by 6 is 5 with remainder 5
> The moving Yao is the fifth line.

As shown in figure 2-4a

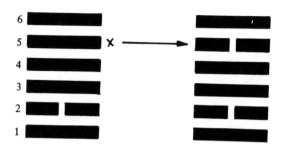

Figure 2-4a

Now we come to a new and important use of the concepts Ti and Yung. We say that the trigram that has the moving Yao is the Yung for the divination, and the other is the Ti. We regard the Ti trigram as being the fundamental one, just as earlier we likened it to the leading role in a play.

An example. Suppose we interpret the inner trigram as ourselves and the outer trigram as the world, other people. And we find the moving Yao is line 4, 5, or 6. Then we find the fundamental change has occurred in others' attitudes, which changes the whole situation for ourselves as Ti. We now respond to the new situation in a different way. Our basic trigram is unchanged, but it has variable aspects, and we select an aspect that harmonizes with the new Ti. If there is none, we are reserved and cautious.

When we use the Hu Tien divination, we deal with events in the present. Using the analogy of our health, we are considering the part of our health that derives from our everyday habits and the way we are presently caring for ourselves.

With the Hu Tien method we must select a subject in the field of life around us to divine with. We do not take any object for divination, but something that is unusual, out of the ordinary. Our guide in this can be sight itself — in a field of unmoving objects, our eyes will instantly spot something that moves. In a view that shows everything moving in a uniform manner, it will pick out the one object that moves irregularly. Our other senses work the same way.

Thus if we see a highway with streams of cars moving along it, there is nothing to divinate with. If we then hear a sudden screech of brakes, there it is. The event may involve a physical object, but it can just as well involve human interaction. Perhaps we are walking along passing people on the sidewalk and suddenly we happen to glance at an old man walking by amd we feel some inexplicably intense impression. Whatever the event is, we observe it quietly and attentively, like a cat watching a bird. It is the subject of our attention and we derive the outer trigram directly from it.

We do this by using what we know about relating the trigrams to anything. We must reflect on what we observed and sense its basic quality. Then we choose the trigram that represents that quality.

We can learn to do this by studying the eight trigrams as well as their symbols, virtues, and specific examples. Some of the examples are traditional and their connection to the symbols and virtues cannot be grasped without knowing more of the tradition. But most of them can be puzzled out with reflection and imagination. For example, we can see with some thought how the telephone with its loud ringing call, and its potential for sending us on immediate errands can be Chen, thunder, a stimulus to movement. Whereas if the postman brings us mail, this is something that penetrates to our attention, but more gently and it can be Sun like wind. Every time we work out one of these connections, we will be adding to our ability to characterize things. This will make the Hu Tien method of divination possible, and just as important, we will be learning to observe any specific event and see the basic general quality that underlies it. Such valuable knowledge in turn will give us guides to our behavior. This kind of work becomes a schooling of the most valuable sort, where we are both student and teacher. Or looking at it another way, nature and life become our teacher.

To use a specific example, the old man will represent Chien, for this is a traditional trigram for an older man.

To select the inner trigram, we use the direction the subject of our attention is in. We use the Hu Tien arrangement, with Li, south, representing our front, Kan, north, representing our back; Chen, east, our left; Tui, west, our right, etc. as shown in figure 2-4b.

If the old man was approaching us along the sidewalk, we have the inner trigram of Li.

Finally, we add the number of each of the trigrams, according to its place in the Hsien Tien arrangement, and add the hour of the day to that number. We divide its sum by 6 to get the moving Yao from the remainder, as before.

Thus the moving Yao is second Yao because of the following:

The number of Chien is 1, the number of Li is 3.

The number of hour is 10.

Total is 1 + 3 + 10 = 14

Divided by 6 = 2 with a remainder 2.

as shown in figure 2-4c.

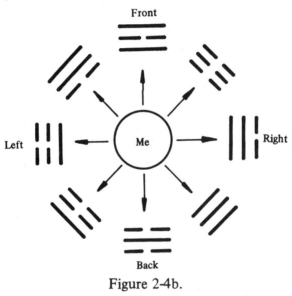

Figure 2-4b.

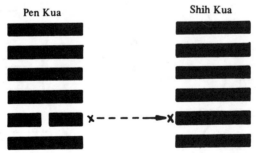

Figure 2-4c

This kind of divination can be applied in many different ways to many situations. Its only limitation is the amount of self-training we have given ourselves and the seriousness with which we divinate. As we work and make some progress with this, we can begin to see that divination is not for passive people who want "easy answers" so they don't have to work hard, and hope for a "good divination" so they can have something to day-dream about and then forget. It is for people who are living actively and who want to cultivate a good orientation towards the life around them, so that their living can be more effective.

2-5 The Hu Tien Method: Shao's marvelous Pillow

Now we will study a few interesting examples of the Hu Tien method of divination. As you recall, in this method, an unusual action or event determines the outer trigram, and the direction of the action in relation to the front of the observing diviner determines the inner trigram as shown in figure 2-5a. Finally, we determine the moving Yao by adding the number of each of the trigrams, according to its place in the Hsien Tien arrangement, as shown in figure 2-5b, and adding the hour of the day to that number. This sum divided by six gives us the moving Yao.

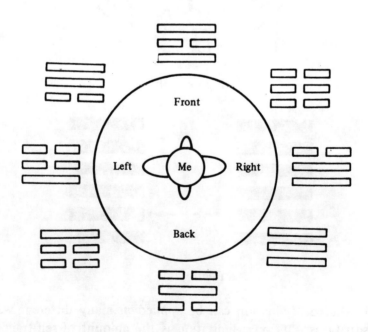

Figure 2-5a

Hsien Tien

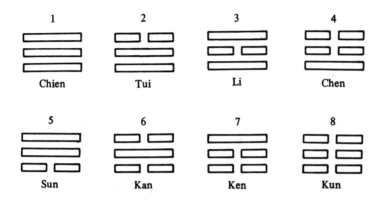

Figure 2-5b

Example One: The old man will die!

Mr. Shao arose early one morning to take a walk along the lake. During his walk, he glanced at an old man just passing him from the other direction and had an odd impression that he could not name, but that was very intense. Shao stopped the old person and asked him, "Has anything happened to you? Are you all right?"

"I've just been walking. Why do you ask?" the old man replied, puzzled.

Shao went home puzzled, too, and consulted the I Ching. For the outer trigram he selected Chien, one of its images being an old man. Then he recalled where the old man was when he noticed him — he was in front of Shao and to the left. The position is represented by the trigram for Sun. The hexagram reads:

Pen Kua

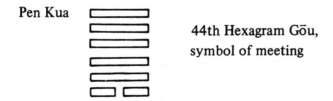

44th Hexagram Gōu,
symbol of meeting

This is the Pen Kua, or original hexagram and Shao next derived the Hu Kua by taking the second, third and fourth lines for the inner trigram, and the third, fourth and fifth lines for the outer:

Hu Kua

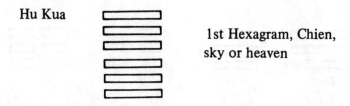

1st Hexagram, Chien,
sky or heaven

The meeting occurred on an early summer morning, not quite 5 o'clock. So the number of the hour is 4. Reading from the Hsien Tien list, the number of Sun is 5 and the number of Chien is 1. Adding these three numbers we have 10. Dividing by 6, we have 1 with a remainder of 4. The moving Yao is the fourth Yao and we use it to derive the Shih Kua from the Pen Kua:

Shih Kua

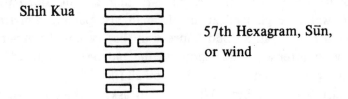

57th Hexagram, Sūn,
or wind

Now we consult the readings to carefully work on a judgment. Gōu has one Yin Yao below and five Yang Yao above. In studying the image of the lines directly, we think of the bottom growing upward, and here this gives an image of Yin growing.

Going further, we think, five Yang lines can be represented by five men and one Yin line by one woman, We read in the Kwa Tsi, "The woman is too bold. Do not take her home with you." It is easy to see how this relates to a crime or trouble between the sexes. But there is nothing of this judgment suggested in the case of the old man. When we have a judgment like this that does not apply, we drop it completely.

We inspect further. The time in the Kwa Tsi for Gōu is autumn. The upper trigram is Chien, or sky, and the lower, Sun, wind. We think of images of a cold autumn wind blowing dead leaves away. We look up the judgment for the moving Yao, the fourth. It is very poor: "There are no fish in the bag. Disaster comes."

The 4th Yao is in the outer trigram, so this is the first Yung Kua. The inner trigram is the Ti Kua. Using the Five Elements, we get the following:

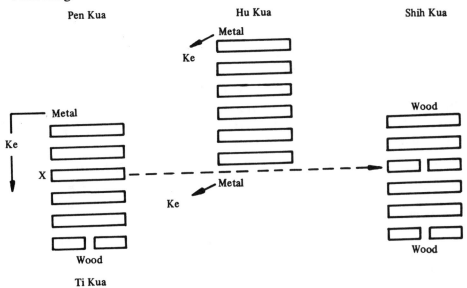

Metal destroys or Ke wood, according to the dynamic principles of the Five Elements. The situation in the Pen Kua, or original hexagram is poor. We go further and look at the Hu Kua, and here both Chien are metal, which intensifies the image even more. Finally we look at the Shih Kua, and both of the trigrams have the symbol of Sun, and the element wood. This corresponds to the Ti Kua in the Pen Kua. This is good, but it is too late.

We see nothing but the repeated strong image of metal destroying wood, Yung Kua destroying Ti Kua. There is nothing close within the trigrams to help. It is like the proverb, "water from afar cannot quench a nearby fire." There is nothing that can be done to evade the bad situation.

We ask, "When will the disaster happen?" The rule is to add the numbers of the inner and outer trigrams and the number of the hour —

5 plus 1 plus 4 — which equals 10. When the subjective diviner is sitting, we say the disaster comes slower and multiply by 2 to get the time. When the diviner is standing still, we take the sum directly. When the diviner is walking, we say it will come faster, and we divide the sum by 2. So we divide 10 by 2 and get 5.

$$Inner + Outer + Hour = Time$$
$$5 + 1 + 4 = 10$$
Diviner walking
$$10 \div 2 = 5$$

Let's return to the story. Mr. Shao determined that within five days the old man will have a disaster. So he visited the old man and warned him that he needed to be very careful in caring for himself the next five days. The old man accepted his advice, but thought, "I am pretty careful in the way I live," so he did nothing special.

On the fifth day, the old man went to a marriage party he was invited to. There was a big banquet, and as he sat eating fish a bone caught in his throat. This was before advanced medical knowledge. There was no doctor, and he died.

It seems mysterious that the old man should die, and it should be so accurately predicted. When we do not understand a whole situation, what happens is always mysterious. It is like a man who has clogged arteries and exerts himself too much one day; his heart fails and he dies. The problem was already there, and the event is not surprising. Yet if we know nothing about it, it seems to be a mystery. And it is just as much a mystery if a man lives to be very, very old.

Example Two. It is a beautiful morning. About 7:40 a.m., Shao is exercising under a tree. Suddenly he hears a cow mooing behind him, and it makes a hoarse sound, different from the sound cows usually make. Shao finishes his exercises, and when he goes home, he does a divination on the cow. The image of a cow is Kun, the outer trigram. The sound came from behind Shao, and this is Kan, the inner trigram. Kun is 8 and Kan is 6 and the hour is 7. This gives 21 and when it is divided by 6, the remainder is 3, so the moving Yao is 3. Thus we have:

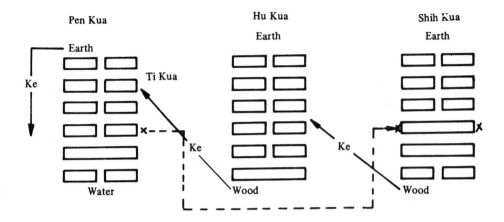

The Pen Kua is the seventh Hexagram, called Shī (師) or army. We read the Yao Tsi for the third Yao, and it says, "To maintain an army without authorization is disaster." The cow is not much like an army, so we know only that the moving Yao is bad. Then we examine the Yung Kua and the Ti Kua for the first hexagram. Just as the hexagram begins with a lower trigram that is "inner", so can we take this beginning Pen Kua as telling us about the "inner" situation for the cow. The cow has troubles. Its Ti Kua of earth destroys its Yung Kua of water. However, in the process of destroying the water, the earth is weakened. This is a case of the Ti Kua being weakened "indirectly" though not "directly". It can be compared to a parent who does not spend a sum of money directly, but spends it by giving it to a son. The parent still has less money in either case. In one the spending is direct; in the other, indirect. Thus, the cow's Ti Kua is weakened "indirectly".

We go on to inspect the Hu Kua and see wood under earth. Here the Wood is another Yung Kua and it destroys the Ti Kua of Earth directly. We look at the Shih Kua and we have Wood under Earth again! The cow is beset with troubles from within and without. Shao adds up the outer trigram number, the inner number, and the number of the hour and gets 21. Shao was standing at the time he heard the cow, and he makes the unhappy conclusion the cow will be killed within 21 days. Later he goes to the farm to find out about the cow. He discovers that after 20 days, someone bought the cow and killed it for beef.

Exercise One. How does Shao know the young man will be married within 17 days?

About 7:30 one morning Shao is standing on the corner of a street. He sees a young man crossing the street and coming towards him. The young man has an expression of great happiness on his face, though there does not seem to be any reason. Shao asks him, "Why do you feel so happy?" The young man replies, "I don't know. I guess I was daydreaming." Shao goes home and does a divination for this young man. He finds out he will be married within 17 days. Dear reader, can you trace this judgment?

Hint. The image of a young man is Ken, and he approaches Shao from the front. This is Li. The answer is at the end of this chapter, on page 88 and 89.

Exercise Two. How does Shao know that the rooster will be killed in 10 days?

It is around 4:30 a.m. Shao is sleeping on his bed when he is awakened by the crowing of a neighbor's rooster. The sound comes from behind him and to the right as he lays in bed. Usually the rooster never crows at night. Shao does a divination when he arises, and concludes the rooster will be cooked in 10 days. How does he know this?

Hint: The image of the chicken is Sun. The direction gives the inner trigram Chien. The answer is at the end of this Chapter, on page 89 and 90.

In working on the exercises, there are simple principles for the student to keep in mind. Divination failure and success can be compared to a superstitious person and a calm person who both hear a strange sound on the other side of a hill. The superstitious person does not listen to the sound calmly and try to notice things about it. He immediately jumps to conclusions: "Oh, it is good!" or "Oh, it is bad!" Since he does not pay attention to the sound, his judgment is based on whatever unrelated feeling he had just before he heard the sound. Once the superstitious person has made such a snap judgment, he then misinterprets and distorts every new sign to fit his preconceived decision. The result is that the person often interprets danger as good news and is harmed, or interprets good news as danger, and runs away from it.

The calm person has inner feelings and hopes, too, but instead pays attention to the sound. He listens to it and tries to discover new things about it. First he hears the sound. Then he notices that the sound is coming closer. It sounds like an animal of some kind. But animals rarely run about and make noises, because it attracts danger to them. So he becomes wary. As he listens more, he notices that the sound is rapidly moving closer. Finally he sees something break through the bushes and immediately sees that it is a wounded, ferocious wild bear. He climbs a tree long before it comes close.

Divination is like this. Even if we are very clever and know all the signs, it is worthless if we do not know how to be calm and observe quietly. We just confuse ourselves. But if we are calm and attentive, we may find our way correctly even if we are not very clever. And because we are calm and look over our work afterwards to correct ourselves and learn more, we increase our knowledge each time we divinate.

In divination, we ask for knowledge from the 4th dimensional world, and we do it within the limits in which we live. This is like extending our intuition, which also comes to us from the 4th dimension.

We learn divination the same way we learn any skill. Did we learn how to drive a car in one day? Did we learn to read and write in one day? No. Each day we learned a little, and gradually added to it.

In learning divination, we study our own life and past and examine ourselves. This gradually teaches us to observe more accurately how we feel and act. Eventually we add to this and learn to correct things we don't like. The more we understand about ourselves, the easier it is to be calm and alert, and to extend our knowledge to other situations.

Eventually we come to have a solid basis from this work to study and learn more about other aspects of life. Suppose we are angry. We study ourselves and learn that often when we get angry we do something rash and get into trouble. So we learn: anger can quickly bring danger. Then we notice that when another person gets very angry, they do not behave as reckless as we did, but become sullen and negative, and remain that way all day. Thus we learn: anger can spoil things very slowly and indirectly. Another time we notice a person who gets very angry, but doesn't do anything special. A day or week later we see the person, and find he has found an opportunity and is energetically doing something to correct the situation that made him angry. Thus we learn: anger can create something good.

When we learn directly this way, by being our own teacher, the learning is much more intense and valuable. This is why the I Ching has the simplest possible structure. It enhances our learning instead of getting in the way of it.

Within this structure of simplicity, there are various ways of divination we can follow. Another way may be more appealing or useful to us. We may also want to advance our knowledge further. Whatever our ultimate goal, we learn the basics first and study them over and over till we master them.

Answer to Exercise One. The young man will marry in 17 days.

The young man represents Ken, the youngest brother, and is the outer trigram. He faces Shao as Shao waits standing at the intersection. Facing is Li, the inner trigram. Using the Hsien Tien numeration, Ken is 7 and Li is 3, and the time is 7, totalling 17. Divided by 6, the remainder is 5, the Moving Yao. This gives —

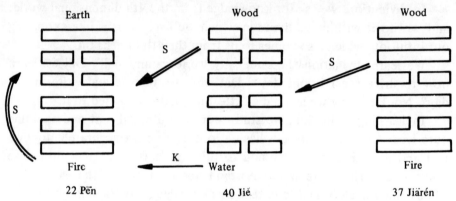

The first hexagram is Pēn or Grace, and part of the judgment is "only small things further." In it we see fire feeding or Sheng the earth of Ken, which is stopping. This suggests the young man giving his enthusiasm to something, and not getting a response. Since he is the "youngest brother" just at the age of starting out in life and being attracted to women, we think maybe he has a girlfriend.

The Yao Tsi for line 5 speaks of a person who rejects empty luxury for simplicity. The person finds a good friend who accepts their very meagre gifts of friendship and reciprocates. This suggests the young man's suit to the girl is finally accepted in the best way. The Hu Kua of Jiě revolves around "lessening of tensions," just like the cloudburst that brings rain lessens the electrical charges in the air and is relaxing. In the Hu Kua we have wood supporting fire and water putting it out, two diverging indications. Since the moving Yao is good, we may assume the young lady's acceptance of her suitor relieves all the tension of his courting her, just as water puts out fire. The final hexagram Jiǔ rén stands for the family, and is a clear indication of marriage. Here we find the water is gone, but the wood remains, supporting the fire of the young man's Ti Kua, which suggests the marriage is a good one. Since Shao is standing when he sees the young man, the number 17 remains, and he decides the marriage will occur in about 17 days.

Answer to Exercise Two. The rooster is Sun, the outer trigram. The direction of his crowing is behind Shao to the right, which is Chien. Sun is 5 and Chien is 1 and the hour is 4. The sum is 10. Divided by 6, it gives a remainder of 4, the Moving Yao. The result is —

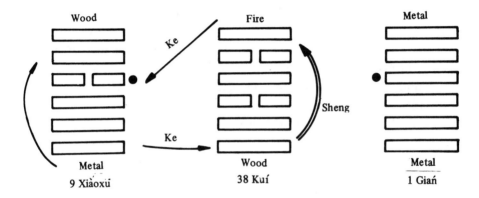

In the Pen Kua, the hexagram is Xiǎoxū, which translates as "taming power of the small." The Ti Kua of the rooster is metal, which is Ke wood. The Pen Kua can be interpreted as the inner environment of the rooster, so it is destroying something that helps it and suffers loss. The moving Yao of 4 speaks about a person in a dangerous situation who restrains a powerful person because they are "in the right." But the rooster is weak in his situation, suggesting he may fail. The Hu Kua is complicated with its wood being destroyed by metal, and its fire destroying metal. One might say "the metal destroys the wood so it cannot feed the fire, so the fire is not strong enough to melt the metal." But the first indication in the Pen Kua is contrary to this idea, and we accept that one and reject this.

Further, the general meaning of the Hu Kua of Kuí is "opposition and conflicts", and this reinforces the notion that the rooster is having trouble. What is the rooster's trouble? It doesn't lay eggs, there are always more of them than are needed for breeding, so roosters make good eating. We think possibly the farmer will kill the rooster for food. In the final trigram of Gia'n there is metal over metal. This suggests

that whatever the fate of the original metal, it is underlined many times
as being what will happen. The rooster was in trouble with a powerful
opposition, and we conclude it was killed and eaten. The original sum
is 10, and Shao is laying down, so we estimate the fate comes slowly,
and multiply by 2 to get 20 days.

2-6 The Hsien Tien Method: Entering the Fourth Dimension

The Hsien Tien method refers to the roots of a situation, which
determine its present and future. To review, we derive a number for the
year by dividing the year by twelve and taking the remainder, or the
number 12 if there is no remainder. To this number we add the number
of the month, and then the day of the month. We divide the sum by
eight and its remainder gives us the outer trigram, if there is no
remainder, the trigram is 8.

To find the inner trigram, we determine the year using the above
formula. We then add to it the month, day, and the hour. We count
the hours of the day from one to twenty-four, and if the time is not a
whole hour, we drop the minutes. For example, 11:47 would be
counted as 11. We then divide our sum by eight to get our inner trigram.

When we get our numbers, we take our trigrams from the Hsien Tien
numeration: 1 − Chien, 2 − Tui, 3 − Li, 4 − Chen, 5 − Sun, 6 − Kan,
7 − Ken, 8 − Kun. The moving Yao is the inner trigram sum divided by
six instead of eight, giving remainders from one to five. We use the
number six for no remainder.

Example One. The wind is whistling, the leaves are flying all about,
and Shao is out taking a brisk autumn walk in the suburbs of his city.
It's around 9:30 in the morning on the 17th of September. As he looks
at the changing colors of the plants and trees and idly thinks of winter
and his warm home, he suddenly notices two sparrows staging a
ferocious mid-air battle for seemingly no reason at all. They finally
break apart and fall to the ground exhausted, neither a winner. The
unusual incident attracts Shao's interest, and he decides to divinate.
Shao lives during the Sung Dynasty, and it is the year Wang Yu 4. (宋仁
宗皇佑四年). This is the year 1,052 in our numeration.

The number for 1,052 is 8 (1,052 divided by 12 is 87 with a
remainder of 8).

The number of September is 9.
The number of the day is 17.
The number of 9:30 a.m. is 9.
The outer trigram is $(8 + 9 + 17) \div 8 = 4$ with a remainder of 2.

Two is Tui ☱

For the inner trigram, we have
$(9 + 9 + 17 + 9) \div 8 = 5$ with a remainder of 3.

Three is Li ☲

The moving Yao is $(8 + 9 + 17 + 9) \div 6 = 7$ Remainder 1.
Line one is the moving Yao.

The Pen Kua or original hexagram, is the 49th, Gé (革).

Metal	☱	Ti Kua
Fire	☲	Yung Kua

We see how the Yung Kua is Li, fire, and the Ti Kua is Tui, metal.
Fire destroys or "Ke" metal, which suggests a problem. We derive the
Hu Kua and Shih Kua by the methods described in page 57 and 53.

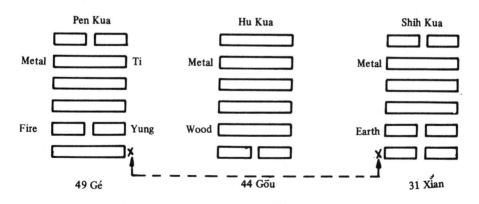

Now we see the situation intensified because the inner trigram of
Hu Kua is Sun, wood . We imagine this Yung Kua as feeding the Yung

Kua in the original hexagram of fire. Wood Shen or feeds fire, making it more intense. But who or what represents the Ti Kua? Shao deliberates and decides it is a young woman, one of the images of Tui, which is the trigram of the youngest daughter. He concludes she will be hurt.

In the Hu Kua, the inner trigram is Sun or wood, while its outer trigram is Chien, metal. Metal destroys Wood, and we know the part of the body of Sun is the thigh, so the young woman will be wounded in the thigh.

We go on to the Shih Kua to learn the final story. Here the inner trigram is Ken, earth, and earth creates or sustains the Metal in Tui, the original Ti Kua. This is a good sign, so Shao decides that the young woman's wound will not be serious.

The next day in the yard next door to Shao's home, a young woman sneaks into the garden and climbs a pear tree to steal some fruit. The gardener sees her and comes running out of his house shouting. The young girl panics and falls out of the tree. As she falls, a broken branch lacerates her thigh, but she is otherwise unhurt. The time is about 2 in the afternoon.

When Shao divinated, he determined this hour as well. First, he added the number of the outer trigram, that of the inner trigram, and the hour of the original event. This is (2 + 3 + 9). He was sitting when he divinated. This means the time comes slower, so he multiplied the sum of 14 by 2, giving 28. He determined that the event would come in 28 hours, rather than days or months or years. Adding 28 hours to 9:30 a.m., we get 1:30 p.m. the following day, the approximate time of the mishap.

Exercise Problem: Do you want to divinate the fortune of your own life?

Hint: Use the numbers of your birth hour, day, month and year to derive your Pen Kua, moving Yao, and the following Hu Kua and Shih Kua. The Pen Kua is the image of your life as a whole, so study the Kua Tsi in the I Ching carefully. The Yao Tsi of the moving Yao gives the present status of your living. A strong Ti Kua in good relation to the Yung Kuas means good fortune, success in your career. Poor indications tell you how to look for your weaknesses and moderate them. In a famous divining book called Pu Shih Yuan Kuei (卜筮元龜), the following characterizations of personality are given for the inner trigram of the Pen Kua:

Chien or Kun — a warm-hearted, benevolent person.
Sun — a cool, heartless person.
Kan — a clever person with sweet, honeyed words.
 a lying, deceitful person.
Chen — a person born at the wrong time, unlucky.
Ken — a person who is always very fair, who doesn't let
 personal feelings sway objective decisions.
Li — a clever, open-minded person, optimistic and good.
Tui — a person with a smiling face, gentle and affable, who has
 good judgment for propriety and moderation in
 speech and behavior.

If we find ourselves with a poor designation, we need not be dismayed, but instead may ask ourselves what we know of our character and what the truth of it is. Perhaps we have Kan for an inner trigram, and we look and find we are always making "promises" and often not keeping them, that we "talk a good show" but don't act so well. Then we know what is meant by Kan. We must realize that this is not necessarily how we will always behave, and there is nothing we can do about it. It simply indicates that this is the kind of weakness we will show when we are weak and careless. In addition, we may learn to find positive aspect of these qualities. For example, we may take a strong Kan character, and use it to become a highly successful "story teller" and writer of fiction. Our ability to use "honeyed words" may someday lead to our talking to someone who wants to commit suicide and convincing him that life has something good to offer, and that he should try to improve his life rather than throw it away.

The same is true if we divinate our fate and find it is a terrible one that gets worse with time! This fate cannot become reality if a person is willing to work and learn. If the reading shows weaknesses, we can exercise our will and spirit to avail ourselves of a corresponding source of energy that "fate" also provides in our situation.

Likewise, if we receive a favorable divination, we must be on our guard. Remember: "A fool and his money are soon parted." If we use the favorable indications as an excuse to be lazy and careless, we can lose our good fortune and have a miserable life. Meanwhile, the person with "bad luck" who learns to equalize his situation, can have a very happy life.

Example Two. The Peonies are trampled by two horses.

It is May 3, 1053. A friend invites Shao to a small luncheon to enjoy the beauty of his peonies. The flowers are famous among the Chinese and have the honorary name of "king of the flowers". Shao's friend has a large house by the canal, and he keeps his backyard planted with flowers. The beautiful show they create each year draws admiring visitors from all over the city. As Shao enters his friend's property he sees the soft light green of leaves opening, hears the birds twittering happily, smells the cold rising from the dank ground mingling with the warm spring breeze. He enters the garden with the peonies in full color and feels he is in an enchanted world. After the small group has lunch they sit and enjoy the weather. They all know Shao specializes in studying the I Ching, and listen alertly when Shao's host says, "The flowers are so beautiful and have such a powerful influence on the enjoyment of our culture, it almost seems equal to many human influences. Do these flowers have a fate, Shao, and can a person like you discover what their fortunes are to be?"

"Everything in the world has its own life cycle and fortune," Shao replies, "I'll check on it for you." The time is about one o'clock in the afternoon. Shao studies briefly and then tells his friends "It seems sad to say this, but the flowers will probably be destroyed by horses tomorrow afternoon." The group of friends is at once sceptical and dismayed, and they part wishing that they had not asked about the flowers.

The next day, at noon, a small group of city officials ride over to Shao's friend's home to look at the famous flowers. Two of the men have army horses just being trained to civil use. One horse nips the other and they start a wild fight that no one can quell, and they trample over half the flowers in the garden.

Let me explain how Shao foresaw this event so precisely.

The number for the year 1,053 is obtained by dividing by 12, and getting a remainder of 9.

The number of May is 5.
The number of the day is 3.
The hour of divination is 12:30, its number is 12.

Summing (9 + 5 + 3) we get 17 and dividing it by 8, we have a remainder of 1. The outer trigram is thus Chien. Doing the calculation for the inner trigram, we begin with (9 + 5 + 3 + 12), and obtain a remainder of 5 or Sun. Dividing (9 + 5 + 3 + 12) by 6, we get a remainder of 5, so the moving Yao is 5.

Thus the Pen Kua is the 44th hexagram of Gōu (姤), and the Hu Kua and Shih Kua derived from it create this arrangement:

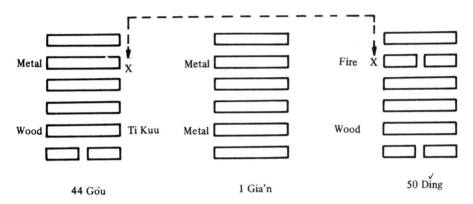

| 44 Góu | 1 Gia'n | 50 Ding |

In the Pen Kua we see that metal destroys or Ke wood, so that the Yung destroys the Ti. The peonies are in danger. In the Hu Kua, there is double Chien, two more Yung Kua of metal, which means great disaster for the Ti Kua. When Shao looks at these three Gian of metal, he thinks: "Gia'n represents horse, it would be easy for the flowers to be trampled by a horse."

Then he looks at the Li in the outer trigram of the final hexagram and thinks "Li is the brightest sunshine, this will happen around noon. But what day? I am divining as we stand here, not walking, so it is not soon, not today. Flowers have a short cycle of blooming, it is tomorrow." If he had divined the time by numbers he would have gotten the number 18, or 6 tomorrow morning, but the Li he judges is a clearer sign, flowers and bright light go together very well.

Exercise Problem..

Each day for several days, pick some topic of interest in your everyday living and divinate and make a judgment by yourself. Take care to do the work in a calm frame of mind. Select a subject that you can check on later to test the accuracy of your work. If it's inaccurate, which it often may be, go over your decisions and see what the correct ones would be.

To make this kind of study we might compare ourselves to a naturalist who has become a novice birdwatcher. He sees a bird flutter in the tree out of the corner of his eye, and he follows it as closely as he can and notes as much as he can of its coloring and pattern, style of flight, size, and song. Then he studies his identification manual and finally narrows down what he believes the bird to be: a robin or a rare warbler.

However, we have a special advantage over the novice birdwatcher, because once the bird has flown away, he can never tell if he was right or wrong in identifying it. For us, when we have divinated, the study is just beginning. We have an "expert friend" to tell us in great detail how accurate our judgment has been. That friend is the event itself.

Using the event we divinated about to improve ourselves, we gradually extend our studies. For example, we divinate and conclude that the active agent in some coming event will be Kan, and that it will be a person. We see Kan means water, and "to entrap", we read "thief" and "boatman". We look at the connected places, bar — maybe a bartender, gas — maybe a gas station attendant, tryst — maybe two lovers. We even extend our thinking: "Thief" could indicate an undercover agent out to entrap a thief instead.

Every indication gives us a clue to narrow down the list of "suspects" in our search. We may read that Kan is the "middle son", and this tells us a lot — if it is connected with a gas station, then the "younger son" would obviously be the person who pumps gas, and the "middle son" the skilled mechanic with the tow truck, and the "elder son" the owner of the business.

There is a bonus in this kind of study, and that is how surprising it is at first to find the event that finally occurs has such close ties to the divination of it — even if we missed or misinterpreted those ties. Once we have seen such a correspondence, any feeling we have that we are dealing with empty imaginings is gone forever.

Example Three. A father is more experienced than his son.

It is a winter night, and snow is whirling about the house. Shao and his son sit and chat around the fireplace. Suddenly someone is knocking at the door. First there is a single knock, after a while, five in a row. Then a voice calls, "Shao, are you home? I want to borrow something from you."

Shao opens the door and the visitor enters with a burst of snow and wind. Shao already has a plan. He wants to see how good his son is with divination. He says to his visitor, "Don't say anything about what you want to borrow, I want my son to figure this out. Here, come over and make yourself comfortable around the fireplace."

Like father, like son — Shao's son is an I Ching student. No doubt he can start with the numbers of hour, day, month and year to develop a Pen Kua, Hu Kua and Shih Kua. But because this is a test of his skill, he wants to develop a new method on his own. He recalls that their visiting neighbor knocked on the door once, then five times. He decides that is his clue, and he calls the first knock the outer trigram, Chien, ☰ and calls the second group of five his inner trigram. Which comes to be Sun ☴. It is past 10 at night, so the hour is 22. To get the Moving Yao he adds one and five and twenty-two to get twenty-eight, and when divided by six, the remainder is four. The moving Yao is 4. His complete divination is:

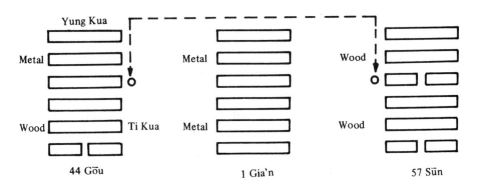

It is a very special case, for of the six trigrams, three are Gia'ns and three are Suns. Gia'n is metal and Sun is wood. So the object their neighbor wants to borrow is related to wood and metal. So the son judges and says, "You want to borrow a hoe."

"You are wrong," says Shao, "he wants to borrow an axe." "What do you want to borrow!?" father and son ask the neighbor, almost in unison.

"An axe," comes the reply.

Shao smiles and explains to his son how he erred. Sun tends to represent something long, like a wooden handle. Gia'n stands for a round shape, especially of metal. A hoe usually is pointed or has a flat edge of metal, an axe always has a curved edge to cut wood better. But the two are close, so Shao looks for another sign to confirm. Is it daytime? Then the visitor may use a hoe in daytime. Nighttime? This is impossible, because there is no light for working outdoors in the garden in the middle of winter. Yet an axe, yes, maybe the neighbor needs to cut up some firewood. He can do this at night. Shao decides for the axe. Its use is acceptable within the time of the divination.

This shows us the role of change in divination. Everything changes, and we adjust our divination to fit what we know of the time. In this way we have a general guide, and the divination gives us more exact direction. We might ask of Shao and his son, "What about a hammer? It has a round head." In Shao's time, what we today call a hammer did not exist. Since it exists in our time, when we divinate we of course, would use this knowledge. Also, follow what strongly impresses us when the question occurs, just as Shao's son had his attention attracted to the knocking sounds at the door and used them to derive the trigrams.

We must begin by using a simple method and working with it, otherwise we become confused with too much. Yet what we are doing is not "dead" or "fixed" but must always adapt a little bit to the circumstances and the time. If we are in a church, we sense one mood; in a park, we sense another; having a snack in our kitchen, we sense another. Can you tell which are the trigrams for each of these? You can tell if you study and think about them. We have only 64 hexagrams to use, and only a few hundred combinations when we divinate with one mvoing Yao. Yet these are like a car with four wheels, it can take us anywhere if we know how to drive. We can learn if we keep a spirit of lightheartedness but always seriousness within it — just like a young man driving in his sports car may smile and wave, but his attention is always focused clearly on the road and the traffic.

Chapter Three:

CRADLE OF CHINESE CULTURE

3-1 How to Read the 64 Hexagrams

The earlier part of this book is an intensive preparation for us to learn to use the hexagrams well. Now we come to the actual hexagrams where we focus all this work. There are several points to consider in learning to make the best use of this section.

*Pinyin. The usual English spellings of Chinese words that are supposed to give a clue to their pronounciation are dropped in favor of the standardized Pinyin spellings, used in teaching the Chinese language to English speaking people. This creates a consistent standard in approaching the pronounciation. If a student wants to learn the correct pronounciation, they can do so easily by getting a language teaching book from the library, or taking a course, and they will find the same standards there.

*Ancient wood block prints for each hexagram. We often say "a picture is worth a thousand words" and today scientists study how a person's "visual mind" is even more complex and powerful than their "verbal mind". In many kinds of learning, words are merely a start for a person to build up a mental picture for themselves. Using pictures directly to work with is very important in developing our whole selves. Not only will we learn to "read directly" from pictures, but it will train us to make better visual images from words.

Look at one of the pictures. Forget the words and don't read them. Look at the picture with all your attention for a minutes, or five or ten minutes. Keep your imagination active and look for the impressions you get from the images. You will find you have all sorts of distinct, personal impressions. This is your personal image. This is what is important – not what someone else tells you are supposed to see there.

Once you have done this, you can then see ways that the picture relates to the event you are divinating about. Suppose we take Hexagram 11, Tái or Positive.

We see a little boy sitting on the clouds.

In the text accompanying the picture, there is a suggestion of possible meanings – "This can be good. A sudden rise to success. Or poor, to aim very high, but to care nothing about developing the fundamentals."

We can see how easily these two images develop. The heavens always represent advanced development, and we expect to see a youngster beginning life near the ground. Here he is high, so it means he has great talents or achievements that have taken him up fast.

Similarly, we can think of the little boy filled with enthusiastic dreams about "what I'm going to do when I grow up" and meanwhile neglecting his homework at school and going nowhere!

There are many possibilities. A pregnant woman who divinates about her child and sees this picture may have a strong impression of realizing she is going to have a boy.

A parent with a sick child may have cause for alarm. The picture may suggest their son will never grow to an adult, but will die and go to heaven.

You may look at the picture and seeing the boy instantly get a strong impression of someone you've just been thinking about. And you may see how the boy's expression and place in the picture define how that person is developing.

To divinate this way can become very powerful as we practice and use all our abilities to unravel the reading. It requires our complete seriousness and sincerity in doing this, as in any serious work where we need to do something well.

Some people may say "This is just superstition!   There is no scientific method to it."

But this is just an insistence that everything in life has only one rigid meaning that can be spelled out on paper.   To correct this, we should look at our daily life, and see how much of it has the deepest meaning, yet it cannot be spelled out.   Suppose you ask your self "Tomorrow is a holiday.   What will I do?"   Is there any standard answer to this?   Even the way we reach our decision is not standardized and cannot be described.   And this is our life with all its order and meaning.

So to practice this divination well, we need to open our mind's eye to the non-standard way we live our daily life, and we can make progress.

*Natural and man-made.   In my book The Tao of Meditation, I describe in greater detail how our activities have an element that is 'natural' and an element that is 'man-made'.   The point in studying meditation is to learn to know the natural clearly, so we can live well and avoid confusion: wherever we find troubles in human living, we always find people with different 'man-made' visions of life conflicting with each other, because each is absolutely convinced theirs is "natural."

We define the natural as that which is completely tied in with the whole of life, the fourth dimensional world that we live in, in a three dimensional way.

When we divinate, we are receiving a fourth dimensional image that is projected into our three dimensional undestanding, and this image is like a blue-print of a building.   It is a complete blue-print of the event, including its beginning and ending.

In divination, we are using some things that are more natural, and others that are necessarily worked out into man-made and personal terms.

For example, the divination tools of Principle Position, Matching, and Middle Position are natural and direct.   Consider Hexagram 11, Tái, or Positive.

Analysis: **The situation is good, because 1st, 3rd, 4th and 6th are all in principle position.

**The match is very good, and this means dealing with other people are perfect.   You can note how 1st and 4th, 2nd and 5th, 3rd and 6th are all one Yang and one Yin.

**The middle position is very poor because the 2nd Yao is Yin and 5th

Principle		
Position		
Yin	▬▬▬ ▬▬▬	Good
Yang	▬▬▬ ▬▬▬	Poor
Yin	▬▬▬ ▬▬▬	Good
Yang	▬▬▬▬▬▬	Good
Yin	▬▬▬▬▬▬	Poor
Yang	▬▬▬▬▬▬	Good

Yao is Yang, neither in principle position. This means you don't have a clear goal, a strong will to promote, develop your goals.

**As a whole, the three Yang Yao below the three Yin Yao mean that Yang is growing up from the bottom to drive away the Yin. This is very active, or very good.

We can see from the above how the natural meanings of the lines form themselves into an abstract pattern that we can directly apply to our human situation.

Now, by contrast, the Hints on Divination where we have the Kwa Tsi and Yao Tsi and 'new' versions of them in our present cultural terms, these are completely man-made. They are there for you to refer to, a stimulus to evolving your own personal ones.

*A final note. The open circle o indicates a Yao is a good one in terms of the whole hexagram, and the black circle ● indicates it is a bad one. If there is no circle by the Yao, it means it is so-so. This is the same whith the notes on the seasons. If we say the hexagram is good in spring, bad in summer, then fall and winter are so-so.

The open circle is derived from the interrelations of all the lines. The seasonal information is derived from application of the trigram cycles to the year. So we can say these indications are more natural.

Qián 乾

Heaven above
Heaven below
The Heaven

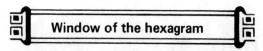

Window of the hexagram

1. A deer on a cloud (天祿) means official rank granted by heaven.
2. The wise man cutting and polishing a piece of shining jade means a person must discipline and educate himself if he is to be a useful citizen.
3. The full moon in the sky means light shining in all directions.
4. An official climbing up the steps of the ladder to watch the moon means rapid and continuous advances in one's career.

Image and Symbol

六龍御天之課，廣大包容之象．

The image is six dragons governing the heavens.
The symbol is of all-inclusiveness.

Kua Tsi (文王彖辭)

(Explanation of the hexagram by King Wan).
乾，元亨利貞．
Qian brings the most profound success. It comes through persistence.

Zhan (占) or hints on divining.

1. This is an April hexagram, good in spring and winter, bad in summer.
2. Qián is double the trigram qian 乾 , so they have the same name, image and characteristics, it is called pure or Chun (純) hexagram. There are eight pure hexagrams in the I Ching. They are:

1.	乾	䷀	Qián Heaven or Chien
2.	坤	䷁	Kun Earth or Kun
29.	坎	䷜	Kán Water or Kan

30.　离　☲　Lí Fire or Li

51.　震　☳　Zhèn Thunder or Chen

52.　艮　☶　Yin Mountain or Ken

57.　巽　☴　Sūn Wind or Sun

58.　兑　☱　Dui Lake or Tui

When we consult the I Ching about an illness, and derive one of these pure hexagrams, it means the condition of the patient is very dangerous.

3.　If you are a woman, Qian tells you that you are too Yang. You need to be more Yin or sweet-natured. Otherwise, there will be trouble. If you are sick, it is related to the brain, lungs or the nervous system.

Yao Tsi (周公爻辭)

Explanation of the separate lines, or Yaos, by the Duke of Chou.
初九・潛龍勿用・
1st Yao the dragon is hidden. Take no action.

 *Zhan* (占)

1.　Be prudent in making statements and careful in personal conduct. Otherwise there will be trouble.
2.　If you are a pregnant woman, the time to give birth to a child is near.
3.　You can emerge successful from a competitive examination.
4.　Your girl friend is too Yang or hard. Perhaps you date someone who fails to appear.

九二・見龍在田・利見大人・○
2nd Yao. The dragon appears in the field. It is a time to see an influential person. ○

Zhan (占)

1. Receive guidence from influential persons to start and develop your own business.
2. A patient's condition is dangerous.
3. To be alert for a fire other disaster from your neighbor.

九三 • 君子終 日乾乾 • 夕惕若 • 厲 • 无咎 • ○

3rd Yao. One is active all day long, and at night worriedly reviews things. There is danger, but one does the right things. ○

Zhan (占)

1. Rain is falling on a dry farmland. It is a good time and worth working on it.
2. Catch the opportunity: it will soon disappear without leaving a trace.
3. Your boy friend is good and reliable, but too Yang.

九四 • 或 躍在淵 • 无咎 •

4th Yao. The flight wavers over the depth. This is all right.

Zhan (占)

1. If you don't know what course of action to take, you will lose the opportunity.
2. Don't underestimate yourself.
3. If you are sick, it is not serious.

九五 • 飛龍在天 • 利見大人 ○

5th Yao. The dragon flies in heaven. It is a time to see an influential person. ○

Zhan (占)

1. Everything goes well.
2. Heaven helps a good person.
3. The condition of a patient will improve tremendously.

上九 • 亢龍有悔 •

6th Yao. The dragon is arrogant and will come to repent.

Zhan (占)

1. Too much is as bad as not enough.
2. It is the right time to retire.
3. One has to stop at the right moment.
4. Remind oneself that things might have been worse.

用九・見群龍無首・吉 ○

All lines change: A flight of headless dragons appears. There will be good fortune. ○

2 ䷁ Kūn 坤

Earth above
Earth below
The Earth

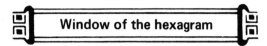

Window of the hexagram

1. Eleven mouths refers to a traditional riddle and the answer is the Chinese character 古 , which means old or ancient. Eleven mouths also means many mouths to feed.
2. An officer sitting on a pile of coins, means to be successful in both politics and business.
3. A god on the raised platform wearing golden armor delivers documents to an officer. This image represents a stroke of genius, coming as if it were divine inspiration.

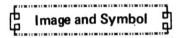

Image and Symbol

生載萬物之課 • 君倡臣和之象 •

The image is to support and contain all things.
The symbol is "all for one, and one for all."

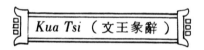

Kua Tsi （文王象辭）

元亨 • 利牝馬之貞 • 君子有攸往 • 先迷後得 • 主利西南得朋 • 東北喪朋
• 安貞吉 •

Kùn brings highest success through cultivation with the persistence of a mare. If a person tries to lead, he is lost. But if he follows, he finds the guidance he needs. It is good to find friends in the west and south, to avoid those from the east and north. Quiet work brings good fortune.

Zhan （占） *or hints on divining*

1. This is an October hexagram. Good in spring and winter, bad in summer.
2. Don't act without either objective or cause.
3. It is good to do something for others.
4. It is one of the eight pure hexagrams. So the patient in a critical condition will recover from illness, but will need a long time.
5. You have a very good wife or girl friend.

Yao Tsi (周公爻辭)

初六 • 履霜 • 堅冰至 • ●

1st Yao. When the first frost is on the ground, the solid ice will be coming soon. ●

Zhan (占)

1. Take care of yourself with the greatest circumspection.
2. Do not be tempted by small gains and suffer a big loss.
3. Old friendships may be completely forgotten with the sudden change of financial expression. This means that even people who are good and long time friends, can have conflits over money. They fight, argure with each other, and forget they are good friends.

六二 • 直方大 • 不習无不利 • ○

2nd Yao. It is straight, square and great. It has no purpose, yet nothing is neglected. ○

Zhan (占)

1. If you are always open and good hearted, people will trust you, and you will be successful in different areas.
2. Some good things will happen unexpectedly.
3. Good luck. Catch the opportunity to develop yourself.

六三 • 含章可貞 • 或從王事 • 无成有終 •

3rd Yao. There are hidden lines. A person can keep persevering. If you serve a king, don't look for visible accomplishment, but work to get things done.

Zhan (占)

1. The right time has not come yet.
2. Forethought brings happiness.
3. Work hard and keep quite like a mare.

六四 • 括囊 • 无譽无咎 •

4th Yao. The sack is tied up. There is nothing to praise, and nothing to blame.

🙪 *Zhan (占)* 🌿

1. Don't try to speculate on the stock market.
2. People will criticize you as a miser.

六五・黃裳・元吉・○

5th Yao. If your lower garments are yellow, you have the greatest good fortune. ○

🌫 *Zhan (占)* 🌫

1. Mind your own business.
2. Attain or develop a new way of life by yourself.
3. A husband is obedient to his wife, and a father to his son.

上六・龍戰於野・其血玄黃・●

6th Yao. Dragons are battling in the meadow. They bleed with sky blue and sandstone. ●

〔 *Zhan (占)* 〕

1. If you think of nothing but your own gain, you will receive censure through your own faults.
2. Don't try to engage in a fight with your allies.
3. He who cannot forbear in small matters spoils great undertakings.

用六・利永貞・

All lines change. Continuing work is a worthwhile thing

🗦 *Zhan (占)* 🗧

1. The symbol is one of dwelling together as husband and wife.
2. If you can exert yourself with dedication, you'll have good fortune.

3 ☵☳ **Tún** 屯
Water above
Thunder below
First Difficulty

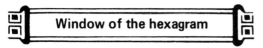

Window of the hexagram

1. A man climbing to the top of a lookout post, means he can see both forward and backward to avoid dangerous situations.
2. A cart sinking deep in the mud, means there is a lot of trouble, everything is mixed up.
3. A dog turns its head backwards. This signifies the Chinese character for crying. (哭)
4. A person shoots an arrow at a document. He uses an ancient bow. This means to hit the bull's eye.
5. A knife is at the cow's head. This means survival is hopeless.
6. A beautiful box with a matching cover means to be united and to work in concert.

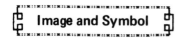

Image and Symbol

龍居淺水之課 • 萬物始生之象 •

The image is a heavenly dragon that decends to a shallow water.
The symbol is of all things starting to germinate.

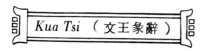

Kua Tsi (文王象辭)

屯 • 元亨利貞 • 勿用有攸往 • 利建侯 •

Tún leads to great success. It is worth persisting. Nothing should be done right now. It is a good idea to get helpers.

Zhan (占) *or hints on divining*

1. This is a June hexagram. It is good in spring and fall and bad in the summer.
2. Tún, a difficult stage, is one of the four evil hexagrams (四大凶卦) in the I Ching. The others are:

29. 坎 ☵ Kǎn Water

39. 蹇 ䷦ Cù Limping

47. 困 ䷮ Kùn oppression

As you can see, these four evil hexagrams are related to Kǎn or water
Tún has trouble at the beginning.
Kǎn has trouble at both the beginning and the end.
Cú has difficulty in the middle stage.
Kǔn signifies the most difficult situation.

3. You draw criticisms with every move you make.
4. Things do not turn out as you wish, so you retire to seclusion and
   examine yourself.

Yao Tsi (周公爻辭)

初九・盤桓・利居貞・利建侯・●

1st Yao. One hesitates on finding a blockage. It is worth persisting
towards the goal. It is worthwhile finding helpers. ●

Zhan (占)

1. Be aware of one's own behavior, and wait for a better opportunity.
2. One worries about one's financial situation.
3. It is not a good time to change a job or position.

六二・屯如邅如・乘馬班如・匪冦婚媾・女子貞不字・十年乃字・●

2nd Yao. Difficulties accumulate, and the horse and wagon come apart.
The person who appears is not a robber, but wants to woo. The young
lady is virtuous and does not agree to the offer. After ten years, she
agrees. ●

Zhan (占)

1. One does not know what course of action to take.
2. A woman indulges in the pleasure of sex.
3. Stick to one's duty, or there will be trouble.

六三・即鹿无虞・惟入於林中・君子幾・不如舍・往吝・●

3rd Yao. A man who goes deer hunting without his guide only gets lost. A mature person reads the signs and decides to do nothing. If he went on, he would just be humbled. ●

Zhan (占)

1. Be content to be what one is.
2. Don't concentrate on details and forget the main purpose.
3. One is unable to return to the proper path after going astray.

六四 • 乘馬班如 • 求婚媾 • 往吉 • 无不利 •

4th Yao. Horse and wagon come apart. One looks for a way to unite them. It is good fortune to do something. Everything favors it.

Zhan (占)

1. One is capable of adapting oneself to circumstance.
2. One has good luck after suffering from unfavorable times.
3. It is a good time to marry.

九五 • 屯其膏 • 小貞吉 • 大貞凶 • ●

5th Yao. It is hard to find good favor. To work mildly and persistently will bring good luck. To push too hard will bring misfortune. ●

Zhan (占)

1. Lack of forbearance in small matters upsets great plans.
2. Don't try to make much of a trifle.
3. It is not a good time to do business, or to change a job.

上六 • 乘馬班如 • 泣血漣如 •

6th Yao. Horse and wagon come apart. Tears of blood flow.

Zhan (占)

1. It is a difficult and hopeless stage.
2. Happy sunny days will bring joy after all the hardships are endured.

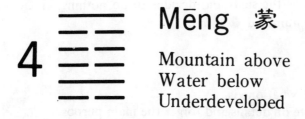

4   Mēng 蒙

Mountain above
Water below
Underdeveloped

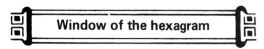

Window of the hexagram

1. A deer and a pile of coins mean to have high official rank, and wealth.
2. A beautiful box with a matching cover means to be united and to work in concert.
3. A twig of a plum tree is snapped. This means there are still other twigs.
4. Two men are rowing on the river in a boat laden with jewelry and coins. This means to return home in glory.

Image and Symbol

人藏祿寶之課 • 萬物發生之象 •
The image is to use one's talent when the time comes.
The symbol is of the initial stage of all things.

Kua Tsi （文王彖辭）

蒙亨 • 匪我求童蒙 • 童蒙求我 • 初筮告 • 再三瀆 • 瀆則不告 • 利貞 •
Mēng is successful. I don't seek out the young fellow, he seeks me. When he asks for an oracle, I tell him. If he asks the same thing two or three times, this is poor manners, and I tell him nothing more. It is favorable to persist in one's goals.

Zhan (占) *or hints on divining*

1. This is an August hexagram. It is bad in spring and autumn, has troubles in winter.
2. The hexagram is water ☵ under a mountain ☶: water becomes fog, so we cannot see the mountain.
3. One considers a matter in an obsessive way.

Yao Tsi (周公爻辭)

初六 • 發蒙 • 利用刑人 • 用說桎梏 • 以往吝 •
1st Yao. To develop an ignorant person, it is good to apply discipline.

Severely rigid restraints should be removed. To go on with these brings disaster.

▌ *Zhan* (占) ▌

1. One is to dispense to reward and punishment impartially.
2. A wise man knows when he is beaten or when to reatreat.
3. It is difficult to please everybody.

六三 • 勿用取女 • 見金夫 • 不有躬 • 无攸利 • ●

3rd Yao.   Do not take up with a woman who throws herself at any strong man. It's a waste of time. ●

▌ *Zhan* (占) ▌

1. Lewdness is the worst of all sins.
2. Only one party is willing.
3. One injures a person already in difficulty.

六四 • 困蒙吝 ●

4th Yao. Getting taken up with impractical dreams brings humiliation. ●

▌ *Zhan* (占) ▌

1. Don't isolate yourself from society.
2. There is much ado about nothing.
3. Truth seldom sounds pleasant, but you have to listen.

六五 • 童蒙吉 • ○

5th Yao. If you are underdeveloped, a childlike attitude is good fortune. ○

▌ *Zhan* (占) ▌

1. Learning is an endless process.
2. One discovers his ignorance only through learning.
3. One should make use of what one has learned.

上九 • 擊蒙 • 不利爲寇 • 利禦寇 •

6th Yao. If you must punish foolishness, it is poor to do it excessively. The good punishment is that which restores order.

Zhan (占)

1. You have to perceive another person's frame of mind through words and expression.
2. In handling one's subordinates, one has to use a proper mixture of severity and gentleness.
3. One needs to take every precaution at the beginning.

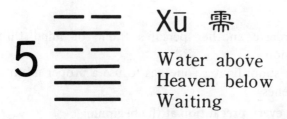

5

Xū 需

Water above
Heaven below
Waiting

Window of the hexagram

1. A full moon means to have the prospect of a very successful career.
2. The one gate means heaven will always leave a door open.
3. A man holding onto a dragon's tail means to try to achieve success by riding on the coattail of a brilliant master.
4. A monk acting as a receptionist means one will be guided by a distinguished person.
5. A grave means twelve is a lucky number.

Image and Symbol

雲靄中天之課・密雲不雨之象・

The image is the sky blotted out by clouds.

The symbol is of dark clouds building up, but no rain comes yet.

Kua Tsi （文王彖辭）

需・有孚・光亨・貞吉・利涉大川。

Xū. If you are sincere, great success will come. It is good fortune to persist. It is a good time to cross the great water.

Zhan （占） *or hints on divining*

1. This is an August hexagram. It is good for spring and winter.
2. The upper trigram Kun or water is evaporating to become clouds in The sky. The farmer waits for clouds to become rain. But this takes time.
3. If a hexagram's 5th Yao is Pien or moving Yao, and the Shih Kua is a pure hexagram, then this hexagram is called qúihún （歸魂） or soul returning hexagram. If we change qúihún's lower trigram, each Yao Yin to Yang or Yang to Yin, we get a new hexagram which is called Yòuhùn （遊魂） or soul wandering hexagram. When one gets qùihùn or Yòuhùn hexagram, it is a bad omen, especially related to illness. These hexagrams are:

	qúihún	pure	yóuhùn	
8. Bǐ				5 Xū
7. shī				36 Mingyi
14. Dàyǒu				35 jiñ
13. Tóng rén				6 Sòng
17. Suī				28 Dàguò
18. Gǔ				27 Yí
53. Jian				61 zhōngfú
54. Guimei				62 Xiaǒguò

Yao Tsi (周公爻辭)

初九 • 需于郊 • 利用恆 • 无咎 •

1st Yao. One waits in the meadow. It is good to continue with what one has at the moment. This is the right attitude.

Zhan (占) or hints on divining

1. Wait a while since the right time has not come yet.
2. Delay your newly conceived plan.
3. Your partner has some trouble, and cannot provide what you ask of him or her.

九二 • 需于沙 • 小有言 • 終吉 •

2nd Yao. One waits on the sand by the river. There is uneasy gossip.

Finally there is good fortune.

Zhan (占)

1. Your friend may have trouble; don't get involved in it.
2. Where whole-hearted dedication is seen, the whole world will step aside to let you by.
3. Calm down. Do not enter a lawsuit.

九三 • 需于泥 • 致寇至。●

3rd Yao. One waits stuck in the mud, and the enemy is attracted.●

Zhan (占)

1. One suffers a major setback because of carelessness.
2. If one does not take care of oneself, one will be beset with poverty and illness.
3. Your girl friend found a new love.

六四 • 需于血 • 出自穴 ●

4th Yao. One waits in blood. Try to get out of the pit. ●

Zhan (占)

1. Don't try to resort too violence.
2. The situation is very dangerous. One must stand fast and let fate take its course.
3. The patient needs an operation.

六五 • 需于酒食 • 貞吉 • ○

5th Yao. One waits while having food and drink. One persists and there is good fortune. ○

Zhan (占)

1. To wait quietly for good news.
2. Good food is not a luxury to you now.
3. You will recover from illness.

上六 • 入于穴 • 有不速之客 • 三人來 • 敬之終吉 •

6th Yao. One falls into a pit. Three surprise guests show up. Entertain them and eventually there will be good fortune.

Zhan (占)

1. The waiting is over. Taking caution in this situation is all that one needs to progress.
2. If three of us are walking together, at least one of the other two is good enough to be my teacher in some area.
3. Three years of hard work is crowned with success.

6 Sōng 訟

Heaven above
Water below
Lawsuit

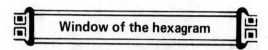

Window of the hexagram

1. Two Chinese characters 口 and 舌 , or mouth and tongue, mean careless talk may land one in trouble.
2. A sleeping tiger lies at the base of the mountain. This means one should guard against losing one's head and panicking.
3. A document in the cloud means something that can be looked at, but not approached.
4. A person standing beneath the tiger means the diviner should be very careful about everything.

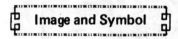

Image and Symbol

飛鷹逐兎之課・水火相遠之象・

The image is the soaring eagle swooping to catch its prey.
The symbol is water and fire cannot coexist.

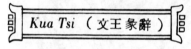

Kua Tsi （文王象辭）

訟・有孚窒・惕中吉・終凶・利見大人・不利涉大川・

Sóng. You have good intention, but find opposition. Stopping halfway brings good fortune, but pushing ahead will bring disaster. It is a good idea to confer with an influential person. It is not a time to cross the great water.

Zhan (占) *or hints on divining*

1. This is a February hexagram. It is good in summer and fall, bad in spring and winter.
2. Think and plan ahead and take precautions against calamity.
3. Nobody wins in a lawsuit.

Yao Tsi (周公文辭)

初六・不永所事・小有言・終吉・

1st Yao. If one dosen't keep up the conflict, maybe there is a little criticism, but in the end there is something good.

Zhan (占)

1. The best thing to do with a conflict is to drop the issue.
2. You may lose money.
3. He who cannot forbear in small matters spoils great undertakings.

九二•不克訟•歸而逋•其邑人三百戶•无眚•

2nd Yao.   One decides conflict is impractical, and one gives it up and goes home.   The 300 households of one's town are protected from disaster.

Zhan (占)

1. Careless talk may land one in trouble.
2. Timely withdrawal prevents evil consequence.
3. There is a bad omen after April.

六三。食舊德•貞厲•終吉。或從王事。无成。

3rd Yao.   Strengthening oneself by studying past virtues creates the ability to persist.   There is danger, but finally there is good fortune. If you happen to serve a king, do not seek conspicuous appointments.

Zhan (占)

1. It is a warning of the danger that goes with an expansive temper.
2. Do not be incited to some action by others.
3. The modest receive benefit, while the conceited reap failure.

九四•不克訟•復卽命• 渝•安貞吉•

4th Yao.   One rejects the conflict, gives it up and accepts what such a fate offers.   One changes one's attitude and finds calmness in persisting in good works. Good fortune.

Zhan (占)

1. Contentment brings happiness.
2. Good naturedness leads to good conditions.
3. Do not plan to compete in an election.

九五•訟•元吉•○

5th Yao.   Giving the dispute to the arbiter is the greatest good fortune.

Zhan (占)

1. One has one's wish fulfilled.
2. Take action as opportunity arises.
3. It is good to seek a spouse.

上九。或錫之鞶帶・終朝三褫之・●

6th Yao.   Even if one happens to get an honorary leader belt, by
noontime it will have been snatched away by others three times.

Zhan (占)

1. One works hard without achieving anything.
2. A triumph is not backed by facts.
3. What one gains cannot offset the losses.

7

Shī 師

Earth above
Water below
Army

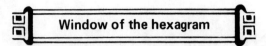

Window of the hexagram

1. It is good in the year of the tiger, horse, and sheep.
2. A general stands on the stage. This means having the authority to make military decisions.
3. The person in charge has an official seal. This means authority or holding power unchallenged.
4. A man kneeling on the stage means to be rewarded, it is a good omen.

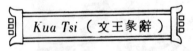

Image and Symbol

天馬出群之課 • 以寡伏眾之象 •
The image is a horse soaring to heaven.
The symbol is of large numbers being overwhelmed by a small group of the enemy.

Kua Tsi （文王象辭）

師 • 貞 • 丈人吉 • 无咎 •
Shī. It takes persistence in the work and a strong leader..
There is good fortune and no feeling of blame.

Zhan （占） 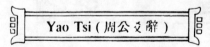 *or hints on divining*

1. This is a July hexagram. It is good in winter and bad in summer and fall.
2. Without good organization nothing can be accomplished.
3. The realization of good things is usually preceded by rough times.

Yao Tsi （周公爻辭）

初六 • 師出以律 • 否臧 • 凶 •
1st Yao. An army must set out well organized. If it is disorganized, misfortune will occur.

Zhan (占)

1. At the beginning of an enterprise, preparation is imperative.
2. Do not plan to oppress your partner to the extreme.
3. Encourage freedom of speech and accept what the other person is saying.

九二・在師中・吉・无咎・王三錫命・

2nd Yao. One is in the middle of the army. This is good fortune and there is no blame. The ruler recognizes this with a triple decoration.

Zhan (占)

1. Better days are coming after all the hardships endured.
2. Share good and bad with your partner.
3. You may have a twin.

六三・師或輿尸・凶・●

3rd Yao. The army carries dead men in the wagon. Bad luck. ●

Zhan (占)

1. An army which is cocksure about its invincibility is doomed to defeat.
2. There is shocking news of a patient.
3. Pursue good fortune and avoid the course of calamity.

六四・師左次・无咎・

4th Yao. Time to retreat. This is blameless.

Zhan (占)

1. The best strategy is to pretend to retreat in order to hide the intention to move ahead.
2. Share bliss and adversity together.
3. Don't be mad at your sweetheart.

六五・田有禽・利執言・无咎・長子帥師・弟子輿尸・凶・

5th Yao. There are animals in the cultivated field. It is good to catch them and there is no blame. The most mature must lead. If the younger person's work leads to his carrying a lot of dead men, then continuing is bad luck.

Zhan (占)

1. Persistent effort can overcome difficult circumstances.
2. He who acts fast will catch the animal first.
3. One is far advanced in one's illness.

上六 · 大君有命 · 開國承家 · 小人勿用 ·

6th Yao. The great prince issues orders on dividing the victory spoils. He gives some of his workers estates to run and others large estates. He does not offer this kind of reward to the inferior and disloyal ones.

Zhan (占)

1. Don't give great responsibility to a man of common ability.
2. To be a founder of an enterprise is very difficult.
3. One should retire after achieving success.

8

Bī 比

Water above
Earth below
Loyalty

Window of the hexagram

1. The full moon in the sky is a metaphor for having the prospect of a very successful career.
2. A scholar drinking in the moonlight means to relax and take one's ease.
3. Drinking deeply means happiness is flawed by sorrow when it reaches an extreme.
4. The pottery jar for cooking medicines is put on a high shelf. This means very good health; you don't need any medicines.
5. A withered old tree puts forth beautiful flowers. This means good fortune that comes after a long spell of bad luck.

Image and Symbol

眾星拱北之課 • 水行地上之象 •

The image is of bright stars encircling the major star of Polaris.

The symbol is of land flooded with water.

Kua Tsi (文王象辭)

比 • 吉 • 原筮元永貞 • 无咎 。不寧方來，後夫凶 。

Bi is good fortune. You should make sure by asking the oracle if you have high standards and constant persistence. If so, everything is good. Uncertain helpers gradually join up. Those who come too late lose out.

Zhan (占) or hints on divining

1. This is a July hexagram. It is good in summer and winter and suggests illness in Spring.
2. You will get help from all sides.
3. Do not do to others what you do not want to have done to you.

Yao Tsi (周公爻辭)

初六 • 有孚比之 • 无咎 • 有孚盈缶 • 終來有他吉 • ○

1st Yao. Hold on in truthfulness and loyalty and then there is no blame.

Truth is like a full earthen bowl. In the end, good fortune shows up from outside. ○

Zhan (占)

1. You start to strive for progress with determination.
2. Sincerity is the basis for forming relationships.
3. If a patient has this Yao, they will recover from illness soon.

六二・比之自內・貞吉・○

2nd Yao. Be loyal in an inward way. Persistence this way brings good luck. ○

Zhan (占)

1. An action impelled by emotion should stop within the limit of propriety.
2. People help those who help themselves.
3. The condition of a patient will be severe.

六三・比之匪人・

3rd Yao. Your loyalties are to the wrong people.

Zhan (占)

1. One always gets blame from somebody no matter how fair and just he is.
2. Do not give a guarantee or promise of money.
3. It is very hard to find something that is up to standard.

六四・外之比・貞吉・

4th Yao. Show your loyalty outwardly. Persistence brings good luck.

Zhan (占)

1. You will be promoted by your boss.
2. Receive advice with sincerity and tact from a good person.

九五・顯比・王用三驅・失前禽・邑人不誠・吉・

5th Yao. An example of holding together. When the king goes hunting, he uses beaters on three sides of the game only. He lets go those that run off in front. People do not need to be forever cautious. This is good.

luck.

Zhan (占)

1. You will break out from a heavy siege.
2. Do not to beat a person when he is already down.
3. To solve the bey issue will expedite the solution of the whole problem.

上六・比之无首・凶・●

6th Yao. A person has no sense for giving loyalty. Bad luck. ●

Zhan (占)

1. There is one trouble after another.
2. Doing something wrong leads to endless regret.
3. The greater one's adversity is, the stronger his fortitude should be.

Xiǎoxù 小畜

9

Wind above
Heaven below
Small Saving

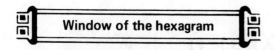

Window of the hexagram

1. A mountain chain represents the Chinese character 出 , "to go out."
2. A man walking up a steep trail on a mountain, means to do something despite the dangers and difficulties involved.
3. A boat grounded on the land means you cannot do anything withit.
4. A lookout post on the grass means something related to grass and trees.
5. There is a decoration of a cow's and a sheep's head on the lookout post means the time of cow and sheep is good.

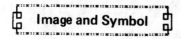

Image and Symbol

匣藏寶劍之課 • 密雲不雨之象 •

The image is a treasured sword resting in its sheath.

The symbol is of weather that is extremely cloudy, but no cloudburst comes yet.

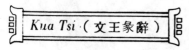

Kua Tsi (文王彖辭)

小畜 • 亨 • 密雲不雨 • 自我西郊 •

Xiaoxù   is successful. There are heavy clouds, but no rain comes from the east.

Zhan (占) or hints on diving

1. This is a November haxagram. It is good in winter, bad in summer and brings quarrels in fall.
2. One Yin Yao governs five Yang Yao; it is a Yin hexagram.
3. The time has not yet come for carrying out one's purpose.

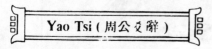

Yao Tsi (周公爻辭)

初九 • 復自道 • 何其咎 • 吉 •

1st Yao. Retrun to your right way. This is blameless. Good luck.

Zhan (占)

1. Be content to be what one is.
2. It is wise not to try to obtain anything by force.
3. One wins battles but loses the war.

九二・牽復・吉・

2nd Yao. He lets himself get drawn out and then returns. Good luck.

Zhan (占)

1. One must listen to good advice.
2. Repentance is salvation.

九三・輿說輻・夫妻反目・●

3rd Yao. The spokes break off the wagon wheels, A man and his wife look at each other with angry eyes. ●

Zhan (占)

1. There is too much urgency to make a wise choice.
2. Haste upsets carefully laid out plans.
3. A married couple should be love each other and be kind to one another.

六四・有孚・血去惕出・无咎・

4th Yao. If you have sincerity, blood and fear vanish. There is no blame.

Zhan (占)

1. This is a principle Yao. It is very difficult for one Yin to govern five Yangs.
2. Do not hide different plans behind the semblance of agreement.
3. There is no danger where there is preparedness.

九五・有孚攣如・富以其鄰・

5th Yao. If you are sincere and have mutual loyalty, you are blessed with many good neighbors.

Zhan (占)

1. Wealth and honor come to us only of their own accord.
2. You gain nothing from a rare opportunity, because you don't take advantage of the opportunity.
3. Although beginning a task from the bottom, one must not forget the ultimate objective.

上九 • 旡雨旣處 • 尙德載 • 婦貞厲 • 月幾望 • 君子征凶 •

6th Yao. The rain comes and people rest. This is due to the accumulating effects of character. To persist in making gains now is dangerous for a woman. It is nearly a full moon, and if a person persists, they have bad luck.

Zhan (占)

1. Accumulation of small amounts results in a huge quanity.
2. A woman shares the fate of the man she married, no matter what he is. (This is a traditional Chinese female virtue)
3. The sun declines after reaching the zenith.

10
Lǘ 履

Heaven above
Lake below
Stepping

Window of the hexagram

1. A bamboo umbrella means one can do something.
2. A damaged document means it has been in use for a long time.
3. A woman means the Chinese character 好 or good.
4. An umbrella means someone you can lean on.
5. A soldier holds a flag, representing a family's coat of arms.
6. There are two Chineese characters on the arch. 千里 means "a thousand miles," signifying that one may have high official rank or a good career.

Image and Symbol

如履虎尾之課 • 安中防危之象 •

The image is trampling on the tail of a tiger.

The symbol is of keeping prepared for possible future perils while enjoying peace.

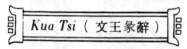

Kua Tsi (文王象辭)

履 • 履虎尾 • 不咥人 • 亨 •

Lu. One steps on the tiger's tail. It does not bite. Success is bad.

Zhan (占) or hints on divining

1. This is a March hexagram. It is good in winter and bad in spring and fall.
2. Lǔ is the image of a nude woman, the third Yao is the symbol of the vagina. One Ying Yao governs five Yang Yaos, so the character of this hexagram is Yin.

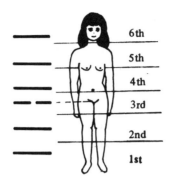

Yao Tsi (周公爻辭)

初九 • 素履往 • 无咎 •

1st Yao. One conducts oneself simply. One makes progress without being at fault.

Zhan (占)

1. It is wise to act independently without seeking company at this time.
2. One should avoid a criminal case involving sex.
3. Where there is a will there is a way.

九二 • 履道坦坦 • 幽人貞吉 •

2nd Yao. One follows a smooth and even course the way a dark man does, and this brings good fortune.

Zhan (占)

1. Do not be so eager to be successful that you see only the immediate advantages.
2. You have talents, but are unappreciated by the world.

六三 • 眇能視 • 跛能履 • 履虎尾 • 咥人凶 • 武人爲于大君 • ●

3rd Yao. A one-eyed man can see and a lame man can walk a little. So he steps on the tiger's tail, and it bites him. This is bad luck. But this is how a soldier fights for his king. ●

Zhan (占)

1. The situation is like that of a sheep attacked by a tiger.
2. Beware of an accident.
3. The realization of good things is usually preceded by rough going.

九四 • 履虎尾 • 愬愬終吉 •

4th Yao. He decides to step on the tiger's tail. He does it with great caution and care. He wins good fortune.

Zhan (占)

1. Do not go beyond your duties to meddle with another's affairs.
2. Errors are likely to occur in haste.
3. Keep distance from the other sex (Do not get involved in an affair.)

九五 • 夬履，貞厲 •

5th Yao. One proceeds resolutely. One persists but with an awareness of the dangers.

Zhan (占)

1. One should make quick decisions in the face of problems.
2. Awareness of the danger makes success possible.
3. There is unexpected income, promotion, etc.

上九 • 視履考祥 • 其旋元吉 • ○

6th Yao. Look back over your conduct and assess the favorable things you did. When everything is well done, good fortune is yours. ○

Zhan (占)

1. You can hit the target with every shot.
2. Mastery comes from long training.
3. Everybody is satisfied.

11

Tài 泰

Earth above
Heaven below
Positive

Window of the hexagram

1. The sweet osmanthus flowers are in bloom on the full moon (月桂). An official climbing up a ladder means to emerge from an examination with success.
2. A deer holding a book in its mouth means something will be given by heaven.
3. A boy sits on the clouds. This can be good, like a sudden rise to success, or poor, like aiming high, but caring nothing about developing the fundamentals.
4. A sheep turns its head back. This is good when the year, month, or day is the image of the sheep.

Image and Symbol

天地交泰之課 • 小往大來之象 •

The image is heaven holding interc   se with earth.

The symbol is of making a very large profit with only a very small investment.

 *Kua Tsi* (文王象辭)

泰 • 小往大來 • 吉亨。

Tài. Small things are fading away and great things are developing. There is good fortune and success.

 *Zhan* (占) *or hints on divining*

1. This is a January hexagram. It is good in spring and bad in summer and fall.
2. The hexagram seen as a moving image shows strong lines coming up from the bottom and weak lines disappearing.
3. The hexagram seen as a closed system of influences shows the strong lines in a position to influence and the weak lines in a place to be influenced.
4. It is a good omen for everything.

Yao Tsi (周公爻辭)

初七・拔茅茹・以其彙・征吉・○

1st Yao. When you pull up a handful of couch grass, you get a handful of sod and roots with it. People are grouped by their common qualities. Being active at this time brings good fortune. ○

Zhan (占)

1. People with similar valuable abilities are in close contact with each another now. When you undertake important work, your helpers will be of the best sort.
2. Your ideas and active work will become more valuable because you share them with others of like mind and get their stimulus.
3. When you need a specialist for an unusual project, people in that person's field will find him for you quickly.

九二・包荒・用馮河・不遐遺・朋亡・得尚于中行・○

2nd Yao. You deal with rowdy people with gentleness. You ford the river with great energy. You never neglect remote matters. You do not look to your friends. In this way you can manage to walk the middle path. ○

Zhan (占)

1. Instead of being lazy and careless because you can get away with it, you do everything the right way. As a result you make the most of your time, instead of wasting it.
2. You love fairness and moderation so much, nothing distracts you from this.
3. If you have the intention to open new land for farming, you will be successful.

九三・无平不陂・无往不復・艱貞无咎・勿恤其孚・于食有福・

3rd Yao. There is no even ground without a hill nearby and no adventuring without a return home. If you remain persevering even when things get dangerous, you never do anything to feel you are to blame. Do not complain about these variations, enjoy what good luck you still have right now.

Zhan (占)

1. There is no perepetual good fortune! things fluctuate. Yet a person who can keep his spirit perpetually positive is always getting the best fortunes life can offer him.
2. The good circumstance does not last long.
3. We should continue mindful of evil; we remain persevering and make no mistakes.

六四 • 翩翩 • 不富以其鄰 • 不戒以孚 •

4th Yao. He flies down, does not brag of his riches, and visits with his neighbor. He has no secret motive, he is sincere.

Zhan (占)

1. There are people with wealth or superior abilities who enjoy being neighborly with any person.
2. A person needs to realize that there are important values every person has to offer as well as the unique values only some possess.
3. Do not be as stubborn as a mule.

六五 • 帝乙歸妹 • 以祉元吉 •

5th Yao. King I marries off his sister. The result is blessings to all and the highest good fortune.

Zhan (占)

1. The king does not give his offspring his power over others, but sends them off to live their own lives and learn their own powers. Instead of becoming a slave to such influence, they have the great good fortune to be free and develop on thier own.
2. A person who cannot stand fluctuations of fortune throws away the good things life offers him.

上六 • 城復于隍 • 勿用師 • 自邑告命 • 貞吝 • ●

6th Yao. The wall falls into the moat. Do not call the enemy up; just keep in touch and command your friends. To persevere in opposition would lead to great losses. ●

Zhan (占)

1. If something collapses completely, trying to save it will waste your time and endanger you. Be quiet and try to keep yourself together and see what fate brings.
2. Good fortune will not last forever.

12

Bì 否

Heaven above
Earth below
Negative

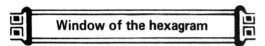

Window of the hexagram

1. A man is bed-ridden with illness, because he is too ambitious.
2. A broken mirror means something that cannot be reunited.
3. A man sitting on the road means the traveller that is coming is a long ways off yet.
4. An arrow is being dropped before it is shot means it has no chance to reach the target.
5. A man clapping and laughing means happiness is followed by sorrow when it is too extreme.
6. The mouth and tongue mean kissing or gossip.

Image and Symbol

天地不交之課 • 人口不圓之象 •

The image is that heaven is not holding intercourse with earth.
The symbol is of people unable to live together.

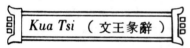

Kua Tsi （ 文王象辭 ）

否之匪人 • 不利君子貞 • 大往小來 •

Bǐ, the evil people are successful. It does not help a good person to persevere with things. Great matters go away and small ones come.

Zhan (占) *or hints on divining*

1. A time of triviality and second-rate things is coming. The weak lines move up from the bottom and the strong ones go out at the top.
2. This is a July hexagram. It is good in spring and bad in summer and winter.
3. You are not strong enough to keep things from collapsing so you stand back and wait the bad times out.
4. Someone who is obviously a corrupt and exploitive person offers to help you, and you smile and say, "No, thanks."

```
┌─────────────────────┐
│  Yao Tsi ( 周公爻辭 )  │
└─────────────────────┘
```

初六 • 拔茅茹 • 以其彙 • 貞吉亨 •

1st Yao. When you pull up a handful of couch grass, you get a handful of sod and roots with it. People are grouped by their common qualities. Inner perseverance will eventually bring good fortune and success.

▌ *Zhan* (占) ▐

1. Some greedy people offer you a chance to make a lot of money, but you look at all the harm they are doing, and realize it is better to be poor and have more valuable dreams right now.
2. You look for activity and see some people doing something, but when you see one of them close up you know the others must be the same and you withdraw because their dreams are not yours.
3. Good-naturedness leads to propitiousness.

六二 • 包承 • 小人吉 • 大人否 • 亨 •

2nd Yao. Others will accept and put up with the good person. This is good fortune for inferior people. But the good man uses the time to stay with himself, and it helps him in the long run.

▌ *Zhan* (占) ▐

1. An accomplished person is approached by shady characters who want his help to further their schemes during hard times. They used to treat him with contempt but now they are very friendly. He turns them down.
2. A good person looks at some people having hard times and has an impulse to help them. They smile and are friendly. But he looks closer and sees they will not do anything truly constructive to help themselves. So he sees it is better to go his own way and develop himself.
3. Do not get involved in a lawsuit.

六三 • 包羞 • ●

3rd Yao. Others are ashamed of themselves but they do not show it outwardly. ●

Zhan (占)

1. A second-rater has gotten a post that is so far above his abilities it is ridiculous. He pushed forward to get it with gusto; now he sees in his heart what a fraud he is, and quails.
2. Even in the most dissolute and vicious person has some small weak realization of how vile and silly he is.
3. It is a bad omen for a patient.

九四 • 有命 • 无咎 • 疇離祉 • ○

4th Yao. The man who follows the commands of the highest sort acts without doing blameworthy things. Others of like mind share this quality with him. ○

Zhan (占)

1. The person who nurtured dreams of good things now has to act. He carries out his dreams in an unselfish way and so does not make mistakes. Those who are drawn to work with him do the same.
2. Instead of following a prearranged personal plan, a person asks "What is the best for this time?" and acts unselfishly, others work with him.
3. You are very much accomplished but behaving modestly.

九五 • 休否 • 大人吉 • 其亡其亡 • 繫於苞桑 •

5th Yao. Stagnation is ending. This is good fortune for the great person. "What if it should fail?" he worries, and so ties his success to a cluster of mulberry shoots.

Zhan (占)

1. When some plants are cut down their strong roots send back a dozen new shoots. The great person worries and looks for something like this to tie his work to, so an accident or two cannot spoil it.
2. A man who failed in something has a chance to start again. This time he uses all his discernment to find an approach that the times will push to success.
3. One fails to achieve success by a very narrow margin.

上九・傾否・先否後喜・○

6th Yao. The stagnation is ended. First there is a standstill, then good fortune. ○

[*Zhan* (占)]

1. The person who persevered thru bad times now finds them ended, and their dreams are still alive. They now reap what they sowed.
2. Yesterday everything went badly for no apparent reason. Now everything is fine again.
3. It is a good time to make a great effort to accomplish something once and for all in order to vaoid future trouble.

13

Tóngrén 同人

Heaven above
Fire below
Fellowship

Window of the hexagram

1. A man holds a document with the Chineese character 心 meaning "mind" on it. This means being blinded by greed.
2. A man shooting an arrow into the mountain means advancement, a high place on the list of people who passed an examination.
3. A deer drinking water, signifies that fame and wealth come in an endless flow.
4. A flowing stream means to have the prospect of a successful career.

Image and Symbol

遊魚從水之課・二人分金之象・

The image is a fish in water, a creature "in its own element."
The symbol is of money being divided between two persons.

Kua Tsi（文王象辭）

同人于野・亨・利涉大川・利君子貞・

Fellowship is out in the open. This is successful. It is good fortune now to cross the great water. The perseverance that an advanced person has acquired will bring success now.

Zhan（占）or hints on divining

1. This is a January hexagram, it is good in summer and fall.
2. If we change the 5th Yao from Yang to Yin, it becomes a pure hexagram of Fire. So Tóngrén is a qúihún or soul returned hexagram.
3. A man wants to start a health and exercise club. When he publicizes his plans, he finds a great many people are interested. He immediately forms the organization and sets in motion advanced goals that the strong interest makes possible to undertake.
4. There have been many break ins in the neighborhood. People get angry and go to the local government to demand action and to work with officals to do something to correct things.

Yao Tsi (周公爻辭)

初九 • 同人于門 • 无咎 •

1st Yao. Fellowship with men entering the gate. There is no blame.

Zhan (占)

1. One plans to attend a class and meets one's fellow students on the way. All work together with good result.
2. One meets others with the same goal just as one starts a big project. Later one finds they have become good friends and allies.
3. It is a good omen for going abroad.

六二 • 同人于宗 • 吝 •

2nd Yao. Fellowship with men in the clan. Humiliation.

Zhan (占)

1. "We must get what we can for ourselves before we think about the others" the small group says. They wind up getting nothing.
2. "Everyone looks out for themselves and we must do the same" the small group says. They get caught stealing what belongs to others and go to jail.
3. Do not wash your dirty linen in public.

九三 • 伏戎于莽 • 升其高陵 • 三歲不興 。 ●

3rd Yao. He hides his weapons in the thick brush and climbs the high hill for a vantage point. For three years he does not rise. ●

Zhan (占)

1. The group of people discovers gold. Immediately they all look at each other with distrust. There is so much disharmony that most of the riches are lost.
2. "We all trust each other," everyone says. Then they go home and make plans for destroying the other person if they make a false move. All their energy goes to this and nothing is done.
3. You will suffer the conquences of your own actions.

九四 • 乘其墉 • 弗克攻 • 吉 •

4th Yao. He climbs up on his wall, but he can not manage an attack.
Good luck.

🀐 *Zhan (* 占 *)* 🀐

1. Two men plan to fight when they meet in a bar, but there are too
   many friendly people there and they can not fight with each other.
   Later there is a chance of reconcilianon.
2. Husband and wife are both spoiling for a fight but then their little
   child had an accident, They are so happy he is unharmed they
   forget all about it.
3. The realization of good things is usually preceded by rough goings.

九五 • 同人先號咷而後笑 • 大師克相遇 • ○

5th Yao. Men who are tied in fellowship first cry and lament, but
they wind up laughing, because after great difficulties they succeed in
getting together. ○

🀐 *Zhan (* 占 *)* 🀐

1. A couple who met and fell in love on vacation return to their homes
   in different parts of the country, and lament. Finally after lengthy
   delays they succeed in shifting their jobs and responsiblities around
   so they can be together.
2. Two people meet at a party and find they have strong common
   goals, and they want to go into business together. But each is tied
   down with many responsibilities. It takes a long time, but they
   finally get together and their enterprise prospers.
3. Another's good suggestion, can help one remedy one's own defects.

上九 • 同人于郊 • 无悔 •

6th Yao. Fellowship with men in the open field. No disappointment.

〔 *Zhan (* 占 *)* 〕

1. A man moves to a new town and finds the people there have nothing
   in common with him. So he gets to know his neighbors and joins

in a community project and makes the best of it.

2. A young woman gets a job at a plant and finds all the people there are older and have little in common with her. She sees they are good natured people and so is able to get along with them in a pleasant and friendly way.

3. It is difficult to please everybody.

14 Dàyōu 大有

Fire above
Heaven below
Great Possession

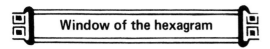

Window of the hexagram

1. A woman releasing the Chi or life-energy from her abdomen means a joyful atmosphere.
2. A baby seen in the midst of the Chi means to have a twin.
3. The presence of king doctors means that during childbirth, the most highly skilled gynecologist is present.
4. A medicine giving off light; represents a drug with very high efficacy.
5. A woman accepting the drug means it's good for her.
6. The presence of a dog means this hexagram is good at the time of the dog.

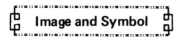

Image and Symbol

金玉滿堂之課 • 日麗中天之象 •
The image is one's house filled with riches.
The symbol is of a time as clear as high noon.

Kua Tsi （文王象辭）

大有 • 元亨。
Dàyou. Possessions on a large scale. The highest success.

Zhan （占） *or hints on divining*

1. This is a January hexagram; it is good in spring and winter and bad in summer.
2. Dàyōu is a qùihùn or soul returned hexagram, one Yin Yao governs five Yang Yaos.
3. A man who has done well at an unimportant job suddenly gets promoted during an emergency to a job that gives full use to all his best abilities.
4. An artist who could think of nothing good to work on suddenly finds himself full of the most advanced creative impulses.

Yao Tsi （周公爻辭）

初九 • 无交害 • 匪咎 • 艱則无咎 •

1st Yao. A person has no relationship with harmful things. Thus there is no blame. If you are always aware of possible problems, you go on this way.

▤ *Zhan* (占) ▤

1. A young man is preparing to take on a big job with great responsibilities. He is careful to act well and thinks over all the mistakes he might get drawn into, so he can avoid them.
2. An ambitious apartment dweller plans to build his own home. He spends all his free time studying every part of the project with great care.
3. Do not be ignorant and boastful.

九二・大車以載・有攸往・无咎・○

2nd Yao. If you have a big wagon for loading things, you can do something. You will have no regrets. ○

▐ *Zhan* (占) ▌

1. A person who has great talents but no way to use them for something good, suddenly discovers a way of using them in a job. He goes ahead and prospers.
2. A small businessman never sells his product very well. Then he risks putting an advertisement in a newspaper and finds out he has orders from everywhere.
3. You will be successful in whatever you do.
4. It is a very bad omen for a patient.

九三・公用享于天子・小人弗克・

3rd Yao. A prince offers his property to the Son of Heaven. A small minded man can not do this.

▥ *Zhan* (占) ▥

1. A man has unusual success, so he sacrifices a lot of it to help his friends. His next door neighbor hoards all his wealth and falls sick from loneliness.
2. A man has a chance to take advantage of the poor and make a lot of money. His friends tell him to go ahead, but he decides to

help the poor with his resources and not charge them.

九四 • 匪其彭 • 无咎 。

4th Yao. A man acts different from his neighbors, and escapes blame.

Zhan (占)

1. A man gets a new job and finds everyone at the office is showing off their status and power. He tries to do his job well and ignore being influenced to imitate them.
2. A young man just out of college joins a research firm as a scientist. The others treat him courteously as an equal but he recognizes he is their inferior in experience and is modest and reserved.
3. One needs to abstain from a bad habit such as drug addiction or carnal pleasure, completely.

六五 • 厥孚交如 • 威如 • 吉 •

5th Yao. A person who offers his powers generously but in a dignified way has good luck.

Zhan (占)

1. A specialist at a new, well-paying job goes out of his way to offer his special talents to all who request help. He finds some of his colleagues begin to take him for granted and treat him inconsiderately. He immediately starts acting more formal and reserved, and the rude ones remember their manners.
2. A mother feeds her children snacks generously whenever they want. She finds they wind up messing up the refrigerator. So she requires them to sit at the table and say "please," and their habits improve.
3. It is a bad omen for a fatient.

上九 • 自天祐之 • 吉 • 无不利 • ○

6th Yao. He is blessed by heaven, and so has good luck. Nothing he undertakes goes patient. ○

Zhan (占)

1. A person achieves great success with the development of his skills. When he thinks of this, he remembers those who gave their energies to teach him and that he should not think all the credit is his. As a

result he is always open to help and influence from others and the new tasks he tries prosper.

2. A man is proud of his achievements, yet remembers that much of their substance came from somewhere else. In relations with others he thinks not only of getting paid well, but of somehow offering to others the chances he had.

15

Qiān 謙

Earth above
Mountain below
Modesty

Window of the hexagram

1. The full moon means things will be fair and square.
2. A man riding on a deer means wealth and official rank will both be achieved.
3. Three people standing on a disordered pile of silk means endless involvement between them.
4. An official holding a mirror means transcending intelligence in making a wise judgment.
5. A Chinese character 公 or "fair" is on the document. This means everything will be in order.

Image and Symbol

地中有山之課・仰高就下之象・

The image is the mountain disappearing into the plane.
The symbol is of hoping to achieve high position but winding up with something much less.

Kua Tsi (文王象辭)

謙・亨・君子有終。

Qiān. Modesty creates success, The good man carries things out thoroughly.

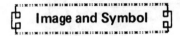 *or hints on divining*

1. This is a September hexagram. It is good in summer, fall and winter.
2. One Yang Yao governs five Yin Yaos. It is the image of a nude man.
3. A man achieves great success, and then he immediately sets out to disperse what he has to enrich others who have too little. People think he is rich, yet no one envies him.
4. Two men think of making a great deal of money, but neither ever thinks of what it is good for. One man fails and is poor, and his whole life is sterile. The other man succeeds and is rich, and his whole life is sterile.

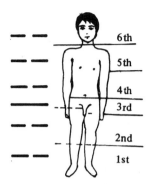

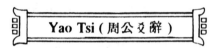

初六・謙謙君子・用涉大川・吉・

1st Yao. A good man who is modest about his life can cross the great water. Good luck.

Zhan (占)

1. An energetic man who "just likes to do good things" happens on an opportunity for a huge undertaking that is in his line. He begins immediately and manages to carry it through. People say, "You must have had great dreams." "No," he says, "I just like to do interesting things and had a chance to do one."
2. A minority group member is hired for an executive job and quickly sees it was done only for appearances. He thinks, so what, I have a chance to learn some things, and when he leaves the job several years later he starts a business of his own that surpasses his former employers.

六二・鳴謙・貞吉・○

2nd Yao. Modesty that comes to expression naturally. To persevere with this brings good fortune. ○

⚍ Zhan (占) ⚍

1. A man sees someone who looks quiet and dour and feels an impulse of sympathy for him. He says something good natured to distract him. The person seems to throw off his gloom. Years later the person tells him he was about to commit suicide and the interruption jarred him out of it.
2. A man who is down on his luck and feels alienated and bitter towards everyone sees someone slip on the icy street and catches him before he hurts himself. The rescued person is so warm and grateful, the bitter man feels "part of the human race again" and his bad mood is destroyed.
3. You will have an occasional joy because of unexpected good luck.

九三 • 勞謙君子 • 有終吉 •

3rd Yao. A good man of modesty and merit carries things out to conclusion. Good luck.

⚏ Zhan (占) ⚏

1. A new man appears on the scene and his work is so good he rises rapidly to prominence. People think "soon he will begin throwing his weight around like the others." They find instead he continues to be courteous and moderate, and they are eager to help him carry out his work to completion.
2. A man starts an ambitious project and soon finds it is tremendously more difficult than he had thought. He thinks "well, I will just go slower and see what I can do, that's all." After a while his capabilities come into focus and it becomes much easier and he completes the project.
3. Do not desire to excel over others, only try to do your best.

六四 • 无不利 • 撝謙 •

4th Yao. There is nothing that does not help modesty in movement and action.

⚏ Zhan (占) ⚏

1. It is good to be like a breeze flowing through a thicket. It opposes

nothing, always finds the open spaces to move through, and is never halted.

2. A person who makes a lot of hustle and bustle to let people know they are there attracts the trouble-makers while a person who helps things to flow smoothly cannot be easily found by them.
3. Remember! Pride goes before a fall.

六五 • 不富以其鄰 • 利用侵伐 • 无不利 •

5th Yao. It is not time to boast of one's riches to one's neighbor. It is a time to attack with energy. There is nothing that will not be favorable in this.

Zhan (占)

1. A man finds himself unjustly opposed. He corrects the situation vigorously, yet offers no offense beyond this.
2. A man in a store is ignored by the clerk when he wants help. He goes and knocks on the manager's door and interrupts him to repeat his request for service.

上六 • 利用行師 • 征邑國 •

6th Yao. Modesty comes to expression. It is good to set armies on the move to correct one's own city and country.

Zhan (占)

1. A man finds people do not treat him with respect. He practices expressing himself more clearly, wears better clothes, and goes out and demands respect.
2. An employer gets upset when he notices his workers no longer work efficiently. He looks at himself and notices he's grown lazy and careless and spends the whole week improving his own habits.

16

Yǔ 豫

Thunder above
Earth below
Joy

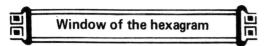

Window of the hexagram

1. Double mountain ranges. This means the Chinese character 出 or "out". The character is formed of two 山 or mountains.
2. An official steals a glance from behind a cliff. This means a time to find what one has been looking for.
3. A deer and a horse mean good fortune.
4. Ingots of gold and silver, piles of coins. Coins mean wealth and riches. This is a very lucky omen.

Image and Symbol

鳳凰生雛之課 • 萬物發生之象 •
The image is a fine son born of a fine father.
The symbol is all things starting to sprout.

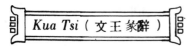

Kua Tsi (文王彖辭)

豫 • 利建侯行師 • ●
Yǔ. It is a time to obtain helpers, and set armies to marching. ●

Zhan (占) or hints on divining

1. This is a May hexagram. It is good in summer and fall, bad in winter.
2. The 4th Yang Yao governs five Yin Yaos, it is a Yang hexagram.
3. You find a community project that needs doing and when you talk to others about it, everyone agrees. It succeeds.

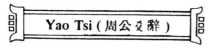

Yao Tsi (周公爻辭)

初六 • 鳴豫 • 凶 • ●
1st Yao. Yǔ that is expressed too much brings poor fortune.

Zhan (占)

1. You talk about your wonderful ideas, but when others want to

say they agree and see some action, you just go on talking. They get
disgusted and leave. Nothing happens.

2. You have a good idea and others agree, but you talk about how
wonderful it is so much, they get bored and lose interest.

3. You are unable to do what you wish.

六二・介于石・不終日・貞吉・

2nd Yao. He is as steady as a stone. Not a whole day passes. Perseverance is good luck.

Zhai (占)

1. Instead of throwing away your energy moving blindly, you watch
circumstances and act only when the times are right.

2. One should constantly make improvements guiding himself with a
new apprasisal of his achievements every now and then.

六三・肝豫悔・遲有悔・

3rd Yao. Yu that only looks upward brings disappointment. He who
hesitates is lost.

Zhan (占)

1. The plans of another person inspire you no end, but you fail to join
the group in time, and get nowhere.

2. The demand exceeds the supply.

3. Relying upon oneself is better than relying upon others.

九四・由豫・大有得・勿疑・朋盍簪・○

4th Yao. You are the source of enthusiasm and can achieve success.
Do not doubt yourself. You gather supporters around you the way a
hair clasp holds hair together.○

Zhan (占)

1. You have the vision to see that you and your friends have what it
takes to do the job. Because of your sureness and clarity, everyone
feels confident and works hard.

2. You will take the right steps and make quick progress.

3. You suffer disgrace in order to accomplish your high-minded task.

六五 • 貞疾 • 恒不死 •

5th Yao. A person is ill and fatigned, yet does not die.

⚹ Zhan (占) ⚹

1. You know you don't have the energy to act and feel oppressed at having to hold back, until you look and see someone who rashly went ahead end in failure. Then you see that your enforced waiting is wise.
2. The greater loss one suffers, the greater fortune one will amass.
3. Long illness makes the patient a good doctor.

上六 • 冥豫 • 成 • 有渝 • 无咎 • ●

6th Yao. He is deluded by enthusiasm. But if he can change when he comes to see this, there is nothing serious lost. ●

Zhan (占)

1. You meet some friends with wonderful plans and think you will all have a great time doing things. Then you find they are all "warm weather warriors" and it's all nonsense. You feel upset, but you realize you still have energy to go on looking for good things.
2. Your plan is like trying to recover a needle from the bottom of the sea.
3. If you abandon yourself to your passions, you will wind in a social position way below where you are now.

17   Sui′ 隨

Lake above
Thunder below
Following

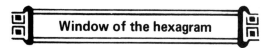

Window of the hexagram

1. A snow goose brings a message through the clouds. This means having good sources of information.
2. A pile of coins means riches.
3. A man sits inside of the red gates. This means being in authority.
4. A person stands outside the red gates. This means to seek fame and wealth.

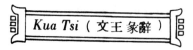

Image and Symbol

良工琢玉之課・如木推車之象・

The image is one of skilled craftsman cutting and polishing a piece of jade.
The symbol is that of using a log to push a car.

Kua Tsi (文王象辭)

隨・元亨・利貞・无咎・

Suí or. Following will have the greatest success. Persistence is advisable. Do what is blameless.

Zhan (占) *or hints on divining*

1. This is a July hexagram. It is good in summer and winter, and bad in fall.
2. If we change the 5th Yao from Yang to Yin, the Suí becomes a pure or Chún hexagram 51 Zhèn or Thunder.
3. You join a group with a strong leader. You find the demands everyone has to meet to keep the good plans working out are very rigorous. When success comes you realize this was important and worth it.

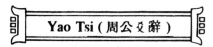

Yao Tsi (周公爻辭)

初九・官有渝・貞吉・出門交有功・ ☺

First Yao. Standards are always changing. Persistence brings good luck.

To go out through the door and find company leads to actions. ○

╏ *Zhan* (占) ╏

1. You find your followers losing interest. You go out and circulate among them and find only their personal aims shifted somewhat and they're ready to follow when you adapt plans to their aims.
2. The methods used may vary, but the principle is the same.
3. A great man knows how to ride the tide of his time.

六二・係小子・失丈夫・●

2nd Yao. She stays with a young fellow, and loses her husband. ●

╏ *Zhan* (占) ╏

1. You stay with a group of nice people who really don't have any clear plans. Later you meet someone from a group that is clearer minded and more active and find out how much you've lost out.
2. One is unable to make up one's mind as to which of two disivable things to choose.
3. Do not be tempted by small gains and suffer a big loss.

六三・係丈夫・失小子・隨有求得・利居貞・○

3rd Yao. If she follows her husband, she keeps away from that young fellow. She finds what she wants through following. It is good idea to persevere. ○

╏ *Zhan* (占) ╏

1. You join a group that is working hard and doing great things, and notice that you now see your old friends less and less and feel sad. Then you realize your life is improving because of your new initiatives.
2. You want something and succeed in getting just that.
3. Always try to criticize yourself so that everything will become perfect.

九四・隨有獲・貞凶・有孚在道・以明・何咎・

4th Yao. Following is successful. Persistence brings bad luck. But to guide oneself with sincerity creates a clear mind. How could there be anything wrong with this?

孟 *Zhan (占)* 製

1. Things go well. Then, when you continue further, they fail. You look over your actions and feelings and find you haven't kept up the best standards and were selfish. Though you take losses in process, you straighten things out, and then feel better.
2. Don't be too complacent about your own manners.
3. To follow what is right is like climbing a very steep slope.

九五・孚于嘉・吉・○

5th Yao. You follow goodness with sincerity. Good luck. ○

製 *Zhan (占)* 製

1. You have ambitious plans for the day, then you see someone who can use some help and you give up your plans so you can help. The other person is happy and you feel you've done something worthwhile.
2. One has to choose what is good and right and stick to it.
3. One has to decide what should be done first.

上六・拘係之・乃從維之・王用亨于西山・○

6th Yao. He meets with a loyal follower, and is brought back into the group. The king presents him to the Western Mountain. ○

Zhan (占)

1. You leave a group to go on your own, but one of them who understands you comes and convinces you to rejoin. Everyone benefits and your contribution is rewarded.
2. Get off to a new start; come out of your shell.
3. Happy events will soon take place in your home.

18

Gŭ 蠱

Mountain above
Wind below
Decay

Window of the hexagram

1. A child sits on a cloud. One day your son will be like a dragon.
2. A snow goose holds a letter in its beak. Good news.
3. A deer. Official rank is indicated.
4. A coin. Wealth.
5. A man and woman hold their hands together and bow to each other. This means congratulations is offered. But thi̇
   of mixed fortunes. Only if one can be alert and wary of one's situation is it good.

Image and Symbol

三蠱食血之課・以惡不久之象・

The image is of three vampires sucking blood.
The symbol is that an evil situation cannot go on forever.

Kua Tsi (文王彖辭)

蠱・利涉大川・先甲三日・後甲三日・

Gú or Decay. There is supreme success possible. It is a time to cross the great water. Before you start, three days pass and after you start another three days pass.

Zhan (占) or hints on divining

1. This is a January hexagram, it is good in summer, bad in fall and worst in winter.
2. If we change the 5th Yao Yin to Yang, Gu becomes a Chùn or pure hexagram 57 Sun. So Gu is a Qùihùn or soul returned hexagram. If you get this hexagram, and feel even a little uncomfortable, the best thing to do is going to your doctor to find out what is happening.
3. Things are run down and going to pieces. You make up a plan to regenerate things, and throw yourself into it with complete dedication, and succeed.
4. You decide you're dissatisfied because your life is "run down" and

make a master plan to renovate everything. You succeed.

Yao Tsi (周公爻辭)

初六・幹父之蠱・有子考・无咎・厲・終吉・

1st Yao. It is a time to correct what has been neglected by the father. If there is a son to do this, no blame comes to the father. Danger. Eventually good fortune.

Zhan (占)

1. You join a group only to find its former high achievements and ideals have regenerated. You set about rebuilding them energetically, and in the end everyone is happy.
2. One should correct one's faults once one is aware of them.
3. Do not withdraw or quit after learning of the difficulties involved.

九二・幹母之蠱・不可貞・

2nd Yao. In setting right what has been spoiled by the other, you must not be too persistent.

Zhan (占)

1. You find yourself in a group that has kept its high standards, but has grown weak and feeble through lack of spirit. You stir things up again, but you're careful not to push people so hard they can't keep up.
2. A wise mother would do everything for the healthly growth of her childern.
3. You cannot accomplish the task without help.

九三・幹父之蠱・小有悔・无大咎・

3rd Yao. In correcting what has been spoiled by the father, there will be some bad feelings, but nothing very serious.

Zhan (占)

1. In your new job as supervisor you reorganize the whole department and for a while most people are worried and angry. Then the new standards begin to improve things for everyone, and it's all forgotten.

2. You have little resources to do as much as you wish.

3. Many possibilities are open to you, just work a little harder.

六四・裕父之蠱・往見吝・ ●

4th Yao. To tolerate what is spoiled by the father. To continue with this guarantees humiliation. ●

Zhan (占)

1. You notice the furnace making a funny noise now and then and you think 'it can't amount to anything serious.' Then in the middle of the night, it blows up and fills the house with smoke.

2. You notice your car seems to drive a little irregularly, ignore it. The next day it breaks down completely in the middle of rush hour.

3. How dangerous is the world where temptations lurk everywhere.

六五・幹父之蠱・用譽・

5th Yao. To correct what has been spoiled by the father. One is praised.

Zhan (占)

1. The used car you buy turns out to be a lemon and you have no money for anything better. You go over it with a fine tooth comb and find lot of things and fix them. After that it runs like a new car.

2. The more the supporters, the greater the achievements of a leader.

3. This is a very bad omen for a patient.

上九・不事王侯・高尚其事・

6th Yao. He does not serve either king or lord. He has higher goals.

Zhan (占)

1. You give up a chance for big money as a talented commercial artist and devote yourself to pure creation. Years later your work is acclaimed as a pace setter for new developments.

2. Get your mind set in the groove it should follow.

3. It's better to sacrifice the few for the benefit of the majority.

19 ䷒

Lín 臨

Earth above
Lake below
Approach

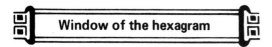
Window of the hexagram

1. A woman flies with the wind. This means one may receive wealth as the result of a relationship with a woman.
2. A flag flies from a car. The flag is a token of authority.
3. A man on a hilltop. This means being in a dangerous position.
4. A tiger sits at the foot of a mountain. This is a warning to take precautions against calamity.
5. A small box. A token that one should cooperate harmoniously.
6. A man shoots an arrow at a tiger. This means to remain attached to an influential person.

Image and Symbol

鳳入雞群之課・以上臨下之象・

The image is a phoenix standing among chickens.
The symbol is standing on a high mountain and viewing the valley below.

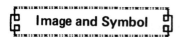
Kua Tsi (文王彖辭)

臨・元亨利貞・至于八月有凶・

Lín or Approach has the highest success. It is a time to persevere. By the eighth month, there will be misfortune.

Zhan (占) *or hints on diving*

1. This is a December hexagram. It is good in fall and winter, bad in summer.
2. You hear it will be a good year for gardeners. You plant a huge garden and work it thoroughly and by the time fall rolls around you have food for the winter.
3. You sense in your business that people are beginning to go for a certain product. You lay in a large supply and at the height of the product's popularity everyone comes to you because they don't have to wait for delivery.

Yao Tsi (周公爻辭)

初九・咸臨・貞吉・○

1st Yao. Joint approach. Perseverance is good luck. Everything favorable. ○

Zhan (占)

1. You want to make your home solar heated and find it is the current fad. You find everything you need easily and help others with the same ideas.
2. Love makes one blind to all imperfections.
3. You have already had a sweetheart in you mind.

九二・咸臨・吉・无不利・○

2nd Yao. Joint approach. Good luck. Everything favorable. ○

Zhan (占)

1. The government announces a limited program to help people renovate their homes. You sign up immediately, and are able to do a thorough job.
2. You and your partner share the same aspirations and have the same temperament.
3. You should make a quick decision when an opportunity offers itself.

六三・甘臨・无攸利・既憂之・无咎・●

3rd Yao. A comfortable approach. Nothing is favorable. If one worries over it, there are no faults. ●

Zhan (占)

1. You find success has been so strong you no longer pay attention to doing your work well. Shocked, you regain your old standards, and there are no troubles.
2. Plots or evil deeds will be exposed sooner or later.
3. You do not practice what you preach.

六四・至臨・无咎・○

4th Yao. Complete approach. There is nothing to blame. ○

Zhan（占）

1. You have developed your talents thoroughly in the past, and someone who realizes their value hires you for a demanding job that you are able to do well.
2. You suffer a loss in one place but make a gain somewhere else.
3. Your lost items are found by others and kept for claimant you.

六五・知臨・大君之宜・吉・○

5th Yao. Wise approach. This is for a great prince. Good luck.○

Zhan（占）

1. Though you're fussy, you leave the people you hired alone instead of constantly bothering them. As a result, they do superior work.
2. It is easier to do a thing than to know the reason why.

上六・敦臨・吉・无咎・○

6th Yao. Your approach is greathearted. Good luck. No flaws. ○

Zhan（占）

1. You see the group you once led has fallen on bad times, and you decide to return to it for awhile to straighten things out. Everyone benefits.
2. You have to be upright in character and diligent in the pursuit of knowledge.
3. The best thing to do is to keep that person at a respectful distance.

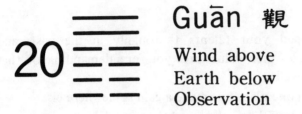

Guān 觀

Wind above
Earth below
Observation

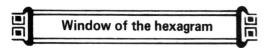

Window of the hexagram

1. Both sun and moon are in the sky. This means the benefits of one's achievements reach far and wide.
2. An official stands beside an incense table. This means to advance in rank.
3. A deer on the mountain means promotion.
4. A god wearing golden armor means to ride the high tide of good luck.
5. An official seal and a weighing scale. This is a good omen.

Image and Symbol

雲捲晴空之課・春花競發之象・
The image is that a clear blue sky is suddenly covered with clouds.
The symbol is all kinds of spring flowers in full bloom.

Kua Tsi (文王彖辭)

觀・盥而不薦・有孚顒若・
Gūan. The ablution is done and the offering not yet made. People look up to him with great trust.

Zhan (占) or hints on divining

1. This is an August hexagram. It is good in fall, and bad in summer and winter.
2. To push oneself ahead by depriving oneself of all daily comfort and subjecting oneself to hardships.
3. The engaged couple and their friends go through the wedding rehearsal the day before the big event. As they do so, the calmness and orderliness of the preacher makes them feel at ease and confident.

Yao Tsi (周公爻辭)

初六・童觀・小人无咎・君子吝・

1st Yao. Childlike observation. For lowly people this is all right, but for a leader this is a disgrace.

Zhan (占)

1. You should not content yourself with a thoughtless view of the prevailing forces.
2. You have to gain something from a rare opportunity.
3. It is as a man with a little learning in the presence of a great scholar.

六二・闚觀・利女貞・

2nd Yao. Take a peep through the door. This is all right for a woman.

Zhan (占)

1. One who avoids seeing trouble does not have to worry about trouble.
2. Don't criticize the others when you cannot do equal or better.
3. You think that is a secret, but it never has been one.

六三・觀我生進退・

3rd Yao. Observation of one's own life. Learn by observing why and when you advance or retreat.

Zhan (占)

1. There is a prospect of a thrilling time ahead for you.
2. To remeber past errors insures against repetition of the same error.
3. When things are at their worst, they will surely mend.

六四・觀國之光・利用賓於王・ ○

4th Yao. Observation of the glory of the kingdom. The king's invitation will be profitable for him. ○

Zhan (占)

1. The financial situation is getting worse, but you may have some unexpected income.
2. You have to learn the truth after investigation.
3. Time and patience beget success.

六五・觀我生・君子无咎・ ○

5th Yao. Observation of one's own life. The superior man is without blame.○

Zhan (占)

1. Where whole-hearted dedication is directed, the whole world will step aside to let you by.
2. It is impossible to predict who will be the winner.
3. The truth comes to light eventually.

上九 · 觀其生 · 君子无咎 ·
6th Yao. Observation of his life. The superior man is without blame.

Zhan (占)

1. One should think of the time of peril at the time of peace.
2. Kind deeds pay rich dividends to the doer.
3. You have to gather his or her frame of mind through his other words and expressions.

21

Hēshi 噬嗑

Fire above·
Thunder below
Bite Through

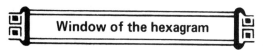

Window of the hexagram

1. The Big Dipper. This is an omen of disaster.
2. A woman offers incense kneeling and worshipping. This is a form of sacrifice performed to exercise evil spirits and bad influences.
3. Half of the Chinese character 憂 which means "worry". This means that the worry goes away.
4. A Chinese character 喜 means happiness.
5. Two snow geese eating the tassel of a rice plant, a coin, and two deer in combination mean a situation that is very gratifying and satisfactory.

Image and Symbol

日中爲市之課・頤中有物之象・

The image is to do business during the midday.

The symbol is the existence of something between the jaws.

Kua Tsi (文王彖辭)

噬嗑・亨・利用獄・

Biting through has success. To put people in jail is profitable.

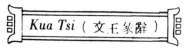 *Zhan* (占) *or hints on divining*

1. This is a September hexagram, it is good in summer bad in spring, fall and dying in winter.

2. The above illustration shows how the mouth biting something duplicates the hexagram.

3. One does not realize the difficulty of an undertaking unless one has experienced it before.

Yao Tsi (周公爻辭)

初九 • 履校滅趾 • 无咎 • ●

1st Yao. His feet are put in the stock and you can't see his toes. There is no blame. ●

Zhan (占)

1. You have good workers, but they gossip too much and don't get the work done. You take them aside and say, "now look, talk at home, the work must get done." After that they regulate themselves, and there is no problem.

2. It is dangerous to hold on to wrong beliefs obstinately.

3. You have to observe all rules and regulations, otherwise you will meet troubles.

六二 • 噬膚滅鼻 • 无咎 •

2nd Yao. He bites through tender meat so far his nose disappears. Nothing to blame.

Zhan (占)

1. You catch an employee stealing some goods and fire him immediately with a great deal of angry shouting. It was basically the right thing to do.

2. In this situation, you can act as circumstances may require without asking for approval from superiors.

3. You have done nothing to make you feel shameful.

六三 • 噬腊肉遇毒 • 小吝 • 无咎 • ●

3rd Yao. He bites on old dried meat and hits something decayed. There is slight humiliation. Nothing to blame.

Zhan (占)

1. You see some juveniles interfering with your neighbor's car and call the police. You go out to confront them and as the police take them away they shout vicious insults at you.
2. Don't adopt measures begond reasonable comprehension.
3. If you do so, it is similar to holding a sword at the wrong end; you will relegate your power to a subordinate unwisely and suffer the consequences.

九四 • 噬乾胏 • 得金矢 • 利艱貞 • 吉 • ○

4th Yao. He bites on dried, tough meat, and gets metal arrows. It is important to be wary of hazards and to persevere. Good luck. ○

Zhan (占)

1. You find out local officials are taking bribes to falsify a building permit near your home. You collect information and get higher authorities to investigate, being careful so the officials don't turn their power against you.
2. Clever birds choose their trees when they nest, which means that capable men should choose the right place to serve.
3. Expert craftsmanship is the result of long practise and hard work.

六五 • 噬乾肉 • 得黃金 • 貞厲 • 无咎 • ○

5th Yao. He bites on dried meat. He receives yellow gold. He is constantly wary of danger. There is no blame. ○

Zhan (占)

1. You find some juveniles stealing. Since they have a responsible background, you want them to have a chance to correct themselves, but realize if you just let them go, this won't happen. Finally, instead of calling the police, you call their parents.
2. As water comes, it forms a channel automatically, which means that the thing takes care of itself.
3. The real value of things lies in what they are made of, not what they appear to be.

上九 • 何校滅耳 • 凶 • ●

6th Yao. His neck is locked in the instrument of torture, we cannot see his ears. Bad luck. ●

[Zhan (占)]

1. You talk to a careless employee privately about doing better work, and the next thing you know he is telling lies about you to others and making them confused and anxious. You wait for him to make some open blunder, and fire him.

2. Your car breaks down and you are stranded for three hours. You fail to get the repairs done that the mechanic recommends, and the next day the wheel collapses and you crash into a pole.

3. It is very stupid to do things like that.

22　Pēn 賁

Mountain above
Fire below
Grace

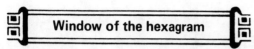

Window of the hexagram

1. Raining means to freshen and purify.
2. A car is being pushed. This means promotion.
3. A boat in full sail means doing a job that is made easy by outside help.
4. An official in uniform is climbing a ladder. This means getting promoted step by setp.
5. A fairy holding a sweet osmanthus plant is standing on the clouds. This represents a maiden first falling in love.

Image and Symbol

猛虎靠岩之課・光明通泰之象・

The image is a ferocious tiger leaning against a rock.
The symbol is of shining in all directions.

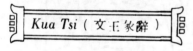

Kua Tsi (文王彖辭)

賁・亨・小利有攸往・

Pēn is successful in small matters. It is good to do something.

Zhan (占) or hints on divining

1. This is a November hexagram. It is good in winter, bad in summer.
2. You and your spouse can't afford to buy a house. So you spend some money and a lot of time and completely renovate your apartment. It looks so good you forget you were ever dissatisfied with it.
3. It looks pretty outside, but inside it is not good.

Yao Tsi (周公爻辭)

初九・賁其趾・舍車而徒・

1st Yao. Pēn or grace to his toes, leaves the carriage, and travels on foot.

Zhan (占)

1. A fellow at work offers to take you to lunch at a posh restuarant in his new sports car, but you know this is way beyond his means, you decline and go to the diner across the street.
2. Who knows it isn't a blessing in disguise?
3. You can enjoy peace and stability both physically and spiritually.

六二 • 賁其須 •

2nd Yao. He gives grace to the beard on his chin.

Zhan (占)

1. You spend all your money on appearances, and neglect more important developments.
2. You should perform the task with full vigor and a sense of urgency.
3. Don't put the cart before the horse.

九三 • 賁如濡如 • 永貞吉 • ○

3rd Yao. Graceful and moist. Continuous perseverance will bring you good fortune. ○

Zhan (占)

1. On your vacation to a tropical island you find things are so comfortable and easy that your have to take long walks every day to keep from just sitting around and drinking too much.
2. You will surpass others by showing your ability and talents.
3. You do the right thing to cope with a new situation.

六四 • 賁如皤如 • 白馬翰如 • 匪寇婚媾 •

4th Yao. Fancy grace or simplicity, which is better? A white horse comes on wings. He is not a robber, he will woo at the right time.

Zhan (占)

1. At the furniture showroom you find yourself gloating over the fancy, high cost furniture. Reluctantly you finally choose some inexpensive furniture that is simple and beautiful. Later you realize the fancy furniture would have made you feel uncomfortable.

2. Have you heard the Chinese saying sophistry that a white horse is not entirely the same as a horse? Why?
3. Good fortune that comes late in one's life after a long spell of bad times.

六五 • 賁于丘園 • 束帛戔戔 • 吝 • 終吉 • ○

5th Yao. Grace in the hills and the gardens. The roll of silk is poor and small, you're humiliated by it. But eventually there is good fortune. ○

※ *Zhan (占)* ※

1. You come from the luxurious urban city and get a poor job in the country that you like better. You feel bad that you can't put on a grand show for your new friends, but later you realize you are all happier living simply.
2. What you hoped to develop with your sweetheart has come to pass.
3. Human fortunes are as unpredictable as the weather.

上九 • 白賁 • 无咎 •

6th Yao. With white grace. Nothing to blame.

[*Zhan (占)*]

1. You see a person who has outstanding achievements which you admire. The person seems impressive. Later you try to remember what clothes be was wearing, and can't remember, because they were the most ordinary street clothes.
2. One who seeks truth is apt to get lost when confronted with too many choices.
3. You can perform the task to perfection.

Bāo 剝

23

Mountain above
Earth below
Peeling

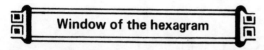

Window of the hexagram

1. A woman is sitting on the bed. This may mean trouble involving sex.
2. A lighted candle is flickering in the breeze. This means something cannot last too long.
3. A bottle-gourd or calabash. These are used for medicine, and suggest sickness.
4. An official is sitting on the mountain top. This can mean retirement, or it can mean a situation getting worse and worse.
5. A disordered bundle is tied with silk. This means a situation that is difficult to resolve or to keep from causing problems and embarrassment.

Image and Symbol

去舊生新之課・群陰剝盡之象・

The image is to replace the old with the new.

The symbol is when things are at their worst, they will surely begin to improve.

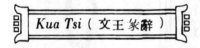

Kua Tsi (文王彖辭)

剝・不利有攸往・

Bāo or peeling. Not a time to go anywhere.

Zhan (占) *or hints on divining*

1. This is a September hexagram. It is very good in Spring, bad in Fall and Winter.
2. Five Yin Yaos grow up from the bottom, driving away Yang Yao at the top. This means the situation is getting worse and worse.
3. Bāo or peeling is a Yang hexagram, It can mean a man with five women in his life. On the one hand, this hexagram means being a "ladies' man" and living a luxurous and sensuous life. On the other hand, it means you dissipate your energy carousing and destroying yourself.

4. You wind up laid off your job, lose your sweetheart, and everything else goes wrong.   So you live quietly and are content simply to be alive.

Yao Tsi (周公爻辭)

初六・剝牀以足・蔑貞凶・ ●

1st Yao.   The leg of the bed is split.   People who persist are destroyed. Bad luck. ●

Zhan (占)

1. The good cause you worked for founders, and exploitive people rush forward to take advantage of it.
2. You should keep all the good and get rid of the bad.
3. You have to stop just before commiting a serious blunder.

六二・剝牀以辨・蔑貞凶・ ●

2nd Yao.   The bed is split where its leg is joined to the platform. People who persevere are destroyed.   Bad luck. ●

Zhan (占)

1. The park where you went to relax is the scene of a riot.   Your friends are scattered.   You hide behind a tree to avoid sticks and stones.
2. You will draw criticism at every turn.
3. The situation is unfavorable.

六三・剝之无咎・

3rd Yao. He breaks off with them.   There is no blame.

Zhan (占)

1. You find the superficial friends you were associating with are headed into some illegal enterprise.   They grumble when you leave them, and you avoid getting-involved in wrong-doing.
2. Do not follow the bad example of others.
3. You have to make proper use of both kindness and strictness in dealing with subordinates.

六四・剝牀以膚・凶・●

4th Yao. The bad mattress is peeling. Bad luck. ●

Zhan（占）

1. You wake up in the middle of the night to hear someone rifling your room in the dark. Scared out of your wits, you remain frozen in terror till the thief leaves.
2. Do not profit yourself at the expense of others.
3. Men of talent and health may decay faster, if they do not take care of themselves.

六五・貫魚・以宮人寵・无不利・○

5th Yao. Like a school of fishes. Good favor comes through the ladies of the court. Everything is good. ○

Zhan（占）

1. Impressed by the strength of your character as a police officer, the head of the local juvenile gang seeks you out for advice, and you get them involved in a positive activity that keeps them out of trouble.
2. If one thrives in calamity, then one can enjoy soft living when old.
3. A wise man knows when he is beaten and when to retreat.

上九・碩果不食・君子得輿・小人剝廬・

6th Yao. A large fruit is left uneaten. The better man gets a carriage. The house of the bad man is split apart.

Zhan（占）

1. The corruption of the small town police force comes to an end with one lieutenant left out. The town council makes him chief, and the others are indicted for accepting bribes.
2. The image is of falling from a high place.
3. You will again take up offical duties.

24 ䷗ Fū 澓

Earth above
Thunder below
Return

Window of the hexagram

1. An official sitting in the car means to have an overseas or very distant assignment.
2. There are two flags flying from the car. This means succeeding in one's first attempt.
3. There is the Chinese character 東 meaning East on the gateway. In the East one generally finds a job and friends.
4. A general holds a sword with a very long blade. This means prestige and influence.
5. A tiger and a rabbit. This is good fortune when it relates to the hour, day, month or year of the tiger or of the rabbit.

Image and Symbol

淘沙見金之課 • 反復往來之象 •

The image is of gold that has been prospected from the sand of a stream. The symbol is of repeated coming and going.

Kua Tsi (文王彖辭)

復 • 亨 • 出入无疾 • 朋來无咎 • 反復其道 • 七日來復 • 利有攸往 • ○

Return is successful. Coming and going without problems. Friends visit without being blamed. The way goes to and fro. On the seventh day return comes. It is a time to have something to do. ○

Zhan (占) or hints on divining

1. This is a November hexagram, it is good in fall, winter and bad in summer.
2. One Yang Yao governs five Yin Yaos, so Fu or return is a Yang hexagram. One Yang is located on 1st Yao which means Yang will start to grow and drive away all five Yin Yaos. The situation will be better and better.
3. After a long siege of progressive bad luck that wore you down to nothing, it seems to be exhausted and your week of darkness is over. An opportunity has appeared, and you are already working on doing

something with it.

Yao Tsi (周公爻辭)

初九 • 不遠復 • 无祗悔 • 元吉 • ○

1st Yao. You return from a short distance. There is no need to feel chagrin. Great good luck. ○

Zhan (占)

1. Your boss is rude and unfair and you begin to think of pilfering. You wake up and realize this is completely stupid. You feel so good the next day you are offered a new job.
2. You have already made careful planning for what you are doing.
3. You always help fulfil another's cherished hopes.

六二 • 休復 • 吉 • ○

2nd Yao. You return quietly. Good luck. ○

Zhan (占)

1. During the holidays you caroused so much you began to get run down and dissipated. Now you realize you'd better pull yourself together. After a few days of this you feel your old self again.
2. You know exactly what is right and what is wrong.
3. Spring returns to the good earth, everything will be going smoothly.

六三 • 頻復 • 厲 • 无咎 • ●

3rd Yao. Repeated Fù or return. Hazardous. Nothing to blame. ●

Zhan (占)

1. You lose fourty pounds overweight, then gain it back, then start over. The constant back and forth is more of a strain than being overweight, but in the long run maybe you have a chance.
2. Don't act without regard for the consequences.
3. You are an individual interested in forward trust and the future.

六四 • 中行獨復 •

4th Yao. Walking surrounded by others, you return alone.

Zhan (占)

1. Your friends all have bad habits, but you have a vision that there it something better and you begin seeking it out.
2. One person cannot handle all the tasks by oneself.
3. You should take a distinctive course or attitude of your own.

六五 • 敦復 • 无悔 • ○

5th Yao. Noblehearted return. Nothing to feel bad about.   ○

Zhan (占)

1. You realize you were rude and unfair to another just because there were unimportant superficial differences. You apologize and change your behaviour.
2. Three years hard work is crowned with success.
3. Think thrice before you act.

上六 • 迷復 • 凶 • 有災眚 • 用行師 • 終有大敗 • 以其國君凶 • 至於十年 不克征 • ●

6th Yao. Missing return. Bad luck. Bad luck inside and outside. If you set armies going this way, you will finally suffer a complete defeat, disastrous for the ruler of the country. For ten years you won't be able to attack again. ●

Zhan (占)

1. You know you have the right idea, and your opponents have inferior notions. A chance comes to make some peace and work together with them. It never occurs to you this might evolve to something favoring the good you know about. You keep fighting instead and finally get totally defeated. It's a long time before you can fight for the "right" again.
2. There is no compromise between the contending factions.
3. It is not a good time to poke your nose into others business.

Wúwàng 无妄

25

Heaven above
Thunder below
Innocence

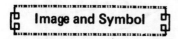

Window of the hexagram

1. An official shoots an arrow at a deer. This means one will be promoted soon.
2. A deer holds a document in its mouth. This means something that is accomplished quickly.
3. A pile of coins in the water. This means wealth that can be seen but not obtained.
4. A rat or a pig. This means good fortune relating to the hour, day, month or year of the rat or the pig.

Image and Symbol

石中韞玉之課・守舊安常之象・

The image is that of a precious jewel concealed inside of a stone.

The symbol is reluctance to accept changes that are not what they appear to be.

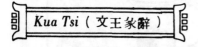

Kua Tsi （文王彖辭）

无妄・元亨・利貞・其匪正有眚・不利有攸往・

Innocence brings supreme success. It is good to persevere. If someone is not he should be, he has bad luck, and it doesn't help to be active.

Zhan （占） or hints on divining

1. This is a February hexagram, it is good in spring and winter; and bad in fall.
2. You will inherit some money or a small piece of land.

Yao Tsi （周公爻辭）

初九・无妄往吉・

1st Yao. Innocent acts bring good luck.

≡ *Zhan* (占) **≡**

1. You feel a direct impulse to do something good, and it works out perfectly.
2. Let nature take its course.
3. Be conservative, cautious and practical.

六二 • 不耕穫 • 不菑畬 • 則利有攸往 •

2nd Yao. If you do not think about the harvest while you are plowing the ground, nor about how you will use the land while you are clearing it from forest, it is worth doing something.

▌ *Zhan* (占) **▌**

1. You study the first lesson of your new course of study with good attention to it, while your friend who can only think of the rewards of graduation cannot concentrate or learn.
2. You will enjoy good health and financial independence.

六三 • 无妄之災 • 或繫之牛 • 行人之得 • 邑人之災 • ●

3rd Yao. Undeserved bad luck. The cow that was tied to graze is the wandering person's gain and the working man's loss. ●

▐ *Zhan* (占) **▐**

1. You leave the keys in your car, and the neighborhood delinquents take it for a joy ride and burn out the engine.
2. There would have been no story to tell or circumstance if not for a chance accurence.
3. You may have an unexpected misfortune.

九四 • 可貞 • 无咎 •

4th Yao. A person who can be persevering will remain without blame.

畀 *Zhan* (占) **畀**

1. Everyone tries to tell you to go this way and go that way but you follow an inner sense of the right way to develop yourself and the result is you don't make serious mistakes.
2. Leave your boat and travel on firm ground.

3. There is true and sincere friendship between you.

九五 • 无妄之疾 • 勿藥有喜 • ●

5th Yao. Don't take medicines for an illness that doesn't come from your own faults. It will pass away. ●

⛧ *Zhan* (占) ⛧

1. You feel lightheaded and shaky and fear the worst. Your doctor tells you its a new kind of flu making the rounds and to go home and sleep it off for a day.
2. You will suffer a setback in trying to take advantage of a situation.
3. If you feel in poor health, don't go to a quack or an unexperience doctor. Sometimes, their treatment or suggestions will give you more trouble.

上九 • 无妄行有眚 • 无攸利 • ●

6th Yao. Innocent action brings bad luck. It is not a time to act.●

Zhan (占)

1. You see the ice is too thin here and know it will be thicker downstream, but somehow this knowledge escapes you and you cheerfully walk out into the middle of the stream and to your surprise crash through the ice.
2. Weather turns foul when some activity requiring fine weather is scheduled to take place.
3. A slight mistake will result in a great error in the end.

26

Daxù 大畜

Mountain above
Heaven below
Great Saving

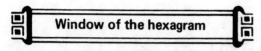

Window of the hexagram

1. A deer and a horse. This means something very gratifying and satisfactory.
2. A document lighted by the moon. This means to pass an examination very easily.
3. An official leans upon the railing. Freedom from restraint.
4. The flowers are pushing through the railing. This means a good omen for finding a job, trying to do business or making money.

Image and Symbol

龍潛大壑之課 • 積小成大之象 •

The image is of a dragon hidden in a solitary glen.

The symbol is that accumulation of small particles results in a mountain.

Kua Tsi (文王彖辭)

大畜 • 利貞 • 不家食 • 吉 • 利涉大川 •

Daxù or Great Saving. It is a good time for perseverance. Not eating at home is good luck. It is a good time to cross the great water.

Zhan (占) *or hints on divining*

1. This is a march hexagram. It is good in spring, bad in summer and fall.
2. After working a long time to develop your new skills, you feel the time has arrived to put them to work, and the feeling is true.
3. Economy in trifies will ensure abundance.

Yao Tsi (周公爻辭)

初九 • 有厲 • 利己 •

1st Yao. Danger, Desist.

≡ *Zhan* (占) **≡**

1. You're all set to cross the stream, and you see the ice is thin. You wait quietly for your chance.
2. A moment's distraction by pleasures can bring endless sufferings to come.
3. He who is in comfortable circumstance knows not the bitterness of misfortune.

九二・輿脫輹・

2nd Yao. The axles are taken from the wagon.

║ *Zhan* (占) **║**

1. You are all set for a week vacation of skiing, but the weatherman says there will be no snow. You cancel your vacation so you can take it later on.
2. It is a good idea to retreat as far as possible in the face of a strong contestant.
3. It is better to seek what is less attractive than your original objective.

九三・良馬逐・利艱貞・日閑輿衞・利有攸往・

3rd Yao. You have a good horse following other. If you're aware of danger and keep persevering, it is favorable. You practice chariot driving and armed defense every day. It is a good idea to have a goal.

▯ *Zhan* (占) **▯**

1. You want to join with others in a great opportunity opening up. You practice the new ambition and how to deal with problems with it every day. Finally you think about what you want to achieve personally. You are all set.
2. Rushness spoils a chance of success.
3. Don't be arrogant because of your ability.

六四・童牛之牿・元吉・○

4th Yao. The horns on a young bull. This is the best good luck.

Zhan (占)

1. You know your friend almost gets crazy when he talks about his job. Every time the subject comes up, you change the subject, or else you talk about his possible future at some new job. One day he notices your deliberation and concern and realizes he could do the same for himself. He does, and is freed of his bad emotions enough to find a way of improving things.
2. You should take precautions against calamity, or to nip trouble in the bud.
3. You try to lower the standard and to be satisfied with the next best qualified.

六五・豶豕之牙・吉・

5th Yao. The tusk of a gelded boar. Good luck.

Zhan (占)

1. You find one of your employees is wild and erratic. You investigate and discover that his supervisor picks on him for no good reason. You transfer him to another supervisor and the problem vanishes.
2. It is like employing a steam hammer to crack a nut.
3. One cannot expect to find elephant tusks in the mouth of a dog, which means a mean fellow never says nice things.

上九・何天之衢・亨・

6th Yao. You attain the way of heaven. Success.

Zhan (占)

1. You work days and go to school evenings for four years of hardship and on graduation you begin a new career that is just what you wanted.
2. Your fortune is as "every road leads to Rome", many ways to reach your goal.
3. Excellence in work is possible only with diligence.

27

Yí 頤

Mountain above
Thunder below
Jaws

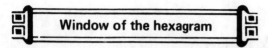

Window of the hexagram

1. A fall of rain. Freshening and purification.
2. Three children. Something accomplished through young people.
3. High noon. After reaching the zenith, a decline.
4. An incense table. To pray for something.
5. A government official wearing a golden robe. One should work hard in order to have a successful official career.

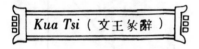

Image and Symbol

龍隱清潭之課 • 近善遠惡之象 •
The image is a dragon hidden in a crystal clear deep pool.
The symbol is to stay close to good acts and stay far away from evil ones.

Kua Tsi (文王彖辭)

頤 • 貞吉 • 觀頤 • 自求口實 •
Yí or Jaws. It is good luck to persevere. Pay attention to providing nourishment, and to what a man seeks to fill his own mouth with.

Zhan (占) or hints on divining

1. This is an August hexagram. It is good in Winter and very bad in Spring.
2. The image of Yí is the mouth and teeth, as shown below.

3. Yí is a Yóuhún hexagram of Gǔ

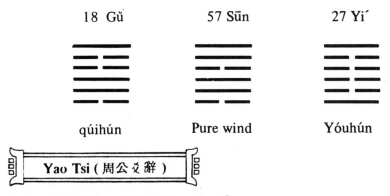

18 Gǔ	57 Sūn	27 Yí
qúihún	Pure wind	Yóuhún

Yao Tsi (周公爻辭)

初九 · 金爾靈龜 · 觀我朵頤 · 凶 · ●

1st Yao. You lost your magic tortise, and look at me with the corners of your mouth pulled down. Bad luck. ●

Zhan (占)

1. You are happy with the good and simple way you live, and then one day your pretentious girl friend drops you for a rich fellow. You think about how lousy it is too be poor, instead of how lucky you are that your simplicity drives bad people away.
2. The reputation is not supported by fact.
3. You will be faced with something at once troublesome and ludicrous.

六二 · 顛頤 · 拂經于丘頤 · 征凶 ·

2nd Yao. Turning to the high summit for nourishment and leaving one's path to get nourishment from the hill. If you keep this up, it brings bad luck.

Zhan (占)

1. You give up the little one-man business you created yourself and go to work for a big corporation. You find you don't have to think or use initiative and in a year's time you feel bored, desperate and atrophied.
2. No one is interested in doing a losing business, but you did!
3. You have a deep interest in all that is artistic.

六三 · 拂頤 · 貞凶 · 十年勿用 · 无攸利 · ●

3rd Yao. Turning away from true nourishment brings bad luck if you persist in it. Don't act this way for ten years. Nothing is worthwhile in this direction. ●

╠ *Zhan* (占) ╣

1. You don't find the friends you like, so you give up looking harder and drift into a group that is always going from excess to excess and calling it "a good time." One night you see one of them almost killed by one of their excesses, and you realize this is death, not life.
2. The image of this Yao is similar to this situation, you love your dog very much and treat it as your best friend, but the dog always bites and barks at you.
3. Don't make false accusations against others.

六四 • 顛頤 • 吉 • 虎視耽耽 • 其欲逐逐 • 无咎 •

4th Yao. You turn to the summit for proper nourishment and this is good fortune. You spy about like a tiger with an insatiable hunger. This is all right.

╠ *Zhan* (占) ╣

1. You decided on an ambitious and difficult enterprise of great benefit to yourself and others. You search like a hungry tiger for allies in your work.
2. One will not go broke if he is frugal.
3. You have to do your job honestly and with dedication.

六五 • 拂經 • 居貞吉 • 不可涉大川 •

5th Yao. He turns away from the path. To remain persevering during this time earns good luck. But one should not cross the great water.

╠ *Zhan* (占) ╣

1. You become aware you just don't have the capability you need to accomplish things, so you turn to someone who has the special skills of character you need for help and learning. As a result you quickly acquire advanced skills, but remember this is not yet your own merit just the influence of help from an advanced person.
2. Happiness lies in rendering help to others.

上九・由頤・厲吉・利涉大川・○

6th Yao. The source of nourishment is here. Being aware of danger is good luck. It is a time to cross the great water. ○

[*Zhan* (占)]

1. Through a life of constant growth you become a spiritual guide and leader to others. The responsibility to be far-seeing and wise is heavy. Your awareness of people's needs leads to great projects, yet the times favor success.
2. You should try repeatedly in spite of repeated failures.
3. You will go through danger as if there were no danger at all.

Dáguó 大過

28

Lake abové
Wind below
Great Passing

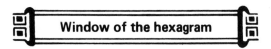

Window of the hexagram

1. An official is sitting on the car with two flags flying from it. This means an overseas assignment.
2. There is the Chinese character 喜 meaning happiness on each flag.
3. Entering the red gates. This means a rich and influential family.
4. An official stands outside of the red gates. This means to be promoted soon.
5. A document. This is a certificate of appointment.
6. A small box. To cooperate harmoniously.

Image and Symbol

寒木生花之課・本末俱弱之象・

The image is a decayed ornamental tree producing flowers.
The symbol is weakness both inside and outside — the Yin lines in the first and sixth Yao.

Kua Tsi (文王彖辭)

大過・棟橈・利有攸往・亨・

Dàguò, or great passing. The ridgepole sags till it almost breaks. It is a time for action, Success.

 *Zhan* (占) *or hints on divining*

1. This is a February hexagram. It is good in spring and bad in fall.
2. Dàguò or great pagging is a Yòuhùn hexagram of Suì or following.

17 Suí	51 Zhèn	28 Dáguò
Qùihún	Pure wood	Yoúhún

3. The weather was perfect and your carefully tended garden is growing

by leaps and bounds. You are suddenly aware that unless you use your imagination and move carefully, most of the great bounty coming will be wasted.

Yao Tsi (周公爻辭)

初六 · 藉用白茅 · 无咎 ·

1st Yao. He spreads white rushes on the ground. There is no blame.

Zhan (占)

1. You and your fiancee will marry soon. You work day and night to arrange everything so it will work out perfectly in settling into your new life.
2. You should take the right remedial steps to correct a shortcoming.
3. He who cannot forbear in small matters spoils great undertakings.

九二 · 枯楊生稊 · 老夫得其女妻 · 无不利 ·

2nd Yao. A dry old poplar has new sprouts at the roots. An older man marries a younger woman. Everything is for the good.

Zhan (占)

1. You were in a rut and feeling old and tired, then a new enterprise came along. You took it up and all your fatigue disappeared and you feel like a new person.
2. One will vainly regret in old age one's laziness in youth.
3. Everyone should take care of one's own aged parents first and then extend the same care to the aged people in general.

九三 · 棟橈 · 凶 · ●

3rd Yao. The ridgepole sags to nearly breaking. Bad luck. ●

Zhan (占)

1. Everything prospers and you ignore advice to slow down and consolidate things. You push ahead, expand more, finally there is so much going on it all collapses.
2. You should make an overall assessment but start with the details.
3. The big mistake has been committed.

九四 • 棟隆 • 吉 • 有它咎 • ○

4th Yao.　The ridgepole is braced.　Good luck.　If you have ulterior motives, you will be upset. ○

Zhan (占)

1.　You get friends to help dig up old bottles to sell at the flea market. You come across a rare treasure worth hundreds of dollars and hide it in your arm for yourself.　Someone notices, and you wind up with no treasure and no friends.
2.　A great man will take time to shape and mature.
3.　You will suffer a major setback due to carelessness.

九五 • 枯楊金華 • 老婦得其士夫 • 无咎无譽 • ●

5th Yao.　A withered poplar grows flowers.　An older woman marries. There is nothing to blame and nothing to praise. ●

Zhan (占)

1.　Instead of thinking of reviving yourself, you think you'll just pretend you're not run-down and tired out.　You do, and nothing comes of it, good or poor.
2.　There will be twists and obstacles if a problem or an issue is not settled promptly.
3.　The setting sun is warm and beautiful, but it will be the cold evening soon.

上六 • 遇涉滅頂 • 凶 • 无咎 • ●

6th Yao.　One has to go through water and it goes over your head.　Bad luck.　But nothing is to blame. ●

Zhan (占)

1.　You see someone in trouble in a burning car in an accident.　You rush to help them but the gas tank explodes and you are nearly killed.
2.　Don't develop bad habits which will destroy you.
3.　Turn the head and you can see the shore, which means that repentance and salvation is at hand.

29

Kǎn 坎

Water above
Water below
Water

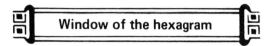

Window of the hexagram

1. A person falls into the well. This means getting into extreme difficulties.
2. The person is pulled out with a rope. This means gaining help in an emergency.
3. An ox and a mouse. Indicate good fortune related to the hour, day, month, and year of the ox or of the mouse.
4. A person has the head of a tiger. This means there is an influential person who can help you to find a job.

Image and Symbol

船漏重灘之課・外虛中實之象・

The image is of a boat which is stranded and leaking to meet additional difficulties.

The symbol is the Yang among the Yin in each trigram.

Kua Tsi (文王袈辭)

習坎・有孚・維心亨・行有尙・

Kǎn twice. If you are sincere, then you interealize success and whatever you do works out.

Zhan (占) or hints on divining

1. This is an October hexagram, it is good in spring, bad in summer and fall.
2. Kan or Water, is one of four evil hexagrams in I Ching. The situation points to difficult in either to proceed or retreat. It is as if two persons (two Yang Yaos) are drowning in the water without any help.
3. You see a difficult and dangerous task yet your inner feeling tells you it must be done and you undertake it in a sober frame of mind. You follow it through to the end and succeed.

Yao Tsi (周公爻辭)

初六・習坎・入于坎窞・凶・●

1st Yao. Double Kan. In the abyss one can fall into a pit. Bad luck. ●

Zhan (占)

1. You get so used to driving your car you forget what a dangerous machine it is, and you have an accident.
2. Whatever is phenomenal is ephemeral, the physical corresponds to the spiritual.
3. A single post cannot support a mansion.

九二・坎有險・小有得・

2nd Yao. The abyss is dangerous. You should work to attend to small things only.

Zhan (占)

1. You get lost in the woods. Instead of rushing about to get out fast, you take your time, look for signs, do only a little bit at a time.
2. One reaps no more than what one has sown.
3. Unless you are absolutely sure that you can succeed in doing something, you should not attempt it.

六三・來之坎坎・險且枕・入于坎窞・勿用・●

3rd Yao.   There is an abyss ahead and one behind. In dangers like this one, pause and wait. Otherwise you will fall. ●

Zhan (占)

1. A vicious guard dog that has gotten loose comes running up and stands snarling at you with rage. If you turn to run, he will attack and if you threaten him he will attack. All you can do is stand waiting alertly until something happens.
2. One does not know what to do.
3. The good circumstances don't last long.

六四・樽酒簋貳用缶・納約自牖・終无咎・

4th Yao.   There is a jug of wine and a bowl of rice, these earthen containers are handed in through the window.   There is nothing at fault in this.

Zhan (占)

1. You meet an ally you can work with in a difficult situation.   There is no opportunity to take him out to dinner to ceremoniously seal the bargain; you both go to work at once.
2. There is a chance to temporarily relieve an emergency or an urgent need.
3. It's the natural outcome of the time and circumstance.

九五 ・坎不盈 ・祗既平 ・无咎 ・

5th Yao. The abyss is not filled to overflowing. It is only filled to the rim. This is all right.

Zhan (占)

1. You get trapped in the small town park with a dangerous looking character waiting for you at the gate. You think about a showdown, then you notice a break in the fence nearby, and your problem of leaving is solved.
2. Contentment brings happiness.
3. May you bear a son!

上六 ・係用徽纆・ 寘於叢棘 ・三歲不得 ・凶 ・●

6th Yao. He is bound with ropes and shut in behind thorn-hedge prison walls. For three years he does not find a way out. Bad luck. ●

Zhan (占)

1. The teller in the bank stole some money   Then he falsified the records to hide that. Then he lied to his supervisor to hide that. Then he stole a car to run away. Now the FBI is after him.
2. Don't injure a person already in great difficulty.
3. You toil all day long just to make both ends meet.

30

Lí 離

Five above
Fire below
Fire

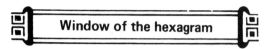

Window of the hexagram

1. A man stands on a tiger's back. This means an awkward position from which there is no retreat.
2. A boat in the middle of a river means you have favorable winds in your sailing.
3. An official holding an arrow stands on the bank of a river. This means something that begins with evil, but ends with good.

Image and Symbol

飛禽振羽之課・大明當天之象・
The image is a flying bird spreading its wings.
The symbol is the sun and the moon in their appropriate places.

Kua Tsi (文王彖辭)

離・利貞・亨・畜牝牛・吉・
Lí or Fire. It is a time to persevere, for doing so brings success. To take care of the cow brings good luck.

Zhan (占) *or hints on divining*

1. This is an April hexagram, it is good in summer bad in spring and winter, may be sick in fall.
2. Lí or Fire is a pure hexagram we can take advantage of fire, for cooking, healing, and so on. At the same time, however, fire can injure as and do great damage. We need to make good use of fire and aviod its dangers.
3. After long work and planning, you now see clearly the path to follow in your activity. You follow it directly, not wasting your energy trying to find shortcuts.

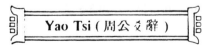

Yao Tsi (周公爻辭)

初九・履錯然・敬之・无咎・ ●
1st Yao. The footprints run crisscross. If you are serious and intent,

there is nothing to blame. ●

░ *Zhan* (占) ░

1. You see several possible routes in and could be confused. But you
   are calmed by your inner strength and you take your time to find
   the correct path.
2. From listening comes wisdom and from speaking repentance.
3. It is often better not to see an insult than to avenge it.
4. To reach a high position, one must start from a low bosition.

六二・黃離・元吉・ ○
2nd Yao. Yellow light is the highest good fortune.

░ *Zhan* (占) ░

1. You see extreme ways to follow but the moderate middle way
   emits with such clearness and force you cannot mistake it following
   it leads to success.
2. Get your mind set. Confidence will guide you on.
3. You will step on the soil of many countries.

九三 ・ 日昃之離・ 不鼓缶而歌・ 則大耋之嗟・ 凶・ ●
3rd Yao. In the light of the setting sun, men either beat the pot and
sing or loudly complain of old age coming. Bad luck. ●

░ *Zhan* (占) ░

1. The party is almost over and some are having a wonderful time
   at the culmination of the whole event. Others are making themselves
   miserable over things they missed, and still others are drinking
   themselves into a stupor trying to forget this.
2. You are deeply attached to your family and home.
3. Consolidate rather than expand business projects in the near future.

九四 ・ 突如其來如 ・ 焚如 ・ 死如 ・ 棄如 ・ ●
4th Yao. Its coming is sudden; it flames up and then quickly dies down
and is discarded. ●

Zhan (占)

1. You are in a restless mood and you suddenly "see the answer" to your situation with great clarity and accuracy. But you fix so intently on it that the inspiration is quickly burned up and destroyed and you are back at zero again.
2. A lifetime of cleverness can be interrupted by moments of stupidity.
3. Please follow more cautiously life's golden rule.

六五・出涕沱若・戚嗟若・吉・○

5th Yao. Tears in bleeding, sighing and lamenting. Good luck. ○

Zhan (占)

1. You reach the great goal you strived for for so long. It is magnificent. The at the height of your happiness you suddenly realize "all the rest of my life is going to be downhill!" and you feel lost and weep. Then a more sober mood comes over you and you realize that all of life is illuminated with equal value and that each different part is to be treasured. Feeling better, you understand how to make the wisest use of where you are now.
2. You are domestically inclined and will be happily married.
3. You have an optimistic faith and confidence in life.

上九・王用出征・有嘉・折首・獲匪其醜・无咎・

6th Yao. The king uses his light to march forth and punish. It is best to kill the leaders and only take captive the followers. There is nothing to blame.

Zhan (占)

1. You have a time of strong clarity in looking at yourself and see it is time to clean your life up. At first you feel so strongly about this you are practically ready to become a monk. Then you realize this would be detrimental to your personality, so you pick out your worst bad habits and set out to correct them.
2. We must always have old memories and young hopes.
3. With integrity and consistency, your credits are piling up.

31 ☰☰ Xián 咸

Lake above
Mountain below
Influence

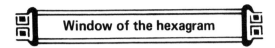

Window of the hexagram

1. A hand is in the sky. Though you never dreamed it would happen, someone will give you a hand and help you.
2. A pile of jewels and coins means riches and wealth.
3. An official stands on the top of a mountain. This means being well versed in both politics and military tactics.
4. A soman climbs up a mountain. When her husband sings to her, his wife follows.
5. A small box means to cooperate harmoniously.

Image and Symbol

山澤通氣之課・至誠感神之象・

The image is the mountains and the water intermingling their influence. The symbol is that utmost sincerity can move even God.

Kua Tsi（文王彖辭）

咸・亨・利貞・取女吉・

Xián or Influence is successful; it is time to persevere. To marry a maiden is good luck.

Zhan（占）*or hints on divining*

1. This is a January hexagram, it is good in spring and bad in fall.
2. It is a good time to arrange a marriage between you and your sweetheart.
3. You realize your life is too empty, so you set out to find some worthwhile goal to cultivate.

Yao Tsi（周公爻辭）

初六・咸其拇・

1st Yao. Xián or Influence shows itself in the big toe.

Zhan (占)

1. You are just about to take a big step. So far nothing of it is visible to others.
2. It is an attempt to do what is far beyond your power, yet if you persist, there is a way to success.
3. Young people fresh from school are uncompromising despite opposition from authority.

六二 • 咸其腓 • 凶 • 居吉 •

2nd Yao.   Influence shows itself in the calves of the leg. Bad luck. Delaying is good luck.

Zhan (占)

1. You feel pushed and pulled by confusing pressures, so you settle down and wait for a clear sign to move.
2. You should wait for a favorable price to sell.
3. The newcomer ends up in front.

九三 • 咸其股 • 執其隨 • 往吝 •

3rd Yao. The influence shows itself in the thighs. It holds on to what responds to it. To continue with this brings an upset.

Zhan (占)

1. Now you feel generous inner impulses to do this, that; and everything. Finally you realize you had better ignore them all and calm down.
2. It is a time to pursue good fortune and shun the course of calamity.
3. The more one tries to cover up something, the more it will become known.

九四 • 貞吉 • 悔亡 • 憧憧往來 • 朋從爾思 •

4th Yao. Persistence is good luck and disappointment disppears. But if you are mentally agitated and your thoughts jump all over the place the only friends who will follow you are the ones you fix your conscious attentions on.

Zhan (占)

1. You find your deepest concern comes from your values, and this becomes your guide. Instead of your thoughts jumping all over and tiring you and everyone else, you have a steady guide.
2. Let's all work together for that worthy project, plan and care for both duties.
3. Don't get into unexpected difficulty.

九五・咸其脢・无悔・

5th Yao. The influence is in the back of the neck. No disappointment.

Zhan (占)

1. You feel a totally stable impression of what your goal is and nothing confuses it.
2. You will impress others by showing your ability and talents.
3. A large tree has its deep root.

上六・咸其輔頰舌・

6th Yao. The influence is in the jaws, Cheeks and tongue.

Zhan (占)

1. Whole kingdoms rise and fall in the words coming out of your mouth in such richness, but the rest of your body reveals.
2. When one is getting old, after the teeth have fallen out, the tongue still works fine. What does this mean?
3. Please, always say good words about others.

Heng 恒

32

Thunder above
Wind below
Constancy

Window of the hexagram

1. The sun is presently behind the clouds. When they pass, the sun reveals good fortune.
2. A phoenix holds a letter in its beak. This means an important letter or communication will come soon.
3. An official is taking a walk. This suggests helping someone.
4. A Taoist priest points to the doorway. This means giving a person good guidance to clear up a confused situation.
5. Two mice. This means good luck related to the hour, day, month and year of the mouse.

Image and Symbol

日月常明之課・四時不沒之象・

The image is of the sun and moon always shining brightly.

The symbol is that the always changing seasons perpetuate the creation of things.

Kua Tsi (文王彖辭)

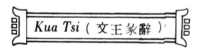

恒・亨・无咎・利貞・利有攸往・

Héng or constancy is successful. There is nothing to blame and it is a time for perseverance and action.

Zhan (占) *or hints on divining*

1. This is a January hexagram. It is good in spring, bad in summer. It means loss of money in the fall.
2. The image of Hèng is the Tao of marriage, the relationship between two lovers.
3. You find yourself with straightforward work of many sorts, instead of a strong focus on some special situation. You follow through steady success.

Yao Tsi (周公爻辭)

初六 • 後恆 • 貞凶 • 无攸利 •
1st Yao. If you seek constancy hastily, you only get persistent failure.

Zhan (占)

1. You decide to "learn persistence," so you work all day like a fiend until you are totally exhausted. The next day you have no energy at all and it all seems nonsense.
2. Be sure to take advantage of an opportunity when it comes along.
3. Small things may cause big trouble.

六二 • 悔亡 •
2nd Yao. Disappointment disappears.

Zhan (占)

1. You know you have the vision to do great things, yet the opportunity is not there. Instead of being upset, you calm your will and adapt to the time.
2. If you make a decision to act, it will soon be too late to regret it.
3. A virtuous man seldom has dreams.

九三 • 不恒其德 • 或承之羞 • 貞吝 •
3rd Yao. If you don't give duration to your character, you will be disgraced and persistenly humiliated.

Zhan (占)

1. You have clear values and goals, but you never think of training your "willpower" to act consistently. The result is that every exterior thing that comes along distracts you or taunts you, and you get nowhere.
2. Man has his will, but woman has her way.
3. As long as your conscience is your friend, you need not be concerned about your enemies.

九四 • 田无禽 • ●
4th Yao. There is no wild game in this field. ●

Zhan (占)

1. You work very hard to find what you want, never finding it; and never thinking about whether you are looking in a place where such things are found.
2. An empty sack cannot stand upright.
3. By spending much time in what is not his proper place, gain cannot be had.

六五・恆其德貞・婦人吉・夫子凶・

5th Yao. When you give duration to your character by persevering, this is good luck for a woman, and bad luck for a man.

Zhan (占)

1. If a man got this Yao, he had worries of trouble at home.
2. When you are serving others you find good luck in constant effort to follow their moves, but when you are following your sense of inner value, you need to give up the outer perseverance.
3. Sincerity can make metal and stone crack.

上六・振恆・凶・●

6th Yao. If you endure in being restless, you bring bad luck. ●

Zhan (占)

1. You just rush ahead all the time, never thinking about your inner nature and so most of your energy is wasted and your judgment is poor.
2. Don't give a promise easily and break it easily.
3. If you act rashly and blindly, you will suffer heavy losses.

33 ≡≡ Tun 遯

Heaven above
Mountain below
Yielding

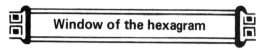

Window of the hexagram

1. A mountain looms the place to go is far beyond the mountain.
2. A river flows the place is far from the river, meaning one must make a long journey to reach it.
3. There is a Chinese character on a bar's flag. This means saying something foolish and rash when drunk.
4. A man steps on a tortise. The Chinese character for tortise (龜) and return (歸) have the same sound. This means a person or object is returning.
5. The moon is half-hidden by the clouds. This refers to the chaos of troubled times.
6. A headdress hangs on a tree. This means to quit or resign a post.
7. A person drinks under a tree. This means to enjoy oneself in ones own way, no matter what others may think.

Image and Symbol

豹隱南山之課 • 守道去惡之象 •

The image is the leopard living in silence in the south mountain.
The symbol is to shun evil and follow the Way.

Kua Tsi (文王彖辭)

遯 • 亨 • 小貞 •

Tun or yielding. There is success. It is a time to persevere in small things.

Zhan (占) *or hints on divining*

1. This is a June hexagram; it is good in spring, bad in summer and winter.
2. Two Yin Yaos below four Yang Yaos, which means that the Yin side is expanding, and the Yang side is yielding.
3. It is evening, and after a long, active day of large projects, you sit at your desk and attend to many small tasks that need doing.
4. Someone wants to attack you socially, but you can see everything

is on their side and you retreat carefully instead — giving your opponent some sharp jabs everytime they overstep themselves and try to break your defenses.

Yao Tsi (周公爻辭)

初六・遯尾厲・勿用有攸往・●
1st Yao. You are at the tail of the Tun or Yielding. This is the most dangerous place to be. You must not think of undertaking any projects.●

Zhan (占) **〓** its on divinati‹

1. You are camping and a bear comes in the middle of the night to steal your food and gets upset and dangerous. You distract the animal with a stick while your friends get away, then you get away, too.
2. If one remains calm upon seeing strange things, the strangeness will be no harm.
3. You are easily moved by what you see or hear.

六二・執之用黃牛之革・莫之勝說・●
2nd Yao. You are held fast with yellow oxhide, and you can't tear yourself loose.●

Zhan (占)

1. You split with your friends in disgust because they always try to browbeat you into behaving like them. But one of them insists you rejoin the group and help them, saying he will defend your side.
2. His motives were not good.
3. You cannot expest to owe the success to good luck.

九三・係遯・有疾厲・畜臣吉・●
3rd Yao. Your retiring is stopped and you are in a tense and dangerous spot. To get the help of people especially servants is a good idea.

Zhan (占)

1. Just as you as driving away from the area where there is rioting, your car gets a flat. You find some rioters who need a ride, and

they fix your flat for you and keep others from attacking your car.
2. Ones folly will bring ones ruin.
3. It's unwise to offend the public.

九四・好遯・君子吉・小人否・

4th Yao. When you yield voluntarily, it is good fortune for the advanced person, but downfall for the inferior person.

Zhan (占)

1. You get driven from your job by greedy and unscrupulous colleagues who fear you for your competence. You leave politely, saying nothing. The business immediately goes into a long-term slump because none of the others have any real skill.
2. Don't expose another person's secrets.
3. It is very hard to make both ends meet.

九五・嘉遯・貞吉・○

5th Yao. You yield in a friendly way. If you persevere now, it is good fortune. ○

Zhan (占)

1. You win some money at poker, and when the players decide to play for very high stakes, you say it is time to go. They heckle you and say you must give them a chance to win their money back, but you are out the door with a smile before they can stop you.
2. Accumulation of small amounts results in large quantities.
3. Knowing someone by his reputation is not as good as meeting him in person.

上九・肥遯・无不利・

6th Yao. You are cheerful in yielding. Everything advances you.

Zhan (占)

1. You thought it over with great care before deciding to move. Now that the moment has come you feel no uneasiness and look forward happily to the path ahead.
2. You will have a high position and good pay.
3. Happiness lies in rendering help to others.

34

Dázhuáng 大壯

Thunder above
Haven below
Great Vigor

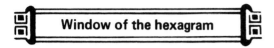

Window of the hexagram

1. The Big Dipper is visible. This is an omen of disaster.
2. A God holds a sword. This is another bad omen.
3. An official kneels and bows. This means to pray for blessings.
4. A monkey, a rabbit, and a dog. The hour, day, month, or year relating to any of these three animals is poor now.

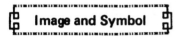

Image and Symbol

牴羊觸藩之課・先曲後順之象・

The image is a ram butting against a fence.
The symbol is crookedness at the start and smoothness later on.

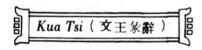

Kua Tsi（文王彖辭）

大壯・利貞・

Dázhuàng or grest vigour. It is a time to persevere.

Zhan（占）*or hints on divining*

1. This is a February hexagram, it is bad in spring, evil in winter.
2. Four Yang Yao advance from below and drive away two Yin Yao on the top, this means great interal vigour.
3. You wanted money to repair your home. Now everything is going right in your business. You impulsively want to spend the money in other ways as well, then you realize this can lead to dissipation and you stick with your plans.

Yao Tsi（周公爻辭）

初九・壯于趾・征凶有孚・

1st Yao. Your Vigor is in your toes. If you continue, you will have bad luck, this is unavoidable..

█ *Zhan* (占) █

1. You meet an old enemy and find him at a tremendous disadvantage. It would be easy to smash him. But he has done nothing wrong, so you go your own way.
2. One has two little power or resources to do as much as one wishes.
3. Don't march fearlessly onward at this critical time.

九二・貞吉・〇

2nd Yao. If you persevere now you will have good luck. 〇

▌ *Zhan* (占) ▌

1. You work for hours without result to solve a problem. Finally, when very tired, you have a breakthrough and see the answer. You consider pushing ahead and finishing the work now, but you realize you are tired and it can wait until tomorrow now that you know the right way.
2. Everyone envies your good luck.
3. Even though you always have good luck, if you try your luck at the gambling tables, you will definitely meet the usual ill luck.

九三・小人用壯・君子用罔・貞厲・羝羊觸藩・羸其角・

3rd Yao. The inferior man thinks only of power, but the superior person does not do this. If you continue this way, it is dangerous. A goat butts his horns against a hedge and finally gets hopelessly entangled.

▌ *Zhan* (占) ▌

1. A fellow develops his physical strength by all sorts of weight lifting and working out, not to make good use of it, but rather to show off to people. His doctor examines him, and finds he has overstrained vital organs and is in a dangerous state.
2. It is said in the theory of Tai Chi Chuan: "Use internal consciousness, not external forms." So, if you practice Tai Chi Chuan, you know what this Yao means.
3. You were able to show great power in solving a difficult problem that came up. You feel elated and that this is the time for gredat

things, but you realize your work is more mundane, so you rest your energies and attend to doing it well.

九四 • 貞吉悔亡 • 藩決不羸 • 壯于大輿之輹 • ○

4th Yao. To persist is good luck and there will be no remorse. The thick hedge opens up and you don't get entangled. Your power depends on the axle of a big cart. ○

Zhan (占)

1. You have tremendous desire to succeed but circumstances are totally against it. So you take every small opportunity that comes along and handle it perfectly and go on to the next, never pushing too hard. Then when things open up, your tremendous motivation comes into full play.
2. It's exactly what you are hoping for.
3. You will get promotion step by step or continuously.

六五 • 羊喪于易 • 无悔 •

5th Yao. You lose the goat easily. There is no unhappiness.

Zhan (占)

1. You were ready to fight for what is right against people with the wrong idea, and to give it all the strength you had. Now you find they have reformed themselves, and you can forget that and relax.
2. Man's determination will conquer nature.
3. You will enjoy happiness and prosperity for the rest of your life.

上六 • 羝羊觸藩 • 不能退 • 不能遂 • 艱則吉 •

6th Yao. A goat butts against a hedge. It cannot back off and it cannot go forward. Nothing furthers. If you note this, you will have good fortune.

Zhan (占)

1. Your car gets stuck in the snow bank and you spin the wheels about. Straining your engine and sinking in deeper. Then you stop. You remember you have a shovel in the trunk.
2. If you go too far you come to a dead end, unable either to advance or to retreat. Whatever you do merely serves to complicate thing

further. The only thing you can do is to calm down and to realize the situation and then come back through the original path.

3. You will make plans to no avail.

35

Jìn 晉

Fire above
Earth below
Advancing

Window of the hexagram

1. A piece of paper has missing words. The situation is incomplete.
2. An officer covers his face and weeps. It is too late to repent, and thus avoid trouble.
3. A ball is stuck fast in the mud. Things do not turn out as one wishes.
4. A rooster's beak holds a weighing scale. One is unable to cry or to laugh.
5. A withered tree grows flowers. This is good fortune that comes after a long spell of bad luck.
6. A letter is held in a deer's mouth. This is a certificate of appointment.
7. There is a pile of gold and jewels. This means riches and wealth.

Image and Symbol

龍劍入匣之課 • 以臣遇君之象 •

The image is the dragon sword kept in its sheath.

The symbol is that one is finally represented with an opportunity to fulfill a goal.

Kua Tsi (文王彖辭)

晉 • 康侯 • 用錫馬蕃庶 • 晝日三接 •

Jin or advancing. The powerful prince is honored with large numbers of horses. He receives an audience with the king three times in a single day.

Zhan (占) or hints on divining

1. This is a March hexagram it is good in spring and winter, and bad in fall.
2. Jin or Advancing is a Yóuhún hexagram of Dáyou or great possession.

14 Dàyou   1. Qián   35 Jìn

qùnhǔm   Pure heaven   Yoúhún

If a patient consults I Ching and gets Jìn, he is in a very serious condition.

3. Finally your worth is recognized and valued accordingly. After three months of failure at learning to juggle, you suddenly can keep the three oranges aloft all the time. Then four, five and six.

Yao Tsi（周公爻辭）

初六 • 晉如摧如 • 貞吉 • 罔孚 • 裕 • 无咎 •

1st Yao. You advance, but are turned back. It is a good time to persevere and win good fortune. If no one has any confidence in you, you should remain calm. This is the right way.

Zhan（占）

1. You start in your new business and when customers find you have no experience, they don't want to deal with you. You keep on confidently until you succeed.
2. Obedience is a better way of showing respect than outward reverence.
3. The spiritual debt is deep and great.

六二 • 晉如愁如 • 貞吉 • 受玆介福于其王母 • ○

1st Yao. Advancing meets with sorrow. If you persevere at this time, you will have good luck. You will obtain great happiness from female ancestor. ○

Zhan（占）

1. Your boss says to make an appointment with his secretary to talk about the special plan you have. But he is always jumping up and going somewhere else when you go to see him. You wonder if he has totally lost interest. You persist and finally see him, discovering he is that much more considerate due to your patience.

2. You should suffer any disgrace and insult in order to accomplish your own project.

六三・衆允・悔亡・○

3rd Yao. Everyone is in accord, and unhappiness disappears.

Zhan (占)

1. You give up your plan to go into business for yourself and take on two partners. To your surprise, you all get along so well that you forget your disappointment completely.
2. You have an ambition for things beyond what is presently available or obtainable.
3. Cooperation and unity make difficult things easy.

九四・晉如鼫鼠・貞厲・●

4th Yao. You advance like a hamster. To persevere in this is dangerous. ●

Zhan (占)

1. You serve as agent for a rich old lady helping her sell her antiques, and you think "no one would know if I took a secret commission on a few deals." But you discard the idea as unworthy. Later you find she had had everything appraised and would have caught you.
2. The good situation doesn't last long.
3. You will make plans to no avail.

六五・悔亡・失得 勿恤・往吉・无不利・

5th Yao. Dissatisfaction disappears. Don't take gain and loss too seriously. To do things is good luck. Everything furthers it.

Zhan (占)

1. Suddenly your special talent is a community asset and you are called on to help again and again. Your friends say you ought to open a business in it on the side and "cash in on it" but you don't have time. When you think it over, you decide "first things first," and you don't feel disappointed.
2. One who avoids seeing trouble does not have to worry about trouble.

上九・晉其角・維用伐邑・厲吉・无咎・貞吝・

6th Yao. It is all right to make progress "with horns" right now, but only to punish your own city. It is good luck to be aware of the danger of this, and there will be no blame. If you persevered too much, then you will take a fall.

[*Zhan* (占)]

1. You are in favor at your job right now and you take advantage of this to "straighten out" a fellow employee who's gotten corrupt. By handling things carefully, you avoid unpleasantness. Someone says you should use this skill outside your job but you realize this way you would overextend yourself.
2. Last minute efforts are useless if no preparatory work has been done.

36

Míngyí 明夷

Earth above
Fire below
Darkening

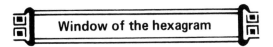

Window of the hexagram

1. A woman is sitting on the well. This symbolizes a trap or being drawn into a hopeless situation.
2. A tiger is inside the well. This means a hero is bullied by a gang of weaklings when his luck is down.
3. A coin is broken. This means loss of money or suffering bankruptcy.
4. A lookout post is broken in the middle. This means not knowing what direction to turn in.
5. The deer is chased by a man. This means to achieve and gain nothing, a very bad omen.

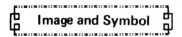

Image and Symbol

鳳凰垂翼之課・出明入暗之象・

The image is the phoenix flying, but with drooping wings.
The symbol is leaving the light and entering into darkness.

Kua Tsi (文王 爻辭)

明夷・利艱貞・

Míngyí. In bad times it is favorable to be persevering.

Zhan (占) *or hints on divining*

1. This is an August hexagram. It is good in winter, bad in summer and fall.
2. Your energies are so intense that, when directed outward they can make your dream come true.
3. Mingyí is Yóuhún hexagram of Shi or Army

7 Shi	29 Kàn	36 Míngyí
quíhún	Pure Water	Yoú hún

If a patient consults the I Ching and gets míngyí, it is a very dangerous condition, needing great care.

Yao Tsi (周公爻辭)

初九・明夷于飛・垂其翼・君子于行・三日不食・有攸往・主人有言・●
1st Yao. Mińgyí.   During flight.   You lower your wings.   You find
no food for three days on your wanderings. But you have a destination.
Your host gossips about you. ●

Zhan (占)

1. You set out with a high and ambitious goal and are struck down
   by a bad fate. Instead of quitting entirely, you make every effort
   to keep your goal alive and suffer hardships while your friends
   say he is crazy.
2. Supposing you grant that be was in his right mind, that was no
   excuse for his conduct.
3. Your mind is superior to being governed by prejudice.

六二・明夷・夷于左股・用拯・馬壯・吉・
2nd Yao. Mińyí.   Hurt him in the left thigh. He helps with the strength
of a horse. Good luck.

Zhan (占)

1. Bad elements where you work have convinced your boss to take
   a stand that is exploitive and second-rate.   You cannot speak out,
   but you never throw away your inner vision of seeing something
   better happening.
2. You and your friends go sailing and the boat is overturned in a
   sudden storm.   You do everything to see your friends are safe and
   that no one is hurt while you wait for help to come.
3. You join a peaceful public demonstration regarding a social ill. But
   the political climate is against it and troublemakers start violence to
   give the demonstration a bad name.   You risk dangers to protect
   your friends and help them get away safely.

九三・明夷于南狩・得其大首・不可疾貞・○
3rd Yao. Mínyí.   During hunting in the south.   Their head leader is
taken prisoner. You should not expect perseverance too soon. ○

Zhan (占)

1. You get involved in a political controversy and by great good luck the opposition leader is discredited in a scandal. Your friends say "we have won now," but you warn them the opposition is supported by many people and can get new leaders easily.
2. If you go south, you will find a job and a friend.

六四・入于左腹・獲明夷之心・于出門庭・

4th Yao. You penetrate the left side of the belly, and get at the deepest heart of Mingyi. You leave the courtyard by the gate.

Zhan (占)

1. You think your more powerful opponent is just misguided and greedy, but by chance you discover his secret plans and find out it is much, much worse. Now that you know, you can get out before disaster strikes.
2. You should take into consideration every aspect of a matter.
3. Birds of different feathers will not flock together.

六五・箕子之明夷・利貞・

5th Yao. The Mingyi is like that of Prince Chi. It is a time for persevering.

Zhan (占)

1. Like Prince Chi you find your relative is involved in evil acts. You will not desert your family, so you pretend to not notice. Discredited, you do not have to do bad things, and you hang around, looking always for a chance to help the good side.
2. A wise person who knows what is best for himself can safeguard against harm.

上六・不明晦・初登于天・復登于地・●

6th Yao. There is no light but darkness. First he raised himself to heaven, then he plunged into the deepest hell. ●

Zhan (占)

1. The bully who dominated your group drove all the good people

away.   No one was left to restrain his rashness and he went
completely berserk.   Now the police have just taken him away and
he will not return.

2. Can you image the situation, If there is no road rising to heaven and
no gate plunging into the deepest hell?

3. To avoid temptation one should maintain presence of mind.

37

Jiàrén 家人

Wind above
Fire below
Family

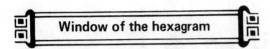

Window of the hexagram

1. A man draws a bow. This means to nurture one's strength in preparation for a challenging task.
2. A repe belt is at the water side. This means dragging through mud and water unable to make a decision.
3. A document is in the clouds. This means imperial graciousness.
4. An official kneels and bows acception the document. This means to express thanks for an assignment.
5. A woman gives her hand to the official. This is a good omen for marriage.

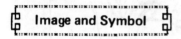

Image and Symbol

入海求珠之課 • 開花結子之象 •

The image is to dive in the deep sea for pearls.
The symbol is flowers turning to fruits.

Kua Tsi (文王彖辭)

家人 • 利女貞 •
The family. The kind of perseverance a woman has will succeed.

Zhan (占) *or hints on divining*

1. This is a June hexagram. It is good in spring, bad in summer and winter.
2. You find your friends have bad ideas and attitudes. You think of attacking, but you look further and find the foundations of their lives are weak and this is where the trouble comes from. Instead you set out to do things to influence them to better their conditions.

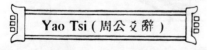

Yao Tsi (周公爻辭)

初九 • 閑有家 • 悔亡 •
1st Yao. There is firm seclusion of the family as a unit. Disappointment

gradually disappears.

Zhan (占)

1. When you and your friends undertake a difficult and adventurous project, you find that initially they can only daydream of success, and you nag them to do the things that are important. Some are very annoyed, but in the long run your group is able to succeed and all else is forgotten.
2. Every family has some sort of trouble.
3. Domestic scandals should not be published.

六二 • 无攸遂 • 在中饋 • 貞吉 •

2nd Yao. She should not follow whims, because she has to take care of the food. Persevering now is good luck later on.

Zhan (占)

1. You feel like doing this and doing that, and then you realize it will mean neglecting your most important duties. You forget your impulses and stick to the important work. You succeed.
2. Don't be a black sheep in your family.
3. You will go with apprehension and return with great enthusiasm.

九三 • 家人嗃嗃 • 悔厲 • 吉 • 婦人嘻嘻 • 終吝 •

3rd Yao. When everyone's temper flares up, to be too severe brings unhappiness. It is the right direction, however. When women and children are disorganized and play too much, it leads to unhappy collapses.

Zhan (占)

1. No one feels like working and a few people get red in the face when you tell them how lazy they are. They go to work sullenly. Later they forget it.
2. A girl should get married upon reaching womanhood.
3. If one grows up in a wealthy enviorment one will suffer more than others who grow up in a poor family.

六四 • 富家 • 大吉 • ○

4th Yao. She is the treasure of the family. The greatest good luck. ○

Zhan (占)

1. One member of your group did nothing but take care of routine things and always keep things in order, but was not appreciated; Then hard times came from outside and everybody suddenly saw they were able to survive only because of this order.
2. One can never fully repay the love and care one has received from one's mother no matter how hard one tries to please her.

九五 • 王假有家 • 勿恤吉 • ○

5th Yao. **You approach your family like a king. No need for fears. Good luck.** ○

Zhan (占)

1. You think first of doing your work thoroughly, and when you work with others of your group, you encourage their good work.
2. A wise mother would do everything for the healthy growth of her childern.

上九 • 有孚威如 • 終吉 • ○

6th Yao. **Your work commands respect. Good luck is coming.** ○

Zhan (占)

1. You did your job well. No one else could use you as an excuse for laziness or poor work. The hard workers felt themselves to be second to you. Everyone is going to benefit.
2. If one accumulates enough good deeds, one will have more than enough blessings to spare.

38

Kui′ 暌

Fire above
Lake below
Opposition

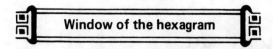

1. A man holds an ax. This means to be in authority.
2. A document is damaged. Means not knowing whether to advance or retreat.
3. There is an ox and a mouse. This is good for the hour, day, month, and year of the ox or of the mouse.
4. The peach tree blossoms. It is spring-time.
5. The gates are closed. A person had returned home.
6. The snow goose flies and cackles. Everything does not turn out as one wishes.

Image and Symbol

猛虎陷阱之課・二女同居之象・

The image is that the ferocious tiger is trapped.
The symbol is that two women are staying together.

Kua Tsi （文王彖辭）

睽・小事吉・

Kuí or opposition. You can have good luck in smaller matters.

Zhan（占） or hints on divining

1. This is a February hexagram. It is good in spring, bad in summer and winter.
2. You find your group split in two by an obstinate dispute. You say nothing, and work on the smaller things that everyone agrees on.
3. There is no way water and fire can coexist.

Yao Tsi（周公爻辭）

初九・悔亡・喪馬・勿逐自復・見惡人・无咎・

1st Yao. Disappointment disappears. If your horse runs off, don't follow it, it will come back on its own. When you see evil people show up, alert yourself against making any mistakes.

Zhan (占)

1. Your friends are angry with you because you took an unpopular stand on an issue that came up. You say nothing and bide your time. One of them brings a couple of unsavory characters to visit. You say nothing and instead are careful to maintain the highest standards of personal conduct. Eventually they go away saying "how dull!" Eventually your friends forget their anger.
2. You will receive a blessing in disguise.

九二・遇主于巷・无咎・○

2nd Yao. You meet your master in a narrow street. There is nothing bad in this. ○

Zhan (占)

1. You stay away from your friend who favors your side of the controversy because others seeing you together become angry. Then you happen on him accidentally in the parking lot, and you exchange a few quick words to fill each other in on what is happening.
2. An ambitous person who constantly shows improvement deserves a new appraisal of his/her achievements every now and then.

六三・見輿曳・其牛掣・其人天且劓・无初有終・●

3rd Yao. You see the wagon dragged backwards, and the oxen brought to a stop, a man's hair and nose cut off. It is a bad beginning, but there is a good end. ●

Zhan (占)

1. Just as you decide to tell your boss his latest scheme is not good you get angry at him for firing another objector! Nonetheless, you know you are right, and you join forces with the fired employee and later see justice prevail.
2. You are secretly interested in one thing while pretending to show interest in another.

九四　睽孤・遇元夫・交孚・厲・无咎・

4th Yao. While you are isolated by opposition, you meet a like-minded person and you know you can associate with him in good faith. Despite dangerous times, nothing regrettable will happen.

Zhan (占)

1. You seem the only one in your group who has any sense, and everyone else is just making trouble. Then you have a chance meeting with a person you didn't know well and find he sees things exactly the same way. You trust each other and as you part, you both feel reassured in your attitudes.
2. You have talents unappreciated by the world.
3. Learning is an endless process.

六五 • 悔亡 • 厥宗 • 噬膚 • 往何咎 •

5th Yao.   Disappointment disappears. A companion bites his way thru the wrappings. If you go to him, it couldn't be a mistake.

Zhan (占)

1. Everyone is against one another because of the controversy. Then a person of the same positive sentiment as yours makes his sincerity visible in his actions, and you join up with the person.
2. You will enjoy the first of the toil of others.
3. Be aware of someone who flatters you while preparing to plant a sword in your back.

上九 • 睽孤 • 見豕負塗 • 載鬼一車 • 先張之弧 • 後說之弧 • 匪寇婚媾 • 往
遇雨 • 測吉 •

6th Yao.   Isolated by opposition, you see your companion as a pig covered with dirt or a wagon full of devils. First you draw a bow against him, then you lay the bow aside. He is not a robber and will court at the right time. When you go to meet him, rain falls, and good fortune comes.

Zhan (占)

1. You see one of your clan acting seeminly irresponsible and foolish and set out to destroy the person's influence. Then you decide to wait and be sure, and the person makes a move towards friendship. When you accept his offer, the tension that had built up

is dispersed and you feel relieved.

2. You will do something inexplicably as if manipulated by super-natural beings.

3. The information you expect is like a fish that dives and never surfaces or a snow goose that departs and never returns.

39 ䷦ Cú 蹇

Water above
Mountain below
Limping

Window of the hexagram

1. The sun shines. This is an image of brightness.
2. There is the Chinese character 喜 meaning happiness printed on a flag. This means someone will surprise you with something that will make you happy.
3. The five drums are the night watchman's drums. This shows a time late at night when everything is quiet.
4. A deer puts its front feet on a drum. This means to become increasingly prosperous.
5. There are two Chinese characters 千 里 meaning "a thousand miles." This is an omen of something very far away becoming a factor.

Image and Symbol

飛雁啣蘆之課 • 背明向暗之象 •
The image is a flying snow goose holding a reed in its mouth.
The symbol is going away from brightness towards darkness.

Kua Tsi (文王彖辭)

蹇 • 利西南 • 不利東北 • 利見大人 • 貞吉 •
Cú or Limping. The southwest is good, and the northeast is not promissing. It is a time to see an influential man. Persevering will being good luck.

 Zhan (占) or hints on divining

1. This is an August hexagram. It is good in fall, bad in spring, suggests you will be getting sick in winter.
2. Cú or limping, is one of four evil hexagrams in I Ching. There is a rolling stream in foreground and a high mountain behind, suddenly you find a tiger gazing at you through the woods. This is the image of hexagram cú or limping.
3. You planned to go on a long vacation and just then you got laid off your job and must save your money instead. You decide to

spend the time studying a long-term skill you want to acquire, and enroll in a course at the community college.

Yao Tsi（周公爻辭）

初六・往蹇・來譽・

1st Yao. Going ahead leads to difficulties, but coming back will earn you praise.

Zhan（占）

1. Just as you are about to ask your girlfriend to marry, you get involved in a terrible argument over some trivial thing that is not important. You decide you better wait awhile and see if you can learn to get along better. It works.
2. Even a lame turtle can travel a thousand miles which means persistence ensures success.
3. A person's true color is revealed only in the long run.

六二・王臣蹇蹇・匪躬之故・

2nd Yao. The king's servant runs into one difficulty after another, yet they are not his fault.

Zhan（占）

1. Your car runs into a ditch, you damage it getting out, then make the damage worse by continuing on, because you are taking a injured person to the hospital.
2. When you go to fix the leaky faucet it breaks open, when you shut the valve off, it breaks apart, then the pipe splits, you wind up rebuilding the whole system since you have no choice.

九三・往蹇來反・

3rd Yao. To go ahead you will find difficalty, so you come back.

Zhan（占）

1. You are able to return to the proper path after going astray.
2. You should retreat as fast as possible in the face of something you don't like.

3. Always remind oneself that things might have been worse.

六四・往蹇來速・

4th Yao. To go ahead you will find difficulty, but coming back will bring unity.

Zhan (占)

1. You want to talk to a friend who is angry and for no reason, but you realize you can't change his mind. You go and talk to his other friends, and you all wait for the chance to do something good.
2. The realization of good things is usually proceded by rough goings.
3. Don't aim too high, while caring nothing about the practical foundation.

九五・大蹇・朋來・

5th Yao. In the middle of the worst difficulties, friends come to help.

Zhan (占)

1. Your neighbor and his family are driven from their apartment by a fire. You call up friends and get them settled temporarily and find clothes for them to wear in the morning.
2. Happiness lies in rendering help to others.
3. Unity of purpose is a formidable force.

上六・往蹇來碩・吉・利見大人・○

6th Yao. Going forward leads to troubles, coming back leads to the best good fortune. It is a time for seeing the influential man. ○

Zhan (占)

1. You retire from your business so you can take up a new and more important pursuit with great enthusiasm. Just as you are getting started, your old partners ask for your help, as they are in trouble. So you give it up for awhile and succeed in helping them reorganize their business with great success.
2. You have the courage to do what is right regardless of consequences.
3. Make up your mind to work from early in the morning till late at night!

40

Jié 解

Thunder above
Water below
Loosening

Window of the hexagram

1. The Chinese character 提 means "to life" as in a flag. This connotes having the intended effect.
2. A sword is stuck in the ground. This means an end to fighting.
3. A rabbit is running. This means to have no doubt.
4. An official is sitting on the clouds. This means a meteoric rise of social position.
5. A crowing rooster is in the yard. This means one will be heard at a great distance.
6. A Taoist priest points at the door with his index finger. This means the way to paradise.
7. A taoist priest offers a book. This means having a good time to offer a plan or advice to others.

Image and Symbol

囚人出獄之課・草木舒伸之象・
The image is a prisoner being released from jail.
The symbol is grass and trees starting to grow abundantly.

Kua Tsi （文王彖辭）

解・利西南・无所往・其來復吉・有攸往・夙吉・
Jié or loosening. The southwest is a good place to look. If there is nowhere you have to go, it is good to return. If you still have some place to go, it is good fortune to complete things quickly.

Zhan （占） or hints on divining

1. This is a December hexagram. It is good in summer bad in fall and winter.
2. Jeí or loosening is like a prisoner being released from jail, or after heavy rain, the weather becomes sunny. Difficulties and troubles all go away.
3. After separating and failing for weeks to settle your squabbles,

you and your wife suddenly come to a time when you see eye to eye. You quickly decide to get together again and resume your regular life.

Yao Tsi (周公爻辭)

初六 • 无咎 •
1st Yao. There is no blame.

Zhan (占)

1. All the arguments have been cleared up, and you resume your regular life, taking it easy at first.
2. You will turn bad luck into good fortune.

九二 • 田獲三孤 • 得黃矢 • 貞吉 • ○
2nd Yao. You kill three foxes in the field and get a yellow arrow. Persevering brings good luck. ○

Zhan (占)

1. Your colleagues tried to talk the boss into a rash scheme that appealed to his greed. You object and you work hard collecting documentary evidence of your view, and it turns the tide.
2. He who caused the dispute is the only one to resolve it.
3. If a patient consults I Ching, getting this Yao, the situation is serious. They may need an operation.

六三 • 負且乘 • 致寇至 • 貞吝 • ●
3rd Yao. If a man carries a heavy load on his back, yet he rides in a carriage, he is going to attract robbers. To persist this way leads to an upset. ●

Zhan (占)

1. You have all sorts of difficult obligations, yet when you get a little money you go out and spend it having a good time. A conman sees what a lazy fool you are and tries to talk you into a scheme to cheat your employers. Shocked, you realize your own bad habits attracted this man.

2. One has a sense of shame and honor only when his livehood is assured.
3. It is good to pretend to hear and know nothing sometimes.

九四 • 解而拇 • 朋至斯孚 •

4th Yao. Get yourself away from your big toe. Then a good person comes along, and you can trust him.

Zhan (占)

1. You have no money and the people you hang around with are stagnant and insincere. You decide it is getting you down, and though it is hard at first, you take up better habits. Then your chance comes along.
2. Financial matters should be settled clearly even between best friends or brothers.
3. Your plan will fail or be discarded before it gets started.

六五 • 君子維有解 • 吉 • 有孚于小人 •

5th Yao. If the only person who can help you is yourself, it is good luck. It proves to second-rate people that you are serious about things.

Zhan (占)

1. You say you want to do better and your friends laugh at you. You think it over and see that they just detract from you, and you resolve to do things on your own. They see your attitude change and you begin to make progress and they leave you alone.
2. Good companions have good influence while bad ones have bad influence.
3. The opportunity seems very near, as if right before your eyes.

上六 • 公用射隼于高墉之上 • 獲之无不利 •

6th Yao. The prince shoots at a hawk on a high wall and kills it. Everything furthers the situation.

Zhan (占)

1. The civic organization you belong to has become worthless, because its leader just likes to play games and do nothing. Appeals fail, so you lay your plans and get him voted out of office the next

election.   He leaves reviling you but the organization begins to become alive again.

2.   It seems too high to be reached, but you will get there.

3.   You are one notch better than average people.

41

Sŭn 損

Mountain above
Lake below
Decrease

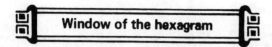

Window of the hexagram

1. Two people sit face to face drinking. This indicates joy and pleasure.
2. The wine bottle has fallen on the table. There is nothing one can drink.
3. A ball is on the ground. Means ones expectations cannot be realized.
4. There are two Chinese characters 再吉 that mean "one cannot expect everything the first time; one has to try again and again for success."

Image and Symbol

鑿地見水之課・握土爲山之象・

The image is drilling underground and finding water.
The symbol is many small particles of earth will make a mountain.

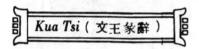

Kua Tsi (文王彖辭)

損・有孚・元吉・无咎・可貞・利有攸往・曷之用・二簋可用享・

Sǔn or Decrease brings the highest good fortune when it is combined with sincerity, and there are no regrets. It is a time to be persevering and to undertake something. How? You can use two small bowls for the sacrifice.

Zhan (占) *or hints on divining*

1. This is a July hexagram. It is good in summer, fall, bad in winter.
2. Two small bowls for the sacrifice means to restrain one's wrath and repress one's desires. If you can do this, God will bless you.
3. You were miserable at your high paying job with all its luxuries and false friends. Finally, in desperation you gave it all up to take a much lesser paying job you really love. The only friends you have left are the ones who were sincere, and when you get together to relax, you do it modestly and have ten times more fun than before.

Yao Tsi (周公爻辭)

初九 · 已事遄往 · 无咎 · 酌損之 ·

1st Yao. To go to help quickly when your tasks are done is blameless. But you have to think about how much you may lesson others in taking help.

Zhan (占)

1. You have a friend who always helps out when you are in need. You decide to learn from this and to be helpful like he is. There is prosperity in helping others.
2. Service begets happiness.
3. Heaven helps those who help themselves.

九二 · 利貞 · 征凶 · 弗損益之 ·

2nd Yao. It is a time to persevere, but not a time to do things on your own. Without decreasing yourself, you can bring increase to others.

Zhan (占)

1. You work for someone else, not yourself. Instead of being too eager to please, you act in a serious and dignified manner, and everyone benefits.
2. It is easy to dodge an open attack but difficult to escape from a clandestine one.
3. One is apt to lose possession of what has been gotten easily.

六三 · 三人行 · 則損一人 · 一人行 · 則得其友 ·

3rd Yao. When three people travel together, the number is decreased by one. When one man travels alone, he finds a friend.

Zhan (占)

1. When you meet with your two friends the conversation always seems to go around in circles when you discuss what to do. When you meet with only one of them, you settle it quickly.
2. If three of us are walking together, at least one of the other two

is good enough to be my teacher.

3. The gain more than compensates the loss.

六四・損其疾・使遄有喜・无咎・

4th Yao. If you decrease your bad habits, it makes the other person come quickly to rejoice. There is no bad féeling.

Zhan（占）

1. You have a good friend, but his constant pessimism and passivity is a disappointment. Then he decides to do something serious about it, and you find he is twice as much fun to know.
2. A true gentleman is glad to admit his own mistakes.
3. You should correct your faults once you are aware of them.

六五・或益之・十朋之龜・弗克違・元吉・○

5th Yao. Someone increases him. Ten pairs of tortoises cannot oppose **this. The highest** good fortune.

Zhan（占）

1. You look for a good mate, but never seem to find anyone you feel is special for you. Then one day this happens, and it is so different and so strong, it is as if fate itself brings it about.
2. You work hard at what interests you, sometimes its goes well, sometimes it plods along, and you persist. Then one day everything falls into place and goes well, and it is as if all the good impulses you've had have come together.
3. It is a most auspicious omen.

上九・弗損益之・无咎・貞吉・利有攸往・得臣无家・○

6th Yao. If you increase yourself without decreasing other people, this is blameless. It is a time for perseverance and undertaking something worthwhile. You find servants, but no longer live in a separate house from them.○

Zhan（占）

1. You decide to study how to live a good life and you succeed and prosper. Then you decide to share what you know with others, and help everyone to prosper.

2. What one accomplishes should not be a private advantage, but rather should be for the public good and available to everyone.

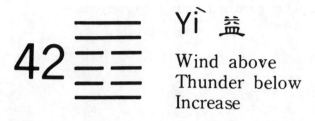

42

Yì 益

Wind above
Thunder below
Increase

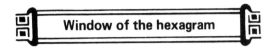

1. An official holds a small box. People adhering to the same principles will map their plans together.
2. A person pushes a wooden car. This means to seize an opportunity.
3. There is a deer and a coin. This is a good omen about wealth or a job, and one should act without hesitation.

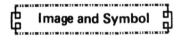

鳴鴻遇風之課・滴水滿河之象・

The image is that a crying snow goose encounters strong headwinds. The symbol is a constant drip of water can fill a river.

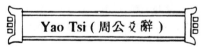

益・利有攸往・利涉大川・

Yí or Increase. It furthers you to do something. It is a time for crossing the great water.

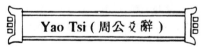 *Zhan* (占) *or hints on divining*

1. This is a July hexagram. It is bad in spring and fall.
2. There are three kinds of beneficial friends: honest friends, understanding friends and learned friends.
3. You have been doing allright in your life, but now you experience a time when everything seems to further your highest visions, and you decide to act on this now while circumstance are propitious.

Yao Tsi (周公爻辭)

初九・利用爲大作・元吉・无咎・○

1st Yao. It is beneficial to accomplish great deeds. The highest good fortune. There is nothing to blame. ○

Zhan (占)

1. Your boss' business is expanding and he gives you an opportunity to develop a new part of it. You work at it with energy, and everyone comes to benefit from it.
2. Your wisdom increases as your age increases.

六二・或益之十朋之龜・弗克違・永貞吉・王用亨于帝・○

2nd Yao. Someone indeed increase him, and ten pairs of tortises cannot oppose it. His constant perseverance brings good fortune. The king presents him before God. Good fortune. ○

Zhan (占)

1. You take up a civic project and there is a sudden surge of interest in it. Instead of relaxing a little, you continue to use all the energy you have to carry it forward, and the end results are beyond what anyone dreamed possible.
2. You will increase your riches.
3. You should straighten up a complicated or messy situation by taking drastic steps and with dispatch.

六三・益之用凶事・无咎・有孚中行・告公用圭・

3rd Yao. You are benefitted by unfortunate events. There is nothing to blame if you are sincere and walk in the middle, and report to the prince with a letter and seal.

Zhan (占)

1. There is an economic depression and the moderate savings you have you can now use to ten times more effect since no one has any money. You use it to start up a business that requires a lot of workers, and thus you profit many others as well as yourself.
2. You will have unforeseen trouble.
3. A determined effort can accomplish any kind of task.

六四・中行・告公從・利用爲依遷國・○

4th Yao. If you walk in the middle and report to the prince, he will follow. It is good for your services to be used in the removal of the capital. ○

🐉 *Zhan* (占) 🐛

1. Your boss decides to move his business to larger quarters and puts you in charge. You coordinate everything, making sure no one is short-changed, and the great change goes well.
2. A change of place is advisable.
3. Advantage will be found in the south east.

九五・有孚惠心・勿問元吉・有孚惠我德・○

5th Yao. If you really have a kind heart, you do not ask questions. The highest good fortune. Kindness will be recognized as your virtue. ○

🦋 *Zhan* (占) 🦋

1. You see someone who needs help and feel sympathy for him. You help him get out of trouble and you never think to ask if he deserves it or is grateful. People see you do this and it makes them less stingy and suspicious.
2. If you persist in working hard, you will suddenly become wealthy and influential.
3. Your stratagem is so wonderful, it seems to be conceived by divine beings.

上九・莫益之・或擊之・立心勿恆・凶・●

6th Yao. He increases no one. Someone even strikes him. He does not keep his heart steady. Bad luck. ●

〔 *Zhan* (占) 〕

1. Your friend has good luck in making money, but it doesn't improve him any. He is even less considerate of people, and wastes his money on luxuries. You see less of him and one day you hear he has fallen in with bad people who stole most of his money.
2. The good circumstance doesn't last long.
3. While two dogs fight for a bone, a third runs away with it.
4. Haughtiness invites losses while modesty brings profit.

43

Kuī 夬

Lake abové
Heaven below
Decision

Window of the hexagram

1. Two people travel together, but before reaching their destination, they encounter water, fire, a tiger and a snake. This means to suffer all the hardships there are.
2. A man uses a sword to kill a snake. This means a brave person.
3. There is the Chinese character 文 meaning "literature" on a flag tied to a post. Below the post there is a pile of coins. This means after enduring hardships one finds fame and wealth.

Image and Symbol

神劍斬蛟之課・先損後益之象・

The image is to use a divine sword to kill a flood dragon.
The symbol is decreasing at first, but afterwards increasing.

Kua Tsi (文王彖辭)

夬・揚于王庭・孚號・有厲・告自邑・不利卽戎利有攸往・

Kui or Decision. You must resolutely make things known at the court of the king, and announce the news truthfully. Danger. It is a time to do something worthwhile.

Zhan (占) or hints on divining

1. This is a march hexagram. It is good in summer and fall, bad in winter.
2. One Yin Yao governs five Yang Yaos, so it is a Yin hexagram. The Yin Yao at the top position, represents a bad man, all of the other five Yang Yaos want to drive this Yin Yao away.
3. You sense that people are so fed up with the dozens of petty burglaries in your community that they are ready to act as one. You go to the newspaper and convince them to print an editorial recommending they avoid wasting money by hiring more police, and get burglar alarms instead, and open a center for rehabilitating juvenile delinquents.

Yao Tsi（周公爻辭）

初九・壯于前趾・往不勝・爲咎・●

1st Yao. You are mighty in your toes. If you go and are not equal to the work, you are making a mistake. ●

Zhan（占）

1. Opportunity is opening up fast and you are ready to rush out and take advantage of it. Then you realize you are unprepared and have no clear ideas of what to do, and you sit down and work things out, and then wait for the right moment.
2. It's better to be the boss of a small group than a top lieutenant in a large organization.
3. Someone will give you a hard time.

九二・惕號・莫夜有戎・勿恤・

2nd Yao. There is a cry of alarm. People carry arms at evening and night. Fear nothing.

Zhan（占）

1. Rumors fly that your company's new advances will be swept away by new tactics from your competitors. But you have been following things closely and know exactly what's going on and how to meet it.
2. There is no danger when there is preparedness.
3. You should carry out an undertaking from start to finish, not giving up halfway.

九三・壯于頄・有凶・君子夬夬・獨行遇雨・若濡・有慍・无咎・●

3rd Yao. To be strong in the cheekbones brings poor fortune. The superior person is strongly resolved. He walks alone and gets caught in the rain and spatter with mud, and people talk against him. There is nothing to blame. ●

Zhan（占）

1. Everyone is attacking corruption right now, but you have your own ideas. You keep up relations with a corrupt person you have

to deal with and show no sign of discontent. This lulls them into a false sense of security and weakens them for the coming attack. Thus while your friends think you betray them, you help them out.

2. When you try to get temporary pleasures, you should first be aware of the adverse consequences.

3. The situation is like the roaring water carrying away the dam.

九四・臀无膚・其行次且・牽羊悔亡・聞言不信・●

4th Yao. There is no skin on his thighs, and it is hard to walk. If he would let himself be led like a sheep, he would lose any bad feelings. But if these words are heard, they will not be believed. ●

Zhan (占)

1. "I must do this my own particular way" your friend says, when you offer him a chance to join with others to get things done. "Joining with us would help you solve your problems easily" you protest, but he glares at you and continues to suffer by doing things the hardway.

2. The rain fell all night and the roof leaked. Now one will meet an added misfortune.

3. Good tools are a prerequisite to the successful execution of a job.

九五・莧陸・夬夬・中行・无咎・

5th Yao   In getting rid of weeds, you have to have strong resolution. If you walk in the middle, you will remain free of blame.

Zhan (占)

1. An exploitive company has been cheating your firm in little ways. You look up the records and find your firm makes alot of income from them. You decide to find ways you can increase business with others, and then get rid of this client.

2. Someone will return evil for your good will.

3. It is still not too late to feel regret and change what you are planning to do.

上六・无號・終有凶・●

6th Yao. There is no cry of warning. Later on there is bad luck. ●

{ *Zhan* (占) }

1. The exterminator gets rid of the termites and you ignore it when you see a couple of survivors crawling around the next day. Then six months later you wake up in the middle of the night and hear them gnawing in the walls again!
2. Because no preventive measures are taken, an endless flow of disasters follow.
3. If you go to the east, you can pursue good fortune and shun the course of calamity.

44

Gōu 姤

Heaven above
Wind below
Meeting

Window of the hexagram

1. An official shoots an arrow at a deer. This means you may have the job you are looking for.
2. There is a Chinese character 喜 meaning happiness on a document. This means it is a good time to create or to write something.
3. Two persons each hold an end of a rope. This means a dispute, or endless involvement.
4. A person with a worn green garment points out the direction for you to follow. This means there will be severe hardship at first, but someone will help you and the road to success will then be smooth.

Image and Symbol

風雲相聚之課・或聚或散之象・
The image is that of the winds mingling with the clouds.
The symbol is either gathering together, or separating.

Kua Tsi (文王彖辭)

姤・女壯・勿用取女・
Gōu or Coming to meet. The maiden is powerful. One should not marry such a person.

Zhan (占) or hints on divining

1. This is a May hexagram. It is good in fall, bad in spring, maybe sick in summer and having arguments and trouble in winter.
2. One Yin Yao grows on the bottom to govern five Yang Yaos. It is a Yin hexagram.
3. It can mean a woman who is very active in social functions or one who has many lovers. It means a marriage needs balance, because either woman or man is too Yang or strong and it is not an ideal couple.
4. You meet a woman who's a flirt in a bar, and you think, this is only harmless fun. Hours later you wake up in the alley out back and

your wallet and your car are gone.

Yao Tsi (周公爻辭)

初六 • 繫于金柅 • 貞吉 • 有攸往 • 見凶 • 羸豕孚蹢躅 •

1st Yao.   It has to be halted with a bronze brake.   Persistence now brings good fortune.   If you let it run its course, you are in bad luck. Even a lean pig has it in him to rage around.

Zhan (占)

1. "Better get a check-up," your wife says when you report a minor pain.   "It's nothing" you think, and forget about it.   Three months later you suddenly turn white, fall on the floor, and begin writhing in pain.
2. Your remarks are not appealing to the other side.   The better way is to change them.
3. Someone will induce you to do something bad.

九二 • 包有魚 • 无咎 • 不利賓 •

2nd Yao.   The fish is in the tank.   This is blameless.   It does not further guests.

Zhan (占)

1. You're the secretary and your boss is in a foul, stupid mood, but he's stuck in his office, busy with some routine work.   You give anyone who comes by a warning look, and they leave him alone.
2. Try to avoid mistakes paining your friends and pleasing your enemies.
3. After observing a person's faults and failings, one will understand what he is.

九三 • 臀无膚 • 其行次且 • 厲 • 无大咎 •

3rd Yao.   There is no skin on his thighs and it is hard to walk.   If he is mindful of the dangers, there is no great mistake.

Zhan (占)

1. You want to go out and party with your dissolute friends in the

worst way, even though you have a heavy load of work to do. But you have no money. Finally you realize this is good luck, and you settle down.

2. The things which cannot be revealed to others will be public knowledge soon.

3. It is very good to cover up another's bad deeds and praise his virtues.

九四 • 包无魚 • 起凶 • ●

4th Yao. There is no fish in the tank. This leads to bad luck. ●

戔 Zhan (占) 彲

1. You are stand offish with the gas station man a block from you home because he's a grimy individual. Now your car won't start, and a tow truck is going to have to come from five miles away and charge a big fee for it.

2. A single post cannot support a mansion.

3. The higher price you have paid is the result of what you have gained.

九五 • 以杞包瓜 • 含章 • 有隕自天 •

5th Yao. A melon is covered with willow leaves. There are hidden lines. Finally it drops down to you from heaven.

戔 Zhan (占) 彲

1. The fellows who work for you are disorganized and poorly motivated. Instead of annoying lectures on conduct and such, you just assign them to their jobs without comment, and do your own job quietly. After a while you discover they have become quite competent and even take a little pride in this.

2. Things take care of themselves when the right time comes.

3. You will get that job. It is for you like catching a bug in a jar. It has no way of escape.

上九 • 姤其角 • 吝 • 无咎 • ●

6th Yao. He comes to meeting with his horns. This is humiliating. There is nothing to blame. ●

┌─────────────────┐
│ *Zhan* (占) │
└─────────────────┘

1. You go to work at a place where your fellow workers are always talking about trivial and boring and even distasteful subjects. You don't pass the time of day with any of them, and they gossip about how there must be something wrong with you. You are very happy with all this because it gives you time for really interesting things.
2. When you climb a mountain, near the peak the road becomes steep, and sometimes disappears entirely. This is the same with an undertakin approching completion. It is the most difficult stage and one needs patience to reach the end.
3. The moon begins to wane the moment it becomes full.

45

Cai´ 萃

Lake above
Earth below
Gathering

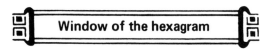

Window of the hexagram

1. A man cuts and polishes a piece of jade. This means to achieve self-renewal by ones inner efforts.
2. A monk points to a child and a fish is on the fire. There is good luck, but not too much.
3. A phoenix hold a letter in its beak. This is a good omen.

Image and Symbol

魚龍會來之課 • 如水就下之象 •
The image is a fish and a dragon gathering together.
The symbol is of water soaking and decending.

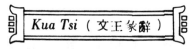

Kua Tsi (文王彖辭)

萃 • 亨 • 王假有廟 • 利見大人 • 亨 • 利貞 • 用大牲吉 • 利有攸往 •
Caí or Gathering. There is success. The king approaches the temples.
It is time to see an influential person, it will bring success. It is a time
for perseverance, and to make great offerings creates success. It is a
time to do things.

Zhan (占) *or hints on divining*

1. This is a June hexagram. It is good in spring and fall.
2. The symbol of caí or gathering is a common carp, the 6th Yao is carp's mouth. The 4th and 5th Yao are the gills. The 1st, 2nd and 3rd Yao are the scales. When the carp jumps over the dragon gate it is an omen of success in service examinations.

3. The whole town gathers together for a special picnic to celebrate a national holiday. You help organize the children to put on a special show, and then clean up all the debris afterwards. They remember the happiness of working and playing together all year long.

初六 • 有孚不終 • 乃亂乃萃 • 若號 • 一握爲笑 • 勿恤 • 往无咎 •

1st Yao. If you are sincere, but not entirely, there will sometimes be confusion and sometimes gathering together. If you call out your distress, then after one grasp of the hand, you can laugh again. There is nothing to regret. Going this way is blameless.

Zhan (占) *or hints on divining*

1. Everyone in your group agrees the time is right for some great undertaking, but discussion wavers back and forth, and nothing is done. Finally someone says, "We need a leader" and someone else says, "I will organize the whole thing!" Everyone is happy and things begin to move.
2. You will find yourself in a very embarrassing situation, at a loss whether to cry or to laugh.
3. Don't seek advice from an ignorant person.

六二 • 引吉 • 无咎 • 孚乃利用禴 •

2nd Yao. Letting yourself be drawn is good luck and blameless. If you are sincere, it is good luck to bring even a small donation.

Zhan (占)

1. You think, "What should I do? This? That?" Then you find yourself being drawn to a group of people who share and share alike.
2. To avoid temptation helps one retain presence of mind.
3. It will happen naturally out of your desire for it.

六三 • 萃如嗟如 • 无攸利 • 往无咎 • 小吝 •

3rd Yao. Gathering together amid sighs. Nothing furthers. But to go is without blame. There is slight humiliation.

Zhan (占)

1. You see a group of people you'd like to join, but the time has passed and everyone is "set" with what they have. You find the person in the group you have most in common with, and you take up a modest relationship with him. Later this person has seen You are allright and introduces others to you.
2. Don't criticize or make comments on something once it is complete. over.
3. Someone will give you a chance to make the best of your abilities.

九四 • 大吉 • 无咎 • ○
4th Yao. Great good luck. Blameless. ○

Zhan (占)

1. You go out and talk to everyone in your apartment about donating some time or money to a community project. People are impressed by your own willingness to help, and the whole thing prospers.
2. The difficult task will finally come to completion.
3. The wise person looks ignorant because be never shows off.

九五 • 萃有位 • 无咎 • 匪孚 • 元永貞 • 悔亡 •
5th Yao. If in gathering together you have a position, this is not blame. If there are some who are not yet sincerely joining the work, then you need sublime and enduring perseverance. Then disappointment disappears.

Zhan (占)

1. The boss gives you a special temporary assignment to direct a project. The people you work with think you have no ability, but they must work with you. You do your best and after awhile they feel you know what you're doing.
2. What's gone is gone.
3. You should think of the better possibilities of that situation.

上六 • 齎咨涕洟 • 无咎 •
6th Yao. Lamenting and sighing; floods of tears. This is blameless.

Zhan (占)

1. You ask your sweetheart to marry you, but she says no, because she thinks you aren't really sincere. When she sees how upset you are at her answer, her eyes are opened, and she agrees to reconsider.
2. You will lead a tranquil life without worldly desires.
3. You have a firm grasp of what is right and wrong.

46

Shēng 升

Earth above
Wind below
Ascending

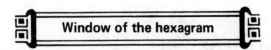

Window of the hexagram

1. A rain falls from the clouds. This means sharing the benefits that someone else produces.
2. A carpenter with a yard stick prepares to saw. This means one should get rid of bad habits, then one will be able to achieve the good.
3. A person polishes a brass mirror. This means to clarify one's thinking so one can see things accurately.
4. A mirror is on a frame. This means to exercise self-control to keep oneself from being drawn into immoral actions.

Image and Symbol

高山植木之課・積小成大之象・
The image is the growing tree in a high mountain.
The symbol is of small things accumulating until they become great.

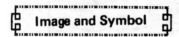

Kua Tsi (文王彖辭)

升・元亨・用見大人・勿恤・南征吉・
Shēng or Ascending has the greatest success. You must see an influential person. Don't worry. Travelling towards the south brings good luck.

Zhan (占) *or hints on divining*

1. This is an August hexagram, it is good in spring and fall.
2. The lower trigram Sūn is wood, the upper trigram Kùn is earth. This is like a seed under the ground to grow a tree, that needs time to push through the resistance of earth and grow. This is Shēng means.
3. You find new opportunities are opening in your career as your skill increases. You put this all to work by setting out to work at a higher level.

Yao Tsi (周公爻辭)

初六 • 允升 • 大吉 • ○

1st Yao. Shēng or Ascending that meets with confidence brings the greatest good luck. ○

Zhan (占)

1. You go to look for a better job and your prospective boss can tell you have the abilities he needs and hires you with a generous salary.
2. You will attain high ranks and acquire great wealth.
3. Wealth and honor come to us only of their own accord.

九二 • 孚乃利用禴 • 无咎 • ○

2nd Yao. If you are sincere, it is worthwhile to bring even a small offering. There is no blame in this. ○

Zhan (占)

1. Your prospective employer says, "He looks a little unconventional and certainly didn't go out of his way to impress me with fancy clothes, but I can tell he knows the job."
2. The moment a pole is erected under the sun, it throws its shadow upon the ground, which means the outcome may be known immediately.
3. One should use one's mental resources to the fullest.

九三 • 升盧邑 • ○

3rd Yao. You advanced into an empty city.

Zhan (占)

1. You reach a point where everything you do prospers and you wonder if it will suddenly end. Then you think "It is more important to concern myself with not wasting any of this time."
2. Everything goes smoothly like walking in a park.
3. Good ideas come at times of crisis.

六四 • 王用亨歧山 • 吉 • 无咎 •

4th Yao. The king offers him Mount Qí. Good luck. No blame.

Zhan (占)

1. You used to believe in yourself no matter what others thought. Now everyone important believes in you, too.
2. When the leaders do not set a good example, how can they expect the subordinate to behave well?
3. It is a lucky occurrence in the course of a disaster, such as in a violent car accident, being only slightly injured.

六五・貞吉・升階・○

5th Yao. Persistence is good luck. You ascend the stairs.

Zhan (占)

1. Things are easy now and if you make little mistakes, no one will notice. But instead you take each step carefully and thoroughly.
2. To reach a high position, one must start from a low position and do one's duties well.
3. You are very skillful in finding a powerful patron to advance your career.

上六・冥升・利于不息之貞・●

6th Yao. Ascending in the dark. You have to be relentlessly persevering.●

Zhan (占)

1. You find you can expand in any direction you look in. Then you remember that the only expansion that will work is one you plan carefully and clearly.
2. It is a very dangerous act, like a blind man riding a blind horse in a crowded street.
3. You are so arrogant that no one is worth anything in your eyes.

47

Kùn 困

Lake above
Water below
Oppression

Window of the hexagram

1. A loose wheel fallen on the ground signifies not knowing what to do.
2. A sick person is lying in bed. You still have a lot of troubles.
3. A pottery jar for cooking medicines means you are always sick.
4. An official pours water into a dry pond to save the fish. An omen of resurrection.
5. Grass grows in the pool. This means having good ideas.

Image and Symbol

河中無水之課・守已待時之象・

The image is no water in the river.
The symbol is to stand on one's own feet and bide one's time.

Kua Tsi (文王彖辭)

困・亨貞・大人吉・无咎・有言不信・

Kùn or Opression. There is success in perseverance. The great person brings good luck. There is nothing to blame. When you have something to say, no one listens to you.

Zhan (占) 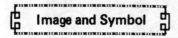 or hints on divining

1. This is a May hexagram. It is good in spring bad in summer and winter, and may indicare an argument or quarrel with other in the fall.
2. Kún or oppression is one of four evil hexagrams in I Ching. The upper trigram Kàn is like a reservoir leaking all its water onto the lower trigram, Kun, or Earth. So the reservoir is empty and cannot irrigate the farms, and supply people with water to drink.
3. The people around you think nothing of your skills and less of your personal influence. You say nothing and pay attention to everything that is happening because you intend some day to be part of it.

Yao Tsi (周公爻辭)

初六 • 臀困于株木 • 入于幽谷 • 三歲不覿 • ●

1st Yao. You sit oppressed under a leafless tree and wander into a gloomy valley. You see nothing for three years. ●

Zhan (占)

1. Fortune goes against you and you fall into a stupor. You become convinced you "don't have what it takes" and likewise that "you can't win in this world." You are destroying yourself and don't even know it.
2. If you want to do a good job, you have to plan thoroughly so as to take into consideration every aspect of it.
3. You seek something from a wrong source, like eliming a tree to get a fish.

九二 • 困于酒食 • 朱紱方來 • 利用享祀 • 征凶 • 无咎 •

2nd Yao. You are oppressed while you sit before meat and drink. The man with the scarlet knee bands is just coming. It is time to offer sacrifices, to set forth right now is bad luck. There is no blame.

Zhan (占)

1. Everything is prospering but you are going out of your mind with boredom and irritability. Then you see a chance — an exciting opportunity appears. But it is not clear how to get hold of it, so you think over your visions and what you really want, and hope to find the way.
2. An innocent man gets into trouble because of his tatents.
3. You have talent but no opportunity to use it.

六三 • 困于石 • 據于蒺藜 • 入于其宮 • 不見其妻 • 凶 • ●

3rd Yao. A man lets himself be oppressed by stone, and leans on thorns and thistles. He comes home and does not even see his wife. Bad luck. ●

Zhan (占)

1. You want to make progress, but every way you turn, you blunder. A small matter convinces you a promising path is no good, and

then you think to find support in something that actually is worth-less. You are so obsessed with yourself, you do not even notice your friends.

2. The symbol of this Yao is like a home in ruins and family members scattered. It is a very bad omen.

3. Domestic scandals should not be publicized.

九四・來徐徐・困于金車・吝有終・

4th Yao. He comes quietly and softly, oppressed in a golden carriage. He is humiliated, but finally reaches his goal.

Zhan (占)

1. You feel sympathy for the poor people who live down the block and want to get to know them and their troubles. You friends tell you they are all bad, and you are acting like a fool. Then one day you feel energetic and follow your impulse, and all goes well.

2. You need to pay the bill, there is no money in the bank; at this critical time, someone helps you.

3. You have plans ready in your mind.

九五・劓刖・困于赤紱・乃徐有說・利用祭祀・

5th Yao. His nose and feet are cut off. There is oppression from the man with purple knee bands. Then joy comes softly. It is a time to make offerings and libations.

Zhan (占)

1. You want to do something to help the poor people in your town, but you find they are in such despair they turn you away angrily. When you talk to the welfare officials, they laugh at you. So you keep your impulse and your vision alive inside of you. Then one day an opportunity comes to act just as you wanted, and you feel joy.

2. You try to be perfect only to receive reproaches.

3. Relying upon oneself is better than relying upon others.

上六・困于葛藟・于臲卼・曰動悔・有悔征吉・

6th Yao. He is oppressed by creeping vines. He moves feebly and says "movement brings troubles." If he feels ashamed at this and pushes himself to start, good luck comes.

Zhan (占)

1. You feel shaken after your auto accident, and stay home all the time. When you go out driving you nearly have a disaster because you are so unsure of yourself. Then one day you get angry at yourself and decide to have no more of this nonsense. Immediately you recover your composure and can drive safely again.
2. The moral of troops will be high if they fight for a just cause. How do we relate this to our daily life?
3. What has that got to do with you?

Jíng 井

Water above
Wind below
Well

48

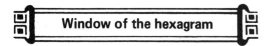

Window of the hexagram

1. A god wearing golden armor holds a secret Taoist talismanic writing. This means to send down blessings from heaven.
2. Two women embrace each other. Good fortune won't last forever.
3. A pile of coins and jewels shines. Wealth.
4. A person falls into a well. This means to charge an innocent **man** with falsehood.
5. An official saves the fallen person with a rope, indicating to escape from danger.

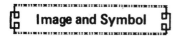

Image and Symbol

珠藏深淵之課・好靜安常之象・

The image is of a pearl hidden in an abyss.
The symbol is to be content, is to be what one is.

Kua Tsi (文王彖辭)

井・改邑不改井・无喪无得・往來井井・汔至・亦未繘井・羸其瓶・凶・

Jiṅg or the well. The town can be changed, but the well cannot change. It doesn't increase or decrease. People come and go to draw from the well. If you get down almost to the water and your rope is not long enough, or if your jug breaks, it's bad luck.

Zhan (占) *or hints on divining*

1. This is a March hexagram. It is good in fall, bad in spring, full in summer and having Chi (氣) or air in winter.
2. Jiṅg is the symbol of drawing water from a well.

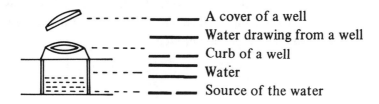

A cover of a well
Water drawing from a well
Curb of a well
Water
Source of the water

3. You feel a joy at simply being alive and getting up in the morning, and realize that this is your motivation and it never changes, and is the same for everyone. When you get into oppressed moods and can't experience this joy, or when you express it poorly, you find this is true bad luck.

Yao Tsi (周公爻辭)

初六・井泥不食・舊井无禽・●
1st Yao. You don't drink the mud of the well, and no animals come to drink at a run down well.●

Zhan (占)

1. You live aimlessly and let your life get run down, and find people are driven away from you by boredom, and no one even knows you exist.
2. It is like crossing a river in a boat of mud; this shows how dangerous the situation is.
3. Your feet sink deep in the mud. It is hard to move, and you get into real trouble.

九二・井谷射鮒・甕敝漏・●
2nd Yao. At the well, people shoot fishes. The jug is broken and leaks.

Zhan (占)

1. You had fine talents but never developed them, and so nothing is drawn out of them. You get so rundown you can't even draw on them anymore.
2. One works hard without achieving anything.
3. It's better to forget about it.

九三・井渫不食・爲我心惻・可用汲・王明並受其福・
3rd Yao. The well is clean, but no one drinks from it. This is my heart's sorrow, for people might draw from it. If the king were clear-minded, this good fortune might be enjoyed by all.

Zhan (占)

1. You have a friend with unusually advanced talents, but he has no connections and cannot find use for them. It seems a shame and you pray that some influential person may some day see him for what he is worth and help him find an outlet.
2. With two hands, one can work miracles.
3. You will do a job made easy by outside help.

六四 · 井甃无咎 ·

4th Yao. The well is being lined. This is blameless.

Zhan (占)

1. You feel your abilities are beginning to get worn and dim, so you take a month off from work and spend the time resting and renovating your whole perspective of things. Then you go back refreshed.
2. It's difficult to serve under two bosses.
3. You will attain two objectives by a single act.

九五 · 井列寒泉食 · ○

5th Yao. There is a clear, cold spring in the well. You can drink from it.○

Zhan (占)

1. You realize that most places you go to for refreshment become empty at times, but there is one place you know that is always fresh and full.
2. Most of your friends you sometimes find very attractive and other times find uninteresting. But you notice one person you know who always leaves you feeling good.

上六 · 井收物幕 · 有孚元吉 · ○

6th Yao. You draw from the well without being hindered. And it is always good. This is the highest good luck.○

Zhan (占)

1. You find among your friends a person who is always fair and full of vitality towards everyone around them. You think about it

and realize this person has a tremendous influence in keeping your
society healthy.
2. One will reach great virtues and magnificent achievements.
3. Everything starts to fall after it has reached its zenith.

49 Gé 革

Lake above
Fire below
Revolution

Window of the hexagram

1. One handle of the cart is new, the other is broken off. If you get
   the new one, then you have a handle to your name, and are known
   for something.
2. There is a rabbit and a tiger. This is good, relating to the hour, day,
   month and year of the rabbit or of the tiger.
3. An official is there to push the car, and there is an official seal
   on the car. This means to get a break after a long period of bad luck.
4. A wide road leading everywhere.

Image and Symbol

豹變爲虎之課 • 改舊從新之象 •

The image is a leopard being transformed to a tiger.
The symbol is to reform the old to the new.

Kua Tsi (文王象辭)

革 • 巳日乃孚 • 元亨利貞 • 悔亡 •

Gé or revolution. Your day comes and you are believed. The highest
success is aided by persevering. Disappointment disappears.

Zhan (占) or hints on divining

1. This is a February hexagram, it is good in winter, bad in spring
   and fall.
2. You have bad habits you want to break but attempts lead only
   to suffering and the frustration of failure. Then a time comes
   when you sense things favor you and it is time to take a chance
   again. You try, and this time you succeed and begin a new and
   better life.
3. After talking for a long time but being afraid to act, you and your
   wife agree your present jobs and life are not what you want, and
   you leave them and move to the country and open a nursery
   business.

Yao Tsi (周公爻辭)

初九 · 鞏用黃牛之革 ·

1st Yao. You are firm as if wrapped in the hide of a yellow cow.

Zhan (占)

1. You plan big changes, but you realize the attempt is dangerous and risky, and the time is not right now. You wait.
2. Don't follow routine, leisurely procedures without thinking about improvement.
3. You should take appropriate measures that suit your special situation.

六二 · 已日乃革之 · 征吉 · 无咎 · ○

2nd Yao. When your day comes, you can have a revolution. Starting is good luck. There is nothing to blame. ○

Zhan (占)

1. You tried for six months to get along better with your boss, because you wanted to be sure the problems weren't your fault. Now you see harmony is just not possible, and you go out and look for a new job.
2. You have a great talent and an attentive mind.
3. You have to do a job while the favorable condition exists.

九三 · 征凶 · 貞厲 · 革言三就 · 有孚 · ●

3rd Yao. Starting right now is bad luck, persevering openly is dangerous. When the talk about revolution has repeated itself three times, you can be sure about making a start, and people will believe you. ●

Zhan (占)

1. There's always random gossip and ill-will towards the boss where you work, but on looking closer it turns out to be just small-mindedness and pettiness. But now you see people are frightened and you hear the same complaint brought up again and again. You find out it is real and you get other workers to join with you in petitioning state authorities to investigate. They find corruption

and unsafe practices and your boss gets fired and you all get someone better.

2. You should forge ahead disregarding of obstructions or failures.   :es.
3. The grudge like a large tree has its deep root.

九四 • 悔亡 • 有孚 • 改命 • 吉 •

4th Yao Disappointment disappears. People believe in him. Changing the government is good luck now.

Zhan (占)

1. The councilman in your town who is always criticizing the others, discovers secret information of misdeeds and publicizes it. Now everyone supports his criticisms, and better people are voted into office.
2. One should estimate one's strength or resources before acting.
3. A talented person will sooner or later distingnish himself despite temporary adversity.

九五 • 大人虎變 • 未占有孚 •

5th Yao. The great man changes like a tiger does. He is believed even before he asks the oracle.

Zhan (占)

1. You get a new boss in your department at the plant and everyone can see he really knows his business and knows how to get good things done. Long before he gets involved in conflicts with other people who want to hamper your department, you are ready to support him loyally and know what to do.
2. A tiger father will not beget a dog son, which means there will be no laggards among the childern of a brave or talented man.
3. Great men appear in response to the call of the times.

上六 • 君子豹變 • 小人革面 • 征凶 • 居貞吉 • ○

6th Yao. The great man changes like a panther, the lesser people molt in the face. Starting big things is bad luck. But to keep perserveving is good luck.

Zhan (占)

1. The corrupt police department gets a new chief, and everyone on the department tries to look better now, and no one dares to be caught in poor practices. The chief can see he doesn't have the best possible department and he settles down to slowly improve its standards and practices.
2. Small resources pooled together can accomplish big things.
3. When the rain stops the sky clears up.

Dǐng 鼎

Fire above
Wind below
Caldron

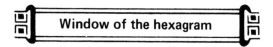

Window of the hexagram

1. When the clouds clear away, the moon shines. This means to rise gradually.
2. A magpie flies southward. Meaning to have an occasion for joy.
3. A child wears a straw hat. This indicates a chance to give birth to a son.
4. A person prepares to slash with a sword to guard against a possible accident.
5. A wise man sits fearless of danger. Heaven blesses the virtuous.
6. There is a mouse meaning to take precautions against calamity.

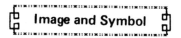

Image and Symbol

調和鼎鼐之課 • 去故取新之象 •
The image is to harmonize a previous relationship with a new one.
The symbol is to leave the old and take to the new.

Kua Tsi (文王彖辭)

鼎 • 元吉亨 • ○
Ding or caldron. The highest good fortune. Success. ○

Zhan (占) *or hints on divining*

1. This is a December hexagram, it is good in spring, bad in summer and fall.
2. The Ding is a huge caldron of bronze with three feet and two ears or handles. It was used in ancient time for cooking or as a sacrificial vessel. It is a national historical treasure; though not many Chinese people can any longer describe what a Ding is or what it looks like.

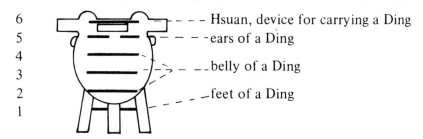

```
6        ---- Hsuan, device for carrying a Ding
5        ---- ears of a Ding
4        
3        belly of a Ding
2        
1        feet of a Ding
```

3. After years of study you are finished with college and enter the field you've chosen to make your life's work. You settle down in your new life happily.

Yao Tsi (周公爻辭)

初六 • 鼎顛趾 • 利出否 • 得妾以其子 • 无咎 •

1st Yao. A caldron with legs overturned helps to dump out stagnant material. He takes a concubine for the sake of her son. There is no blame.

Zhan (占)

1. You lose your old job and cannot find one like it because of changes in industry. You decide there is no use in living in the past, and take up learning a new skill. You take a great loss in pay, but before a year is passed you are receiving raises and beginning to establish yourself.
2. Do not give others cause to talk about you.
3. You will establish a home and make achievements.

九二 • 鼎有實 • 我仇有疾 • 不我能即 • 吉 •

2nd Yao. There is food in the caldron. My fellows resent me, but they can't hurt me. Good luck.

Zhan (占)

1. You make sacrifices and devote yourself to excellence, only to find less hard working people resent you for it. But it doesn't matter, because the skills you are developing are taking you somewhere.
2. A standard of comparison comes from all quarters.
3. You have to handle something without rigid application of dead rules.

九三 • 鼎耳革 • 其行塞 • 雉膏不食 • 方雨虧悔 • 終吉 •

3rd Yao. The handle of the caldron is altered. You are impeded in your way of life. The fat of the pheasant goes uneaten. Once it rains, disappointment is exhausted. Good luck comes.

Zhan (占)

1. You are excellent at your job, but no one notices because those skills aren't highly valued at the time. Instead of being embittered, you resolve to continue developing yourself. Then one day you see a job opening where your skill is greatly needed, and your fortune is made.
2. To think deep and far ahead leads you to success.
3. You ought to make amends as quickly as possible.

九四 • 鼎折足 • 复公餗 • 其形渥 • 凶 • ●

4th Yao. The legs of the caldron are broken. The prince's meal is spilled and he is soiled. Bad luck. ●

Zhan (占)

1. Ambitiously you win a high post for yourself in a new company, and feel your fortune is made. Two months later you discover you are over your head in problems more difficult than you can handle and that your complacency was your downfall.
2. You should take every precaution at the beginning.
3. You ought to lower the standard and to be satisfied with the next best or less advanced situation.

九五 • 鼎黄耳 • 金鉉 • 利貞 •

5th Yao. The caldron has yellow handles, gold rings. It is a time to persevere.

Zhan (占)

1. When you get promoted to head your department, all the men you worked with as equals before are happy to support you, because You know how to communicate with them. You think things over and realize your success depends entirely on their happiness in being treated fairly and resolve never to lose sight of this.
2. It is like a heroic deed performed by a straightforward man.
3. Honest advice aften grates on the ear.

上九 • 鼎玉鉉 • 大吉 • 无不利 • ○

6th Yao. The caldron has rights of jade. The highest good luck. There is nothing that is not helpful. ○

┌〜〜〜〜〜〜〜〜〜〜┐
│ *Zhan* (占) │
└〜〜〜〜〜〜〜〜〜〜┘

1. You have a difficult task to carry out but it is so important to
   you, you show the greatest patience and moderation in working
   on it with others, while inside yourself you maintain the highest
   and most rigorous standards. Everything prospers.
2. As soon as a thing reaches its extremity, it reverses its course.
3. Even though you are in a state of the highest good luck, you have
   to understand that what happens to a small part may affect the
   whole.

51

Zhèn 震

Thunder abore
Thunder below
Thunder

Window of the hexagram

1. A man stands on the crag. This means to be in a dangerous position.
2. The flowers are in full bloom and a document hangs from a branch. Spring is a good time to write.
3. A man pushes a car with a book in it. One needs special express service.
4. A pile of coins and jewels is the omen of fame and wealth.

Image and Symbol

震驚百里之課‧有聲無形之象‧
The image is a tremendous clap of thunder.
The symbol is what can be clearly heard but cannot be seen.

Kua Tsi (文王彖辭)

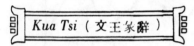

震‧亨‧震來虩虩‧笑言啞啞‧震驚百里‧不喪匕鬯‧
Zhén or thunder is successful. Thunder comes – startlement! People laugh uneasily. The thunder terrifies things for a hundred miles, and he does not drop the sacrificial spoon and chalice.

Zhan (占) or hints on divining

1. This is an October hexagram, it is good in all four seasons; but especially good in summer.
2. Zhén or thunder is a pure hexagram. The image is of shock, authority and movement. People are startled by the thunder; it is trying to do something good so as to offend heaven.
3. You are out of work six months and everyone in the house is uneasy. Get a job, anything. Your wife tells you. A week later you come home with the news that you've found a new, higher post at a company 500 miles away and you will all have to move. Everyone is in a furor of upset and turmoil at adjusting, and you are careful to see to it that everything is done right and nothing goes amiss.

Yao Tsi (周公爻辭)

初九 • 震來虩虩 • 後笑言啞啞 • 吉 • ○
1st Yao. Zhén or thunder comes upset. Then happy laughter follows. Good luck.○

Zhan (占)

1. You find your two year old child who has been lost in the woods 18 hours. Everyone runs in alarm to see if he is hurt, and laughs in relief that he is all right.
2. How can one expect to accomplish great feats without taking risks?
3. It is purely a personal matter. There is no need to let others know.

六二 • 震來厲 • 億喪貝 • 躋于九陵 • 勿逐 • 七日得 •
2nd Yao. Zhén or thunder comes and brings threat. A hundred thousand times you lose your treasures and have to climb the nine hills. Don't go looking for them. After seven days you will get them back.

Zhan (占)

1. Your girlfriend tells you she is leaving you for another fellow. You are terribly upset but decide you must accept this. You throw yourself into other activities so as not to become obsessed with your loss, and it works. After a couple months you feel all right. Later on — you find someone you like even better.
2. You always speak and behave as others do without views of your own.
3. The sparrow's nest is occupied by a pigeon.

六三 • 震蘇蘇 • 震行无眚 • ●
3rd Yao. Zhén or thunder comes and you feel distraught. If it pushes you to action, you will be free of bad luck. ●

Zhan (占)

1. You work very hard at your new job, and do all right. Then after your probationary period is over, you're fired. For days

you are totally depressed. Then you remember what the employer told you — it wasn't your fault, the company had to cut back. You push yourself into finding a new job, and the hard work you did previously sets you up to do well in the new job.

2. Ruin falls only on those who have weaknesses.

3. The head of an ox does not match the mouth of a horse.

九四・震遂泥・●

4th Yao. Zhén or thunder is stuck. ●

Zhan（占）

1. You make a breakthrough of great importance in your work. You are all set to use it, you look around but find there is nothing happening to favor it or even oppose it. For the time being, your treasure is totally hidden.

2. Don't stop your task halfway.

3. You should shun the extremes and to maintain the middle course.

六五・震往來厲・億无喪有事・

5th Yao. Zhén or thunder comes and goes. Danger. But nothing is lost, and there are things to be done.

Zhan（占）

1. Fate attacks you from a dozen directions, one attack at a time, like a madhouse. Somehow you sense the only wise thing to do — adapt to each surprise as it comes, and after it is all passed, you will have survived to do something worthwhile.

2. Every person has weakness as well as strengths, so the important way is how to take advantage of the good side and avoid or correct the weak side.

3. There is no way of telling his or her real intentions.

上六・震索索・視矍矍・征凶・震不于其躬・于其鄰・无咎・婚媾有言・

6th Yao. Zhén or thunder brings ruin and people gaze about terrified. To go ahead is bad luck. If thunder has not yet touched you, but it has already reached another, there will be nothing to blame. Although one's friends will be gossiping about you.

Zhan (占)

1. You go to work Monday morning and find everyone running about in a disorganized way because the plant will close down. You calmly gather together your personal possessions, call the employment agency, and leave for an immediate appointment. Your co-workers think you are callous and unfeeling.
2. There will be twists and obstacles if your problem or issue is not settled promptly.
3. It is a miserable end which you are driving towards.

52

Yín 艮

Mountain above
Mountain below
Mountain

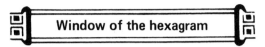
Window of the hexagram

1. A monkey offers a letter with the two Chinese characters 東北 meaning northeast on it. One will be finding friends in the northeast.
2. A monkey holds a document. The information one is anxiously awaiting will be received on the day related to the monkey.
3. An official holds a mirror. This means a virtuous official, as the mirror was often used as a salutation to the judge in old China. (明鏡高懸)
4. Three people are tied to each other with rope. This means a lot of trouble and conflict until the day of the monkey, when there will be an opportunity to resolve it.

Image and Symbol

遊魚避網之課・積小成高之象・
The image is of a fish trying to escape from a net.
The symbol is being at a giddy height, which continues to get higher, little by little.

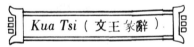
Kua Tsi (文王彖辭)

艮其背・不獲其身・行其庭・不見其人・无咎・
Yiń or mountain. He keeps his spine still like a mountain so he no longer feels his body. He goes into the courtyard and does not see his fellows. There is nothing to blame.

Zhan (占) *or hints on divining*

1. This is an April hexagram, it is good in winter, bad in spring and fall.
2. Yiń is a pure hexagran. In traditional Taoist meditation it is used as a guide to cultivating Chi energy and concentration of in the back and spine.
3. You have taken up personal meditation for some mouths now, and one day you find the calmness you have sought. You feel

alive, yet somehow unbothered by anything, you see things that
before excited your sense of conflict but now appear as just the
movement of life.   When you take your place actively in all this,
you are calm and make no mistakes.

Yao Tsi (周公爻辭)

初六・艮其趾・无咎・利永貞・
1st Yao.   He keeps his toes at rest.   There is no blame.   Continued
persevering works well.

Zhan (占)

1. You enter a room full of people at a party.   You stand there motion-
    less, looking around you and taking in all the activity.   Then you
    see some people whose activities and talk attract you, and you
    push over there to see what is going on.
2. Mastery is the result of long practice or training.
3. One does not realize the difficulty of an undertaking unless one
    has experienced it before.

六二・艮其腓・不拯其隨・其心不快・
2nd Yao.   Keeping his calves motionless.   He can't save the person
he follows.   His heart is not happy.

Zhan (占)

1. You go out with some friends to celebrate.   For some reason they
    get in a rowdy mood and decide to make a disturbance.   You
    instantly see it will end badly and pull back, but you can do nothing
    to stop them.   You feel sad to see the trouble they get themselves
    into.
2. There is too little meat for so many wolves.
3. Don't be too ambitions at this time!

九三・艮其限・列其夤・厲薰心・ ●
3rd Yao.   He keeps his waist at rest.   He makes the sacrum bone of
his spine stiff.   Danger.   The heart stifles. ●

⚏ *Zhan*（占）⚏

1. You decide to reform yourself seeking absolute perfection immediately. You eliminate bad habits, such as smoking, drinking and overeating. There are no exceptions. After three days, you feel like your body and mind are being torn apart by the pressures, and you have to do something – even revert to bad habits! – to bring yourself back into some kind of balance.
2. The only way you can make decisions is let bygones be bygones.
3. Since we are already here, let's make ourselves at home.

六四 • 艮其身 • 无咎 •

4th Yao. He keeps his trunk at rest. There is nothing to blame.

⚏ *Zhan*（占）⚏

1. You have learned to maintain a kind of composure that requires an effort of force, but just a little. You are making progress.
2. When your nasty mother-in-law comes to visit, you exert your will power to "be empty." So as not to be bothered. This is a little artificial, but it is a lot better than when you used to bicker with her.
3. It is not a good time for vacation or traveling.

六五 • 艮其辅 • 言有序 • 悔亡 •

5th Yao. He keeps his jaws still. His words are orderly. Remorse fades.

⚏ *Zhan*（占）⚏

1. You used to babble a lot when you were under pressure, but you've reached a stage now where you control yourself a little more. And this gives you a little more of an edge in keeping trouble away.
2. You can be a very successful orator, a pastor or a lawyer. Because you are very eloquent, your statement will be received with respect.
3. When speaking of the devil the devil appears.

上九 • 敦艮 • 吉 • ○

6th Yao. You keep still like a mountain in a noblehearted way. Good luck. ○

｛Zhan (占)｝

1. The struggles and sufferings and mistakes you went through to learn composure are all in the past now, and you live fully by a standard you previously only only dream of.
2. The suspicions have dissolved completely.
3. Do not employ a person one distrusts. One must trust the person he employs.

53

Jian 漸

Wind above
Mountain below
Gradually

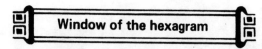

Window of the hexagram

1. A lookout post is set on a high place. The purpose is to try to see things more clearly.
2. A pottery jar for cooking medicinal concotions is on the ground. One should take protective measures in advance.
3. An official climbs a ladder. This means to soar higher and higher.
4. A branch of flowers lays on the ground. This means to flunk a competitive examination for a job or, be denied admission to a school.

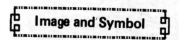

Image and Symbol

高山植木之課・積小成大之象・

The image is to plant trees in the high mountains.

The symbol is to accumulate the small until it is developed into the large.

Kua Tsi (文王家辭)

漸・女歸吉・利貞・

Jian or Gradually. The maiden is offered in marriage. Good luck. It is a time to persevere.

Zhan (占) *or hints on divining*

1. This is a January hexagram, it is good in spring, summer and fall, bad in winter.
2. Jian means to follow in proper sequence, to plant one's feet on solid ground, to do a job honestly and make gradual progress.
3. If we change Jian's 5th Yang Yao to a Yin Yao, it becomes a pure hexagram, Yin or Mountain. So jian is a quihún hexagram.

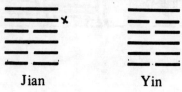

Jian   Yin

If a patient who consults I Ching gets the Jian, it is a very evil omen.

4. A friend who has contact with a big company gets them to make a small order from your firm.   "This is just the start," he warns, and sure enough, after a year of small orders, they decide they trust your integrity and shift a lot of business to you.

Yao Tsi (周公爻辭)

初六 • 鴻漸于干 • 小子厲 • 有言 • 无咎 •

1st Yao.   The wild goose gradually comes near to the shore.   The youngest son faces danger.   There is a lot of talk.   There is nothing to blame.

Zhan (占)

1. You take up a new venture, neither your friends nor your family will support you, and you go on alone, a little worried, but determined.   Because of your personal determination you finally win through to success.
2. A promise has barely been made before it is broken.
3. Over-confidence in one's skill may bring him disaster.

六二 • 鴻漸于磐 • 飲食衎衎 • 吉 • ○

2nd Yao.   The wild goose gradually nears the cliff.   There is food and drink in peace and sharing.   Good luck. ○

Zhan (占)

1. On the first anniversary of your new venture you have a dinner party for your friends to share your happiness with them concerning your successful fortune.
2. There is still much to learn after one has grown old.
3. If a patient gets this Yao, he is in a very serious condition.

九三 • 鴻漸于陸 • 夫征不復 • 婦孕不育 • 凶 • 利禦寇 • ●

3rd Yao.   The wild goose comes over the pleateau.   A man goes forth and never returns.   A woman is pregant but has a miscarriage.   Bad luck.   It is a good idea to fight off thieves.●

Zhan (占)

1. Your business is successful but a friend comes to try to draw you into a "big venture" where you'll make "ten times more money." You look it over, realize you're poorly prepared for it and that if you fail, you will be bandrupt.   You stick with your present business and concentrate on getting people to pay their bills more promptly.
2. It is a dilemma, difficult both to proceed and to retreat.
3. You will lose much more than you gain.

九四 • 鴻漸于木 • 或得其桷 • 无咎 • ○

4th Yao. The wild goose comes upon a tree. Maybe it will find a flat branch. Nothing to blame. ○

Zhan (占)

1. You and your wife move to a motel near your new job, and find there is no housing available.   You scour the neighborhood thoroughly and finally find a suitiable apartment you can settle in for row.
2. The wild goose chooses a tree when it comes to rest, so one should choose the right place to be or the right leader to serve.
3. It's too late to take corrective measures when a crisis has already developed.

九五 • 鴻漸于陵 • 婦三歲不孕 • 終莫之勝 • 吉 • ○

5th Yao. The wild goose gradually comes toward the summit. For three years the woman has no child. Fianlly, nothing can stop her. Good luck.○

Zhan (占)

1. You get a job from a man you've known socially for years and been friendly with. Now all of a sudden he is aloof and reserved and does nothing to encourage your hard work. A year later he suddenly becomes friendly again, and you find out one of his trusted employees told bad stories about you, and finally got found out.
2. The trees in the mountain are felled because timber is useful. This

is the same as a talented person; his ability may be his own ruin.

3. You always feel grateful for a kind act and plan to doublely repay it.

上九・鴻漸于陸・其羽可用爲儀・吉・○

6th Yao. The wild goose gradually comes near the high plains. Its feathers can be used in the sacred dance. Good luck. ○

Zhan（占）

1. You retire from your job and take up engrossing personal interests, having a healthy old age. Years later you return to your former workplace for a visit and find stories still circulate of spirited things you did.
2. Your reputation is well supported by fact.
3. You will become famous all over the nation.

Guīmèi 歸妹

Thunder above
Lake below
Marrying Sister

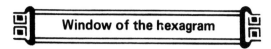

Window of the hexagram

1. An official rides on a deer's back and points at the clouds with his index finger. This means to have an ambition for things that are not presently available or obtainable.
2. A fawn follows its mother. To advance smoothly in officialdom.
3. The Chinese character 文 meaning "literature" is on a flag hanging from a lookout post. This means the information one is anxiously expecting will be coming soon.
4. A man stumbles and falls on thorns, his passenger helps him get out. People help those who help themselves.

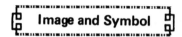

Image and Symbol

浮雲蔽日之課・陰陽不交之象・

The image is the sun obscured by threatening clouds.
The symbol is a time when Yin and Yang have no interrelation.

Kua Tsi (文王彖辭)

歸妹・征凶・无攸利・

Gūimèi or the marrying sister. Doing things now is bad luck. There is no enterprise that will go well.

Zhan (占) *or hints on divining*

1. This is a July hexagram. It is good in summer and winter, bad in spring and fall.
2. If we change Gūimèi's 5th Yao Yin to Yang, it becomes a pure hexagram Tuí or Lake, so Guimèi is a qùihún hexagram.

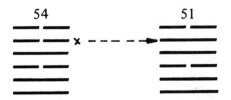

If a patient asks I Ching and gets Gūimèi, the condition is very serious.

3. To do your civic duty you get yourself elected to the school board. After the first meeting, seeing the intense and complex business being handled, you realize it will be a year or so before you can fit into the group well and take on any important assignments.

Yao Tsi (周公爻辭)

初九 • 歸妹以娣 • 跛能履 • 征吉 •

1st Yao. The marrying sister as a concubine. Like a lame man who is able to walk. Doing things is good fortune.

Zhan (占)

1. Frankly you got the job because you were a friend of the boss' son. Everyone knows you are a worker, too, and you are treated with friendliness but not yet accorded any respect. You do your simple chores quietly without showing off, and now and then you have a chance to earn a little merit when an opportunity occurs.
2. Even a lame trutle can travel a thousand miles; this means persistence insures success.
3. Your doing is enough for you to be proud of.

九二 • 眇能視 • 利幽人之貞 •

2nd Yao. A one-eyed man who can still see. It is a good thing for a solitary man to persevere.

Zhan (占)

1. You signed up for the job because there was opportunity opening up in that department. Then a sudden turn of fate made things completely unfavorable. You sit around and have almost nothing to do. Still, you keep things orderly and devote what good work you can to your employer.
2. The eyes cannot see the eyelashes, which means that one does not have a correct appraisal of one's own ability.
3. Some are blind in the eyes but not in the mind.

六三 • 歸妹以須 • 反歸以娣 •

3rd Yao. The marrying sister as a slave. She marries in the role of a concubine.

Zhan (占)

1. You were going to buy a rig and become and independent trucker. But you didn't have the money. You wound up deciding to drive a milk truck for a big firm. It has none of the freedom, independence, and chances to make money, but is a steady job. You don't know whether you like it or hate it.
2. You are a woman of great capability, but don't have a good marriage.
3. One should retire when one has ridden the crest of success.

九四 • 歸妹愆期 • 遲歸有時 •

4th Yao. The marrying sister goes beyond the allotted time. Then a late marriage comes along.

Zhan (占)

1. You never made the grade as a writer the way you wanted to in your younger years, and decided to go into a different business rather than just be one of the thousands of "hacks." Now in your middle years, the chance you always wanted comes along, and you take it.
2. It is better to live in retirement and wait for a comeback in public life.
3. A change of place is advisable.

六五 • 帝乙歸妹 • 其君之袂 • 不如其娣之袂袂良 • 月幾望 • 吉 • ○

5th Yao. The King I gave his daughter in marriage. The princess' embroidered gowns were not as pretty as those of the servant girl. The moon that is almost full brings good luck. ○

Zhan (占)

1. No one knows your wife came from a rich family and gave up a fortune to marry you. They see how happily you get on together and are sure that must mean she came from a simple background like you.
2. A large capital will yield a large profit.
3. The leaves of firs and cypress are always the last to fall.

上六 • 女承筐无實 • 士刲羊无血 • 无攸利 • ●

6th Yao. The woman holds a basket that has no fruit in it. The man stabs a sheep and no blood flows from it. Nothing is worth doing. ●

[*Zhan* (占)]

1. A couple you know marries and they seem to do it just because they have nothing better they can think of to do. You don't think much of the marriage and are not surprised when they have all sorts of troubles after a couple years.
2. Good tools are prerequisite to the successful execution of a job.
3. A smart young woman has a much older, dim witted man for a husband.

Fēng 豐

Thunder above
Fire below
Prosperity

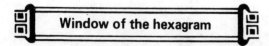

Window of the hexagram

1. The bamboo tube is burned to ashes. Good luck in springtime.
2. The dragon and snake contrast each other. This is sign of changes.
3. An official wearing a uniform is standing there. This means wait for something that is imminent.
4. There is a small box. This means harmony.
5. A man plays a Sheng (笙), a Chinese musical instrument. This means to be beside oneself with happiness.
6. To ride on a tiger is a very dangerous situation.

Image and Symbol

日麗中天之課 • 昔暗囬明之象 •

The image is to be as bright as the sun at noon.
The symbol is to step into the brightness of today and say good-by to the darkness of the past.

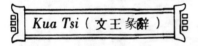

Kua Tsi (文王彖辭)

豐 • 亨 • 王假之 • 勿憂 • 宜日中 •

Feng or prosperity is successful. The king earns abundance. Don't be sad. Be like the sun at high noon.

Zhan (占) *or hints on divining*

1. This is a Septmber hexagram, it is good in spring, bad in fall.
2. When the sun has reached meridian, it begins to decline. When the moon has become full, it begins to wane. This principle exists even move with the affairs of men!
3. Your boss is so skilled that when an unusual demand for your company's product comes along, in a few months you sell more than you have the past three years. Everyone is busily occupied and happy, for there is a special bonus coming along. In another month the "boom" will be over, but everyone thinks of the present.

Yao Tsi (周公爻辭)

初九・遇其配主・雖旬无咎・往有尚・

1st Yao. When a man meets his fated king, they can be together ten days and it isn't a mistake. To go out and do things will lead to recognition.

Zhan (占)

1. You plan to go fishing alone, but you meet an old-timer and strike up an imprompt friendship with him. He tells you of a secret fishing hole where the catches are good and you both go there, coming home with the biggest catch of the year.
2. You can act as circumstances may require without asking for approval from superiors.
3. You have done nothing to make you feel shameful.

六二・豐其蔀・日中見斗・往得疑疾・有孚發若・吉・

2nd Yao. The curtain is so thick that the polestars are visible at noon. Through going out you will meet with distrust and hate. If you arouse him through truth, good fortune comes.

Zhan (占)

1. You join a sports club, but there is so much bickering you cannot join up with another outstanding athlete you see who you'd go well with. You say nothing and when there are trials, you perform at your best and he sees for himself you're suited as a good player.
2. After work is done, those who did the work are layed off.
3. A single tree cannot make a forest which means one person cannot handle all the tasks by himself.

九三・豐其沛・日中見沫・折其右肱・无咎・●

3rd Yao. The underbrush is so thick that the small stars can be seen at noon. He breaks his right arm. No blame. ●

Zhan (占)

1. You joined the protest demonstration because you sincerely

favored the good, but now you see it has degenerated into a show of total anarchy for undiciplined negative types. You hold back trying to do anything because there is nothing to be done, and go your way.

2. Discipline tends to get lax as time goes by.
3. You ask about something you already know.

九四・豐其蔀・日中見斗・遇其夷主・吉・

4th Yao. The curtain is so thick that the polestars can be seen at noon. He meets his ruler; who is the same kind of person. Good luck.

Zhan (占)

1. The club you belonged to collapsed of its own bad conduct and laziness. As you leave, you meet one of the members who had been a sincere worker. You join and talk of the possibility of someday getting a better group together.
2. You should avoid someone as if he or she is the plague.
3. What is done cannot be undone!

九五・來章・有慶譽・吉・○

5th Yao. Lines are appearing, blessing and fame are appearing. Good luck. ○

Zhan (占)

1. Your club elects a new leader who is unusually responsive to good advice. All the right people show up to let him know of opportunities opening up. He knows how to bring them to fruition, and everyone benefits greatly.
2. The first prize will go to the nimblest.
3. Haste makes waste.

上六・豐其屋・蔀其家・闚其戶・闃其无人・三歲不覿・凶・

6th Yao. His house is full of prosperity. But he screens himself off from his family. He peers through a crack in the gate and no longer sees anyone. He sees nothing for three years. Bad luck.

Zhan (占)

1. Your friend made a lot of money and purchased luxuries for himself

and will no longer talk equally to anyone. Everyone is disgusted with him and won't have anything to do with/him. He is lonely and dangerously out of touch.

2. The more one tries to cover up a secret, the more it will become known.

3. Neglected matters must be dealt with.

56 ䷷

Lú 旅

Fire above
Mountain below
Traveler

Window of the hexagram

1. There are three stars. The lucky star shines brightly.
2. A high-ranking person fishes from the platform. This indicates transcending material desires.
3. A monkey and a ship. Good luck related to the hour, day, month and year of the monkey or of the ship.
4. A stream runs. This means to have the prospect of a very successful career, with its riches coming in an endless flow.

Image and Symbol

如鳥焚巢之課 • 榮極衰生之象 •
The image is like a bird's nest that was set on fire by somebody.
The symbol is flourishing followed by withering when it reaches an extreme.

Kua Tsi (文王彖辭)

旅 • 小亨 • 旅貞 • 吉 •
Lu or the traveller. Success is won through smallness. Persevering is good luck to the traveller.

Zhan (占) *or hints on divining*

1. This is a May hexagram. It is good in spring, bad in fall and winter. It may mean lost money in summer.
2. Lu tends to refer to travel, but this is not the kind of travelling we know today where we usually think of excitement and enjoyment. In ancient times, travel meant great danger and hardship. We need only think of the settlers of the American west travelling in their covered wagons and facing possible starvation, no water, and attack by Indians to get an idea of what is meant by Lu.
3. You go on an overseas vacation, renting an auto and travelling by yourself rather than choosing a "package tour."

Yao Tsi (周公爻辭)

初六 • 旅瑣瑣 • 斯其所取災 • ●

1st Yao. If the traveller involves himself with petty things, he brings bad luck to himself. ●

Zhan (占)

1. You meet a good natured ruffian on your travels and go drinking with him and he steals your wallet.
2. Water flowing out in a trickle takes a long time to be exhausted.
3. Can you imagine and understand outside of the sound the musical instrument is making?

六二 • 旅即次 • 懷其資 • 得童僕貞 •

2nd Yao. The traveller comes to the inn. He has his goods with him. He wins the loyalty of a young servant.

Zhan (占)

1. You find yourself be friend by good people who are impressed by your manners. A young fellow who is travelling trows in his lot with you for a few days.
2. Friendship lasts as long as money does.
3. If you put an awl in a bag it may be temporarily hidden but will eventually pierce the bag and show itself.

九三 • 旅焚其次 • 喪其童僕 • 貞厲 • ●

3rd Yao. The traveller's inn burns down. He loses the loyalty of his young servant. He is in danger. ●

Zhan (占)

1. You argue with some people you meet who you hardly know, for no good reason. Your young companion sees your rudeness and deserts you, taking their side.
2. It is like using gas to put out a fire, which means to make things worse.
3. He who has wealth suddenly speaks louder than others.

九四・旅于處・得其資斧・我心不快・●

4th Yao.   The traveller rests in a stopping place.   He gets his property and an ax.   His heart is not pleased. ●

🌿 *Zhan (占)* 🌿

1. Your trip goes well and brings you riches, yet you always want more and make yourself unhappy with your discontent.
2. You have to forge ahead in disregard of obstrcles and failures.
3. An ice sheet of three feet in thickness takes more than one cold day to forms which means the grudge or animosity has a deep root.

六五・射雉・一矢亡・終以譽命・○

5th Yao.   He shoots a pheasant and it drops with the first arrow shot. This comes to bring him both praise and occupation. ○

🌿 *Zhan (占)* 🌿

1. You are looking for things to do.   You meet people who are impressed by your courtesy aｎd when they hear of your particular skills, they offer you some work and friends for a while.
2. You will win an enduring fame that spreads throughout the world.
3. Many buckets of water will make a river.

上九・鳥焚其巢・旅人先笑後號咷・喪牛于易・凶・●

6th Yao.   The bird's nest burns.   The traveller laughs first, then winds up lamenting and weeping.   He loses his cow through carelessness. Bad luck. ●

🌿 *Zhan (占)* 🌿

1. You spend all your day enjoying yourself and having fun without a thought of anything else and then when night falls it is too late to find a place to stay, and you spend the night on a cold bench.
2. You are busy all day long for nothing.
3. One should start thinking about changes when one is in an extremely distressed or difficult state.

57

Sūn 巽

Wind above
Wind below
Wind

Window of the hexagram

1. A person kneels to accept a piece of cloth granted by a high-ranking official. This means hoist the sail when there is wind.
2. A snow goose has brought a message from the clouds. This means to sing in joy.
3. A person rides on a tiger's back. This is an awkward position from which there is no retreat.
4. A person hits the tiger. This means having fear now, but safety later.
5. A tiger runs away. A dangerous situation has passed away.

Image and Symbol

風行草偃之課 • 上行下效之象 ●

The image is when the wind blows, the grass bends.
The symbol is that the deeds of the superior person are imitated by lesser people.

Kua Tsi (文王彖辭)

巽 • 小亨 • 利有攸往 • 利見大人 •

Sūn or the wind brings success through what is small. It is a time to be active and to see an influential person.

Zhan (占) *or hints on divining*

1. This ia an April hexagram. It is good in summer and winter, bad in fall.
2. Sun is a pure hexagram, it can be like a strong storm that wrecks a ship. If a patient gets this hexagram, he is in a very dangerous condition.
3. You buy a fine horse that no one can manage and that has harmed people. Each day you patiently approach the beast and wait. After many days it sees you will not harm it and begins to become your friend.

Yao Tsi (周公爻辭)

初六 • 進退 • 利武人之貞 •

1st Yao. In advancing and retreating, the perseverance of a warrior is what to cultivate.

Zhan (占)

1. You see an opportunity that is not quite right yet and are drawn to it, then retreat a little, then you back and fill indecisively. Finally you make up a clear plan of just how you will act according to circumstances. Now you know how to be.
2. You have too little power or resources to do as much as you wish.
3. You will draw criticisms at every move.

九二 • 巽在牀下 • 用史巫紛若 • 吉 • 无咎 •

2nd Yao. Sun or the wind. Penetrating under the bed. You use a large number of priests and magicians. Good luck. Nothing to blame.

Zhan (占)

1. Suddenly people seem a little cold towards you for no reason. You ask a friend and he says something vague and unfriendly. You become determined and ask and ask and ask. Finally you discover someone has told lies about you that superficially fit your disposition, and no one knows whether to trust you anymore. You bring out the real truth with proofs, and people become more at ease again.
2. Let everybody mind his own business.
3. Your talent is like a pearl left in the deep sea.

九三 • 頻巽 • 吝 •

3rd Yao. Repeated penetration. You are at a dead end.

Zhan (占)

1. You investigate a course of action, then the next day you are unsure and go over it again thoroughly. You feel unclear and go over it again. Time passes and finally the opportunity is completely lost.

2. It's your fault. The only thing you can do is to keep quiet and bear the insults.
3. You have ambition for things beyond what is presently available or obtainable.

六四・悔亡・田獲三品・○

4th Yao. Disappointment disappears. During hunting, three kinds of game are caught. ○

Zhan (占)

1. You undertake a project that suits your abilities with great care and energy. Everything works out well.
2. Things are seemingly peaceful and people live thoughtlessly with an illusory sense of security. You realize lurking dangers could appear and you remain sobere and cautious.
3. The whole plan may be ruined by a last minute mistake or negligence.

九五・貞吉・悔亡・无不利・无初有終・先庚三日・後庚三日・吉・○

5th Yao. Persevering is good luck. Disappointment disappears. There is nothing that does not help. There is no beginning without a completion. Before you change, three days, after your change, three days. Good luck. ○

Zhan (占)

1. You see your fortunes are failing, yet the basics are good. It is time to fine tune improvements, and you deliberate carefully before acting, and then keep careful track when things are set in motion to see they work right. Good fortune results.
2. Only people of similar character and disposition can become good friends.
3. Don't try to remember the good deeds you have done for others. Instead, remember what others have done for you.

上九・巽在牀下・喪其資斧・貞凶・●

6th Yao. Sün or the wind penetrating under the bed. He lost his property and an ax. He has bad luck. ●

{ Zhan (占) }

1. You should go to your parents' place in order to seek their sincere advice.
2. It is like trying to kill a fly with a long spear.
3. Worms breed only when things have already started rotting.

58

Dùi 兌

Lake above
Lake below
Lake

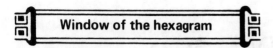

Window of the hexagram

1. A person sits on a yoke used for carrying things on the shoulders. This means to relax a little, to lay down one's responsibilities.
2. The moon in the sky is an omen of a union.
3. A woman stands by a small box. This is an ideal time for a wedding.
4. An arrow is placed on a document. This means to be the first name on the list.
5. A scholar steps onto the pavilion. Means to make a sudden rise in one's career or social position.

Image and Symbol

江湖養物之課・天降雨澤之象・

The image is that of lakes and rivers providing nourishment and refreshment to everything.

The symbol is a seasonable rain that has fallen everywhere.

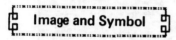

Kua Tsi (文王彖辭)

兌・亨・利貞・

Dùi or the lake is successful. Now is a time to persevere.

Zhan (占) *or hints on divining*

1. This is an October hexagram, it is good in spring and fall, bad in summer, means possible sickness in winter.
2. Dui or the lake has the meaning of joyousness. It is a pure hexagram.
3. After working hard and doing well, you see the opportunity for an interesting short vacation, and instead of merely dissipating yourself, you go out and have a wonderful time.

Yao Tsi (周公爻辭)

初九・和兌・吉・○

1st Yao. You feel contented joyousness. Good luck. ○

Zhan (占)

1. You work very hard, yet things around you are stimulating and good. Your desires are simple and fulfilled.
2. A good-natured person has a good chance of getting rich.
3. Obedience is a better way of showing respect than outward reverence.

九二 • 孚兌 • 吉 • 悔亡 •

2nd Yao. You are sincere in joyousness. Good luck. Disappointment disappears.

Zhan (占)

1. Friends tell you, you should want lots of money for luxuries, but you see you already have what you want and this would only buy you dissipation and unhappiness. They finally see this and give up bothering you.
2. Lack of forbearance in small matters upsets great plans.
3. A lie, if repeated often enough, becomes a truth to the listener.

六三 • 來兌 • 凶 •

3rd Yao. Joyousness comes to you. Bad luck.

Zhan (占)

1. You never have any mind of your own, and the minute you finish working, you take any distraction that offers itself. The result is you become even more distracted and characterless.
2. The cart is worn down and the horse is weary.
3. You have good fortune or success in love affairs.

九四 • 商兌未寧 • 介疾有喜 •

4th Yao. Joyousness that weighs things is not peaceful. After getting rid of his mistakes, a man is joyful.

Zhan (占)

1. You can't decide which kind of diversion to pursue during your free time. Finally you look at them and see they are different

kinds of empty glamour that can't bring you any satisfaction. Then you begin to see what you really like, and feel relieved and happy.

2. You ought to pursue good fortune and shun the course of calamity.
3. It is like someone who tries to avoid a small pit only to fall into a deep well.

九五・孚于剝・有厲・

5th Yao. Sincerity towards dissipating influences is dangerous.

Zhan (占)

1. You meet some very pleasant, interesting people, but as you begin to get to know them you see that none of them develops any sense of personal purpose, they just wander. You realize this can't make you happy, and you let them go.
2. What you are doing is cheating yourself and others.
3. When a big tree comes down, all the monkeys on it will disperse.

上六・引兌・

6th Yao. Joyousness that is seductive.

Zhan (占)

1. You are drawn by first one kind of pleasure, then another. You never exercise your own initiative or try to discover what you want. People say "nothing will ever become of him" and they are right.
2. One has to think about the unfavorable rather than the favorable possibilities of a situation.
3. No use crying over spilled milk.

59

$\equiv\!\equiv$

Huàn 渙

Wind above
Water below
Dispersion

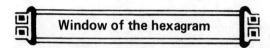

Window of the hexagram

1. A temple is in the mountain. This means to be extremely aloof from mundane affairs.
2. A monk. Symbolizes a peaceful and pure person.
3. A person follows the monk. This represents availing oneself to a life of leisure.
4. A ghost follows this person. This suggests being prudent in making sta'ements and careful in personal conduct.
5. A 'god wearing golden armor. This means receiving Heaven's help.

Image and Symbol

順水行舟之課 • 天風吹物之象 •

The image is to sail a boat with the current.
The symbol is strong wind sweeping things away.

Kua Tsi (文王象辭)

渙 • 亨 • 王假有廟 • 利涉大川 • 利貞 •

Huàn or dispersion brings success. The king comes to his temple. It is a time to cross the great water. It is a time to persevere.

Zhan (占) or hints on divining

1. This is a March hexagram, it is good in summer and winter, bad in fall.
2. Huán or dispersion is like wind blowing over water. It disperses it, changing it into mist and foam. It is the same with our minds. Through hardness and selfishness, we become rigid, the rigidity leads to separation from others. We need warm spring breezes to dissolve the rigidity, when a boat is crossing a river, all hands must unite in joint task.
3. Friends invite you to join a party out in the country to "celebrate spring." It sounds silly to you, but when you go, the day is so beautiful and everyone is so happy that you come home feeling twice as alive and full of good feeling as when you left.

Yao Tsi (周公爻辭)

初六・用拯・馬壯・吉・

1st Yao. He brings help and has the strength of a horse. Good luck.

Zhan (占)

1. Your friends are inspired with a grand idea and project and as they begin to work out the arrangements they start to argue. You quickly join the discussion, and work unceasingly to clear away trivial disagreements so the plan can go forward.
2. You work very hard like travelling on horseback without stopping.
3. Even with a team of four horses, it is difficult to overtake carelessly uttered words.

九二・渙奔其機・悔亡・

2nd Yao. At the dissolution, he hurries to join that which supports him. Disappointment disappears.

Zhan (占)

1. You find yourself dwelling on your fortunes and discontented with the help others give you. Then you think, I am just in a bad mood, and you go out and visit good friends and find your viewpoint is healthy again.
2. You will suffer a setback in trying to take advantage of others.
3. One loves what is his own.

六三・渙其躬・无悔・

3rd Yao. He dissolves himself. No disappointment.

Zhan (占)

1. You take up a project that is so important to you that you give up your personal impulses of like and dislike, and follow whatever furthers the work. Your inspiration has such strength you find this possible, and you prosper.
2. One should be prepared for possible future perils while enjoying one's life.
3. A withered old tree suddenly puts forth new sprouts.

六四・渙其羣・元吉・渙有丘・匪夷所思・○

4th Yao. He dissolves his links with his group. Highest good luck. The dispersion leads again to accumulation. This is something common people never think of. ○

Zhan (占)

1. Your interests begin to take you outside your circle of friends, and you let this happen without worrying. Later you find you've developed further as a person, and are more interesting to old friends and new alike.
2. There is nothing wrong or improper about it.
3. It is like having a sweet shower after a long drought. You will get something urgently needed after being deprived of it for a long time.

九五・渙汗其大號・渙王居・无咎・○

5th Yao. His loud cries dissolve things like sweat. Dissolution. A king goes without blame. ○

Zhan (占)

1. One of your group gets a superior idea for a project for all and will not ignore it. Others hear and are drawn to the notion, and the old stagnation that prevailed is dissolved.
2. There is no passing the buck.
3. Don't destroy the bridge after you have crossed the river, which means to discard a person after he has outlasted his usefulness.

上九・渙其血・去・逖出・无咎・

6th Yao. He dissolves the blood. Leaving, or keeping at a distance or going away is without blame.

Zhan (占)

1. You and your friends are relaxing in the park, when you see suspicious looking characters approaching. You alert them, and while someone goes to call police, the rest of you retreat to a safe place.
2. It is not wise to concentrate on details while forgetting main purpose or objective.

3. One may give financial aid to others in an emergency but should not do so if they are perennially in need of money.

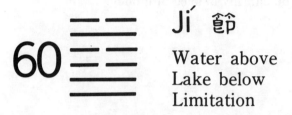

60

Jí 節

Water above
Lake below
Limitation

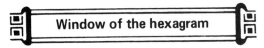

Window of the hexagram

1. It rains cats and dogs. To give contributions to charity in every direction is suggested.
2. A fish jumps out of the fire. This indicates an escape from death by a narrow margin.
3. The sun's eyelashes — when the clouds open up, one sees the light of the sun. This means a turn of fortune for the better.
4. A cock stands on the roof. To crow is to give everyone the news.
5. A dog is in the well. A person is bullied by others when he is down on his luck.

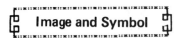

Image and Symbol

船行風息之課・寒暑有節之象・

The image is sailing a boat without wind, Nothing happens.
The symbol is the change of seasons.

Kua Tsi (文王彖辭)

節・亨・苦節不可貞・

Jí or Limitation is successful. Excess limitation should not be pursued with.

Zhan (占) *or hints on divining*

1. This is an October hexagram, it is good in spring and summer, bad in fall and winter.
2. Jí is the symbol of a bamboo joint as shown below.

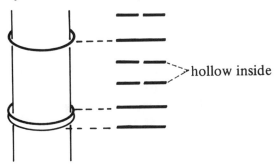

hollow inside

3. You set up a new plan for regulating your life better. When you find it is a little bit too harsh, you soften it just a little, and hold to that.

初九・不出戶庭・无咎

1st Yao. Do not go out the door and the courtyard is blameless.

Zhan (占)

1. You see an opportunity that can improve your skills, but when you look at it closely, you see it would overtax you and maybe lose all. You keep with what you are working on.
2. Wealth and treasure is of secondary importance compared with time.
3. While there are things for which a foot is too short a unit of measurement, there are things for which the inch can be long enough. This means that every person has weak points as well as strong points.

九二・不出門庭・凶・

2nd Yao. Not going out the gate and courtyard brings bad luck.

Zhan (占)

1. The "just right" opportunity you wanted is here. If you do not move now, you are cheating yourself.
2. Those who obey the mandates of nature will prosper while those who defy it will perish.
3. The flying moth is forever attracted by the flame.

六三・不節若・則嗟若・无咎・●

3rd Yao. He who doesn't follow limitations will lament. No blame. ●

Zhan (占)

1. You got so enthused at the party that you ate and drank as if there was no tommorow. Now tomorrow is here.
2. Those who are discriminated against will complain.
3. You will realize the matter to be as urgent as your eyebrows catching fire.

六四・安節・亨・○
4th Yao. Contented limitation is successful. ○

Zhan (占)

1. The limitations you have worked out for yourself fit you so well and naturally, you are quite pleased with things.
2. Every limitation has its value, which requires persistent effort in order to lead to success.
3. You enjoy peace and stability both physically and spiritually.

九五・甘節・吉・往有尚・○
5th Yao. Sweet limitation is good luck. To act this way brings respect. ○

Zhan (占)

1. You told your friends what you were planning to do, but you asked no special help of them, and did it on your own the best you could. They see what you've achieved, and want to do the same now.
2. Great men appear in response to the call of the times.
3. One has a sense of shame and honor only when his livelihood is assured.

上六・苦節・貞凶・悔亡・
6th Yao. Excessive limitation. Persevering brings bad luck. Disappointment disappears.

Zhan (占)

1. To catch up in your studies for an examination you worked day and night all week long. In this way you were able to pass, but afterward you resolve to study more regularly and not have to do this again.
2. He who is in comfortable circumstances knows not the bitterness of misfortune.
3. A moment's relief or pleasure can bring endless sufferings to come.

61

Zhōngfú 中孚

Wind above
Lake below
Central Sincerity

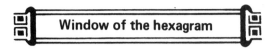
Window of the hexagram

1. To hope one's son will have his name on the document. This means that where whole-hearted dedication is involved the whole world will step aside to let you by.
2. A person beats the night watchman's drum and copper gong. This means to take precautions against calamity.
3. An official drags a deer with a cord. If one devotes oneself to the fullest, one will continue to have the prosperity one presently has.
4. A snow goose holds a letter in its beak. Good news will come soon.

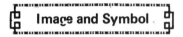
Image and Symbol

鶴鳴子和之課・事有定期之象・

The image is the crane calling out and her young ones responding.
The symbol is things changing with the passage of time.

Kua Tsi (文王彖辭)

中孚・豚魚吉・利涉大川・利貞・

Zhongfú or central. Pigs and fishes. Good luck. It is a time to cross the great water. It is a time to persevere.

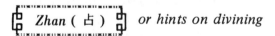
Zhan (占)   *or hints on divining*

1. This is an August hexagram, it is good in fall and winter.
2. Zhongfú or central sinceity is symbolized by an egg. The 1st and 6th Yao are the eggshell, 2nd and 5th Yao are the white of an egg. The 3rd and 4th Yao are the yolk as shown below.

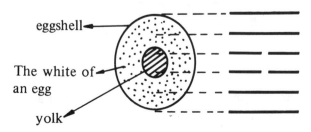

3. Zhongfú is an yóuhún hexagram of 53 Jian.

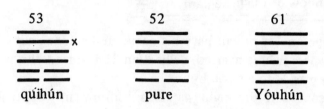

| 53 | 52 | 61 |
| qúihún | pure | Yóuhún |

If a patient consults the I Ching and gets Zhongfú, it is a very bad omen.

4. When you took the job of teacher you thought it would be boring. But now you find that to communicate things about life to people and to get them to pursue their own learning is a great pleasure and inspiration.

Yao Tsi (周公爻辭)

初九・虞吉・有他不燕・

1st Yao. It is good luck to be prepared. If there are secret designs, it becomes distracting.

Zhan (占)

1. You plan a public campaign for a good purpose and the newspaper editor tells you privately not to worry, he will give it strong editorial support. Halfway through your work you realize you have been easing off the intensity because of the expected support, and that you don't really know if you will receive it.
2. You should stick to what you are suited for.
3. You have spent your best years without any achievement.

九二・鳴鶴在陰・其子和之・我有好爵・吾與爾靡之・○

2nd Yao. A crane calls in the shade and its young one replies. I have a good glass, I will share it with you.○

Zhan (占)

1. Someone sees you doing something helpful to others out of a natural impulse. It reminds them of their own impulses, and they join with

you.

2. You are like a crane standing among chickens, which means greaty surpassing the others.

3. One can drink more than usual with a bosom friend.

六三 • 得敵 • 或鼓或罷 • 或泣或歌 •

3rd Yao. He finds a comrade. Now he beats the drum, now he stops. Now he cries, now he sings.

Zhan (占)

1. When you were alone, you worried about yourself. Now you have friends, and you worry about them, or you feel good because of them.

2. Good fortune that comes after a long spell of bad luck.

3. You should reject evil ways and start on the right track.

六四 • 月幾望 • 馬匹亡 • 无咎 •

4th Yao. The moon is nearly full. The horse in the team strays off. There is nothing to blame.

Zhan (占)

1. You never think yourself best, for that is excessive. When you look about to see how others are doing, you lose your own train of activity for a moment and stagger, then regain it.

2. The arrival of fortune or misfortune is unpredictable.

3. Careless talk always lands one in trouble.

九五 • 有孚攣如 • 无咎 •

5th Yao. He has truth, and it links together. Nothing to blame.

Zhan (占)

1. Your group never seems to have any trouble, because your leader radiates self assurance, and everyone else sees and has it, too.

2. It is sooner said than done.

3. You work laboriously only to earn criticisms.

上九 • 翰音登于天 • 貞凶 •

6th Yao. The cockcrow reaches to heaven. Persevering brings bad luck.

[Zhan (占)]

1. You depend on good words too much to nurture support. They can only do a small part of the job.
2. Even if you were given wrings you couldn't fly away from this kind of situation.
3. Don't profit yourself at the expense of others.

62 Zráoguò 小過

Thunder above
Mountain below
Small Passing

```
┌─────────────────────────────────────┐
│  ▦     Window of the hexagram    ▦  │
└─────────────────────────────────────┘
```

1. A full moon is in the sky. When the bad days are over, everything goes back to normal.
2. A man flips his cap under a tree. You will get a job with the government.
3. A person is trapped by a net. Another uses a knife to cut him loose. This means the end of a boundless hardship.
4. A watch post is set on a hilltop. This points to the prospect of a very successful career.

```
┌──────────────────────┐
│  Image and Symbol    │
└──────────────────────┘
```

飛鳥遺音之課・上逆下順之象・

The image is the sounds that come down from a flying bird.

The symbol is that to ascend is going against the current, while to descend is natural and right.

```
┌────────────────────────────┐
│  Kua Tsi ( 文王象辭 )       │
└────────────────────────────┘
```

小過・亨・利貞・可小事不可大事・飛鳥遺之音・不宜上宜下・大吉・

Xiǎoguò or small passing. Success. It is a time to persevere. Small things can be done, but not great things. The flying bird brings a message that it is not good to strive upward at this time. It is good to remain below. The greatest good luck.

```
┌──────────────────┐
│  Zhan ( 占 )      │  or hints on divining
└──────────────────┘
```

1. This is a February hexagram. It is good in spring, summer and fall, not too bad in winter.
2. Xiǎoguó or small passing has the symbol of a bird on the wing. The 1st, 2nd, 5th and 6th are the wings, 3rd and 4th are the body of a bird as shown below left.

Xiaoguó also has the symbol of a soldier on guard at the door. The upper trigram Zhèn is a soldier, lower trigam Yín is the gate as shown in picture above right.

3. Xiáoguò is an Yóuhún hexagram of 54 Guimèr.

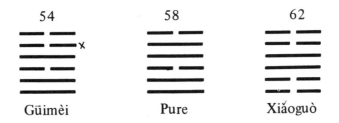

It is a very evil omen for a patient.

Yao Tsi (周公爻辭)

初六 · 飛鳥以凶 · ●

1st Yao. The bird meets with bad luck due to flying. ●

Zhan (占)

1. You could have remained at the lodge, but you loved to go skiing, so you went out when the conditions were obviously bad, and had a bad fall.
2. A hungry person will eat whatever food is available.
3. Your are in a situation where you can neither proceed nor retreat.

六二 · 遇其祖 · 過其妣 · 不及其居 · 遇其位 · 无咎 ·

2nd Yao. She passes by her ancestor and meets her ancestress. He fails to reach his prince, and so meets the official. Nothing to blame.

Zhan （占）

1. Your boss is busy with important things when you go to see him about something. Rather than interrupt, you take up the matter with his assistant, acting with as much authority as you have at the time to keep things going.
2. You are unable to do what you wish.
3. An unfair contest brings no honor to the victor.

九三・弗遇防之・從或戕之・凶・●

3rd Yao. If you are not extremely careful, somebody may come up behind you and strike you down. Poor luck. ●

Zhan （占）

1. You learn your enemies will make an all-out attempt to attack you tomorrow. You think, "I shouldn't concern myself with such petty people, my behaviour has been correct." Then you think, well, they may try to seize on some meaningless point and blow it out of proportion and fool everyone, maybe I had better be very careful.
2. Your friend is a wolf in sheep's clothing.
3. One who has done something bad secretly, cannot look others in the eye.

九四・无咎・弗過遇之・往厲必戒・勿用永貞・●

4th Yao. There is nothing to blame. He meets him without passing by. To go out is dangerous. You must be on guard. Don't act. But be persevering. ●

Zhan （占）

1. You find strong and hostile opposition to the project you are working on. You yield to it and become inactive, while you continue to constantly look for ways to forward it when the right time comes.
2. One will get nowhere if he lacks single-mindedness and perseverance.
3. To do evil deeds frequently will bring ruin to the doer.

六五・密雲不雨・自我西郊・公弋取彼在穴・

5th Yao. There are dense clouds, but no rain from the western lands. The prince shoots and hits the man who is in the cave.

⫷ *Zhan* (占) ⫸

1. In local politics you get yourself placed in exactly the influential position you want. But you find you can do nothing because you have no good helpers. You start to look for them, aiming for people who have true ability, not flashy appearances.
2. The greater fortune one amasses, the greater the loss he will suffer.
3. It is better to leave a deficiency uncovered than to have it covered.

上六・弗過遇之・飛鳥離之・凶・是謂災眚・●

6th Yao. He passes him by, not meeting. The flying bird leaves him. Bad luck and injury. ●

[*Zhan* (占)]

1. You did an excellent job repairing your auto. But you decided you wanted even better results. You took it all apart again, and now all you have is a mess on your hands.
2. Instead of pretending to understand everything, one should listen more to others.
3. Although beginning a task from the bottom, one must not forget the ultimate objective.

63

Jìjì 既濟

Water above
Fire below
Finished

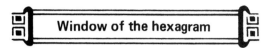

Window of the hexagram

1. A man stands on the bank watching a boat approach. This means to receive timely assistance.
2. There is a pile of coins symbolizing riches and wealth.
3. The rain is following. To receive favors.
4. Two children walk in the rain. One is young, but successful in one's career.
5. There is a document as an omen of luck.

Image and Symbol

舟楫濟川之課 • 陰陽配合之象 •

The image is many boats making a river a prosperous one.
The symbol is the Yin matching the Yang.

Kua Tsi (文王彖辭)

旣濟 • 亨小 • 利貞 • 初吉終亂 •

Jíjí or finished. There is success in small things. It is a time to persevere.
At the start there is good luck, at the end, there is disorder.

Zhan (占) or hints on divining

1. This is a January hexagram. It is good in winter bad in summer.
2. The Yin Yao and Yang Yao are correctly arranged, each in its appropriate place. For it is just when perfect balance has been reached that any movement may cause order to revert to disorder. We should take thought of misfortune and arm ourselves against it in advance.
3. You reformed the politics in your small town. There is nothing big to do now, just keep things going. You know that things will slowly start to fall apart and become corrupt again, but you also know that with constant care you can make it be a long time before this happens.

Yao Tsi (周公爻辭)

初九・屯其輪・濡其尾・无咎・●

1st Yao. He brakes his wheels and gets his tail in the water. Nothing to blame. ●

Zhan (占)

1. Your friends were so inspired by achieving an important common goal, they immediately set off to try to achieve another too far advanced. You hold back and have to put up with the nonsense that results, but do not get yourself in trouble.
2. You will suffer a major setback due to carelessness.
3. Heaven will always leave a door open.

六二・婦喪其茀・勿逐・七日得・

2nd Yao. The woman loses the curtain of her carriage. Don't run after it. On the seventh day, you'll get it back.

Zhan (占)

1. After the big company merger you go to your superiors to get approval for some important work, and find they are careless and can't be bothered to listen to you. You accept their judgment and hold back, a time will come when they see how important it is and come after you very quickly.
2. You will suffer a loss in one place but make a gain somewhere else.
3. Time makes all the difference.

九三・高宗伐鬼方・三年克之・小人勿用・

3rd Yao. The Kao Tsung disciplined the Devil's Country. After three years, he conquered it. You must not employ inferior people.

Zhan (占)

1. After lengthy efforts, you finally succeed in expanding your chains of stores into poorer areas of the great city. You find out soon after your assistants are assigning all your least talented people there. You tell them to clean house instead and put good people

there or the territory will be lost.

2. A great man will take time to shape and mature.

3. You have already made careful plans for what you are doing.

六四・繻有衣袽・終日戒・●

4th Yao. The finest clothes can turn to rags. Be watchful all day long. ●

Zhan (占)

1. There's a break-in in the neighborhood and you get alarmed and think of installing an alarm system. Then you forget about it, and a week later, five homes are broken into. Yours is one of them.

2. Psychological offense is the best of tactics.

3. Do not criticize or comment about something that is already over.

九五・東鄰殺牛・不如西鄰之禴祭・實受其福・

5th Yao. The person in the east who slaughters an ox does not get as much happiness as the fellow in the west with his small offering.

Zhan (占)

1. The rich people down the road have a big, flashy Christmas celebration and lots of luxuries, but no real friends. You find you are many times happier attending the smaller celebration of your poorer friend.

2. If you always think thrice before you act, what you have hoped to happen comes to pass.

3. No mather how capable one is, he needs the help of others to do more or better work.

上六・濡其首・厲・●

6th Yao. He gets his head in the water. Dangerous. ●

Zhan (占)

1. You move heaven and earth to win through the hardships that are now past. You find yourself looking back at this in awe, while present conditions change without your paying attention to them.

2. You have to handle something without rigid application of rules.

3. A leopard leaves behind its skin when it dies.

64

Wèijì 未濟

Fire above
Water below
Unfinished

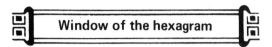

Window of the hexagram

1. A man holds a long knife in his left hand and an ax in his right hand. This means prestige and influence built up by keeping good faith.
2. A tiger sits on the ground. This means to suffer a drastic fall in one's prestige.
3. A flag is waving on the mountain. This symbolizes winning the first match.
4. A man holds a flag. This is a token of authority.

Image and Symbol

竭水求珠之課 • 憂中望喜之象 •
The image is emptying the lake to find the pearl.
The symbol is that worry proves a blessing to most people.

Kua Tsi（文王彖辭）

未濟 • 亨 • 小孤汔濟 • 濡其尾 • 无攸利 •
Wèijì or unfinished. Success. But if the little fox gets his tail wet after nearly crossing the stream, it doesn't further anything.

Zhan（占） *or hints on divining*

1. This is a July hexagram. It is good in wint bad in fall.
2. As you reach your driveway after driving through a long and dangerous snowstorm you feel so relieved that you relax your caution and immediately lose control and end up in the ditch.

Yao Tsi（周公爻辭）

初六 • 濡其尾 • 吝 • ●
1st Yao. He gets his tail in the water. Humiliation. ●

Zhan（占） Hints on divining

1. The moving van has left and your possessions are scattered around

your new home. You decide you'll surprise your wife, and order things without waiting for her help. She arrives to tell you the 200 pound couch you just dragged upstairs belongs downstairs.
2. You have too little power or resources to do as much as you wish.
3. A single moon is much lighter than a thousand stars, which means quality is more important than quantity.

九二 • 曳其輪 • 貞吉 •

2nd Yao. He brakes the wheels. Perseverance brings good luck.

Zhan（占）

1. You hold off, but are ready to move at a moment's notice.
2. It is too urgent to make a wise or careful choice. Rashness spoils chances of success.
3. To solve the key issue will expedite the solution of the whole problem.

六三 • 未濟征凶 • 利涉大川 •

3rd Yao. Wèijì or unfinished, attack is bad luck. It is a time to cross the great water.

Zhan（占）

1. Your plans are blocked by strong opposition. You pull back, call in your helpers, and plot an entirely new course of action to take you through to the goal.
2. One can be austere if he has no selfish desires.
3. You have to do something no matter what the consquences.

九四 • 貞吉悔亡 • 震用伐鬼方 • 三年有賞于大國 • ○

4th Yao. Persevering brings good luck. Disappointment disappears. Use shock to discipline the Devils Country. For three years, great realms are given out. ○

Zhan（占）

1. Your side finally gets its chance and you all work with great energy to "clean house" in your debilitated company. It works because no one faltered, and is followed by a period of regeneration and extended prosperity.

2. A wise person who knows what's best for himself can safe guard his personal security.
3. The opportunity is ripe, now or never.

六五・貞吉・无悔・君子之光・有孚・吉・○

5th Yao. Persevering brings good luck. No disappointment. The light of the advanced man is true. Good luck.○

🗱 Zhan (占) 🗱

1. The battle is over and won, good things can happen now.
2. The Heaven has complied with man's wishes.
3. You have a great talent and an attentive mind.

上九・有孚于飲酒・无咎・濡其首・有孚失是・

6th Yao. There is drinking wine in an atmosphere of real confidence. Nothing to blame. But if you wet your head, you lose it, truthfully.

[Zhan (占)]

1. Everything is all set for the new time and all you have to do is wait and relax with friends. But if you get carried away and drunk, you may spoil what you worked so hard for.
2. One should know how to submit to the proper regulatives.
3. We might think Jiji is appropriate for the last hexagram of the 64, since it means finished, or completion. But such an arrangement would give us a view of living as something static, having an end. The I Ching sees life as an endless cyclic process, constantly going from Wu Chi to Tai Chi and then to a new Wu Chi and a new Tai Chi. Thus the last hexagram is Weiji or unfinished, and it tells us that the completion of one cycle is the beginning of a new one.

Here's Good News······
THE TAO SERIES
by *Jou, Tsung Hwa*
Wonderful Gift Books!

THE TAO OF
TAI-CHI CHUAN
Way to Rejuvenation

The best-selling Tai-Chi book. It covers the following:

*Discussions of the Tai-Chi Philosophy, moving beyond mere physical forms and including information available from no other sources — even Tai-Chi books written in Chinese.

*Authoritative pictures of the original Chen, Yang and Wu Forms presented to help the Tai-Chi community develop a "standard alphabet" in communicating and understanding the variety of Tai Chi forms.

*Detailed instruction on the practice of the Chi Kung (米功) or Breathing Exercise, and the development of the Chan Ssu Chin (纏絲勁). Two methods indispensible to the student seriously concerned with advancement but never before developed and explained clearly. For the first time the origin, purpose and practice of these exercises are presented as an essential part of Tai-Chi.

*Translations of The Classics of Tai-Chi Chuan, writings of the great masters that provide the most authentic guides possible to Tai-Chi progress and development.

*Definitions of a student's level of progress in terms of the three powers: humanity, earth and sky. Principles for the beginning student and the natural progression of practice for the more experienced student are described.

*The theoretical foundations of Push-hands and practical exercises used to develop this art.

THE TAO OF
MEDITATION
Way to Enlightenment

Everyone can be enlightened by this inspiring and informative book. This book now makes available the basic principles of enlightenment in different forms of meditation as well as practical exercises based on traditional Chinese methods.

The book is presented in three parts:

Part One explains the philosophy of all forms of meditation. The uses of the Tai-Chi symbol and the concepts of Yin and Yang are described.

The philosophical ideas of space and time are discussed to open the reader's mind to the fourth dimension. This fourth dimensional view of our three dimensional world has never before been explained so clearly. It is truly the way to enlightenment. The need for students to create their own personal discipline is stressed.

Part Two describes in detail a series of twelve breathing exercises or Chi Kung that can be used to lead and circulate the Chi energy to every part of the body. These exercises are extremely valuable to serious martial arts students and to all who desire to reach higher levels of health and self-awareness.

Part Three deals with the Lien Ching Hwa Chi (練精化炁) or the transfer of sexual energy to psychic energy. Enlightenment through meditation is taken out of the realm of superstition and presented in a realistic, practical way. Detailed guidance to the life-long study of this traditional Chinese method, which is one of the paths leading to the fourth dimensional world, is provided.

THE TAO OF
I CHING
Way to Divination

For the first time in English the I Ching is presented in such a revealing light and told with such elegance through the use of pictures and vivid imagery to finally "Raise the veil of mystery" and encourage personal, practical use of this most valued work of Chinese culture.

The book describes the following:

*How the meaning of Yin and Yang evolved from the Tai-Chi diagram. The basic principles of the I Ching's structure is explained so that the student can determine the meanings of the trigrams directly from the central concept of Yin and Yang.

*Methods of divination including yarrow stalks or coins, but, most importantly, the direct interpretation of time and personal life events. You can use the I Ching to predict coming events and to adjust your behavior to attain harmony in your daily life.

*Three-part divination. The principles of the Five Elements are used for interpretation. Specific examples and exercises to illustrate each divination method are included.

*Pictures based on traditional Chinese wood block prints which are used to summarize the qualities of each hexagram visually instead of in words. This approach enhances the learning of creative, nonverbal, concepts in understanding the I Ching.

*How the traditional meanings of the hexagrams can be translated into relevant, personal terms. Included here are also many details on the lore of divination as applied to the specific hexagrams.

*As a whole, this book takes the reader away from the perception of the I Ching as a series of sayings by some wise person arrived at by a mysterious method and back to its roots as a timeless method of cultivating self-awareness and improving the quality of life.

Tai Chi Foundation
7199 E. Shea Blvd. Ste 109-225
Scottsdale, AZ 85254
Fax: 480 609 8663 email: Taichilj @aol.com

Name:_____

Address:_____

City:_____State_____Zip_____

____ Check or ____ Money Order Enclosed.

Yes, Please send me the book listed below:

Qty.	Code	Title	Price	Total
	To1	The Dao of Taijiquan: Way to Rejuvenation 7th Edition, softcover, updated information and pinyin system or romanization.	$21.95	
	To2	The Dao of Meditation: Way to Enlightenment Softcover. Covers theory of Daoist meditation under Northern School approach	$17.95	
	To3	Tao of I-Ching: Way to Divination Probably the most complete book available on the Yijing. A very intellectual work. Softcover	$24.95	
Total Order				
Shipping/Handling*				
Total Order				

* Please add $3 shipping/handling per book. Foreign orders MUST be in U. S. currency from a bank with a branch in the US to avoid service fees. Foreign order must add $12 per book airmail, or $4 per book service mail